P9-CFG-526

PREACHER

Book Six

Garth Ennis Writer
Steve Dillon John McCrea Artists
Pamela Rambo Patricia Mulvihill Colorists
Clem Robins Letterer Cover Art and Original Series Covers by Glenn Fabry

Preacher created by Garth Ennis and Steve Dillon

Axel Alonso Editor – Original Series Scott Nybakken Editor
Robbin Brosterman Design Director – Books Louis Prandi Publication Design

Shelly Bond Executive Editor – Vertigo Hank Kanalz Senior VP – Vertigo and Integrated Publishing

Diane Nelson President Dan DiDio and Jim Lee Co-Publishers Geoff Johns Chief Creative Officer
Amit Desai Senior VP – Marketing and Franchise Management Amy Genkins Senior VP – Business and Legal Affairs
Nairi Gardiner Senior VP – Finance Jeff Boison VP – Publishing Planning Mark Chiarello VP – Art Direction and Design
John Cunningham VP – Marketing Terri Cunningham VP – Editorial Administration
Larry Ganem VP – Talent Relations and Services Alison Gill Senior VP – Manufacturing and Operations
Jay Kogan VP – Business and Legal Affairs, Publishing Jack Mahan VP – Business Affairs, Talent
Nick Napolitano VP – Manufacturing Administration Sue Pohja VP – Book Sales
Fred Ruiz VP – Manufacturing Operations Courtney Simmons Senior VP – Publicity Bob Wayne Senior VP – Sales

PREACHER BOOK SIX

DC Comics. 1700 Broadway, New York, NY 10019. A Warner Bros. Entertainment Company.
Printed in the USA. First Printing. ISBN: 978-1-4012-5279-3

Library of Congress Cataloging-in-Publication Data is Available.

Table of Contents

There is no intro for this one. Garth had a half an idea about writing a kind of last-word-on-PREACHER thing, but it turned out half was all he had. Steve suggested a back-and-forth piece between the two of us, an e-mail exchange about our memories of the book, but it was tacitly agreed that stuff like that makes sensible people cringe themselves into oblivion. So we've got nothing.

Instead, we decided to dedicate this sixth and final PREACHER hardcover to you, the readers. This book is for everyone who's ever bought PREACHER, whether it was a single issue, the whole run, all nine trades or all these latest editions, or whatever combination of same. It's for anyone who's ever talked about us, written about us, blogged about us, generally spread the word by whatever means were available. It's for the people who come up to us at signings with those tell-tale dog-eared copies of GONE TO TEXAS — the ones we know instantly have been passed around to a dozen or more friends, sparking imaginations, getting them going too. *Hey, man, I told my buddy about this and he doesn't read comics, but he checked it out and now he's reading PREACHER...* It's for every single one of you. You know who you are.

Cheers,

— Garth Ennis & Steve Dillon

September 2011

PREACHER

Book Six

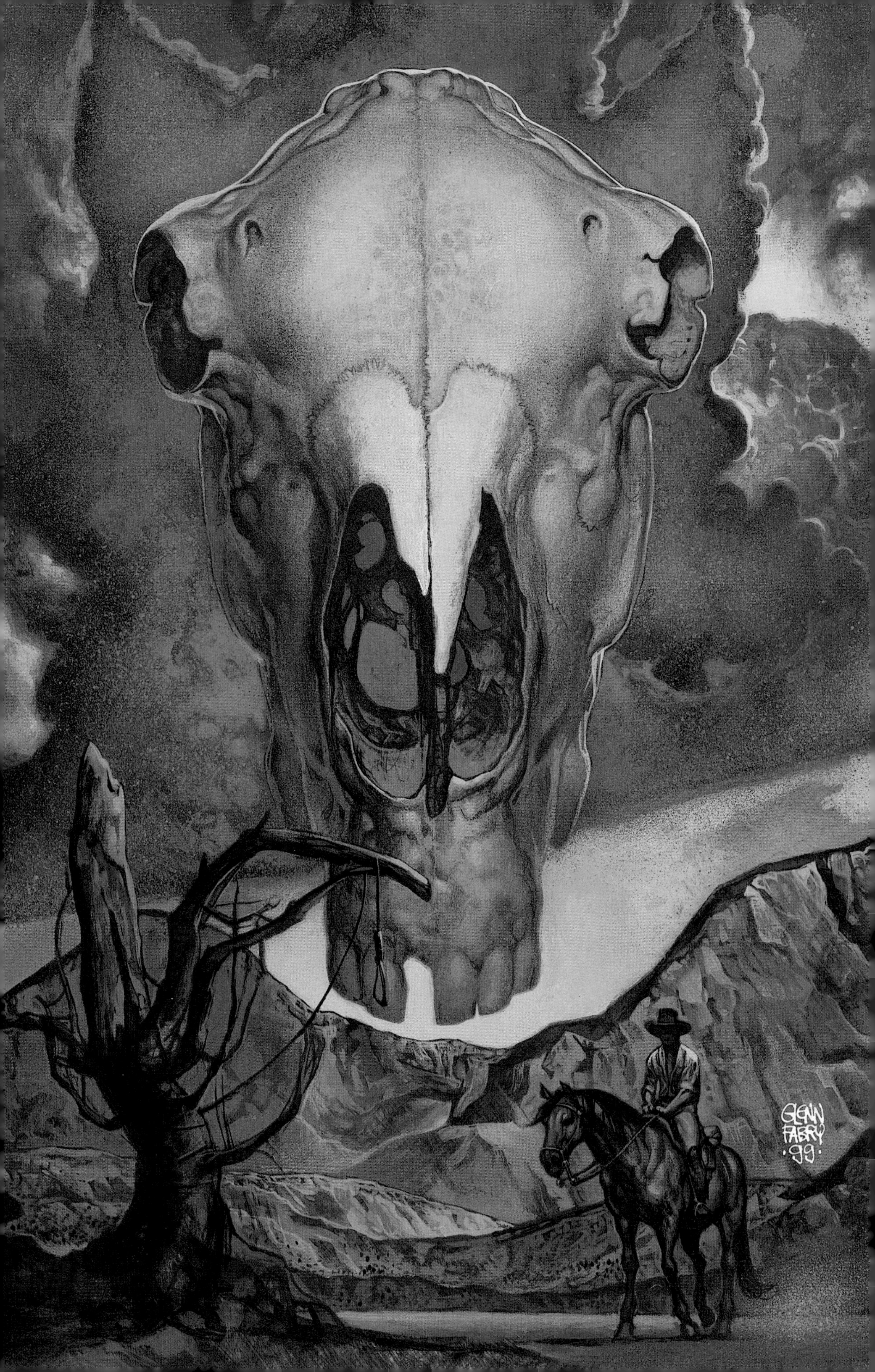
GLENN
FABRY
·99·

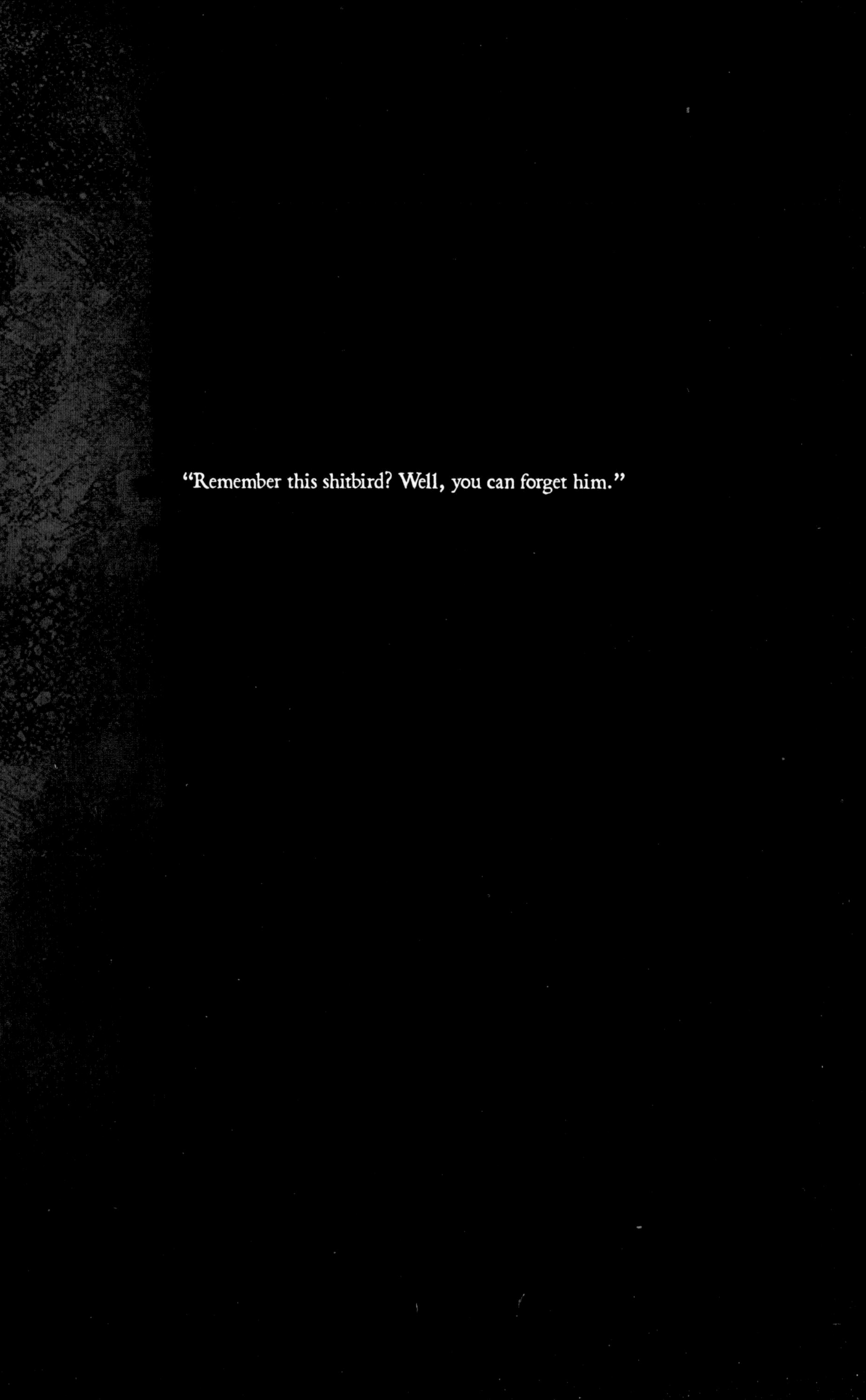

"Remember this shitbird? Well, you can forget him."

TALL IN THE SADDLE

GARTH ENNIS
STEVE DILLON
JOHN McCREA
PAMELA RAMBO
CLEM ROBINS

OH, YOU AIN'T...

WELL YOU MIGHT WANNA THINK ABOUT THAT, CUSTER. MIGHT WANNA THINK ABOUT DOIN' WHATEVER THE HELL MR. LANGTRY TELLS YOU TO DO...
SHUT UP, DONNY.
DON'T HAVE TO STEAL 'EM. ALREADY BEEN STOLE. ALL YOU GOTTA DO'S DRIVE A TRAILER LOADA THE DAMN NAGS I GOT WAITIN' DOWN IN MULESHOE.

MAKES NO DIFFERENCE TO ME, LANGTRY. I AIN'T HAVIN' NO TRUCK WITH STOLEN HORSES.
AN' TELL YOUR BOY HERE TO BACK OFF, 'FORE I KICK HIS ASS SO HARD HIS BALLS START RINGIN' OUT DIXIE...

WELL WE GONNA SEE--
SHUT UP, DONNY.
CUTTIN' YOU A BREAK HERE, CUSTER. OWE ME A LOTTA MONEY, ON THEM CARS YOU LOST.

STILL AIN'T TOLD ME HOW YOU LOST 'EM, NEITHER.

NOR DID HE EVER. BUT HERE'S HOW:
WHEEE-HEE-HEE-HEE! LOOK AT MY TITS!!

YOU'LL NEVER TAKE ME, LAWMEN! NO PRISON WALLS CAN KEEP ME! NO CHAINS CAN HOLD ME DOWN!

OH LORD...!

OH, SHIT!

SHIT-SHIT-SHIT-SHIT-SHIT!

AW NO--

WE REALLY CAN'T STOP, BABY--
SO DON'T.

BOBBY, WAIT!
LIKE HELL!

THAT WAS THE *HIGHWAY PATROL,* AMY! I MEAN JESUS CHRIST, OKAY?
BUT THEY DIDN'T GET THEM, BOBBY! THEY NEVER DO! AND THEY WON'T GET US, EITHER!
THERE'LL BE MORE! I'M NOT GETTING BUSTED, NOT FOR ANYONE! I AM *GONE!*

HOLY JESUS--
OH, THIS IS *NOT* THE STRANGEST PLACE WE'VE EVER DONE IT...

...CRAZY. I MUST HAVE BEEN OUT OF MY MIND TO LET YOU TALK ME INTO THIS!
BOBBY, YOU'RE SCREWING EVERYTHING UP! ALL LANGTRY WANTS IS ONE MORE CAR TO MAKE THE BUY, AND JESSE AND TULIP HAVE GOT IT!

THE HELL WITH JESSE AND TULIP! SHE'S ADDICTED TO GODDAMN G.T.A., AND HE'LL DO ANYTHING FOR KICKS! HE'S A TOTAL PSYCHO, AMY!
AT LEAST HE'S NOT A WHINING LITTLE PUSSY! PULL OVER, DAMMIT!

STOP THIS TRUCK!
OH GOD-- OH YES--OH JESUS--

LOOK, DON'T CALL ME A PUSSY, OKAY?!
YOU'RE MESSING UP A MILLION-DOLLAR DEAL! YOU'RE STARTING TO CRY! YOU WET THE BED! I THINK I'LL CALL YOU WHATEVER THE HELL I LIKE!

I DO NOT WET THE BED!
NO, NOT YEEEIIIGGHH!!

OOOOOOH-- OOOOHH
I DON'T *BELIEVE* THIS...
OH ME EITHER, BABY--

I CAN'T STAND IT! NO! **NO!**
BOBBY!
WE'RE ALL GONNA DIE!

WHAT--
HOW--
HOLD TIGHT, BABY.

AW NO!

I--I--
I'M SORRY I WAS A BAD PERSON...

I'M SORRY I LAUGHED AT MY DAD WHEN MY MOM RAN AWAY WITH A LESBIAN...I'M SORRY I STOLE FROM THE RICH AND NEVER GAVE TO THE POOR...
AMY!

JUMP, AMY! IT'S GONNA GO OVER! YOU'VE GOTTA JUMP NOW!
WH-WH-WH--?

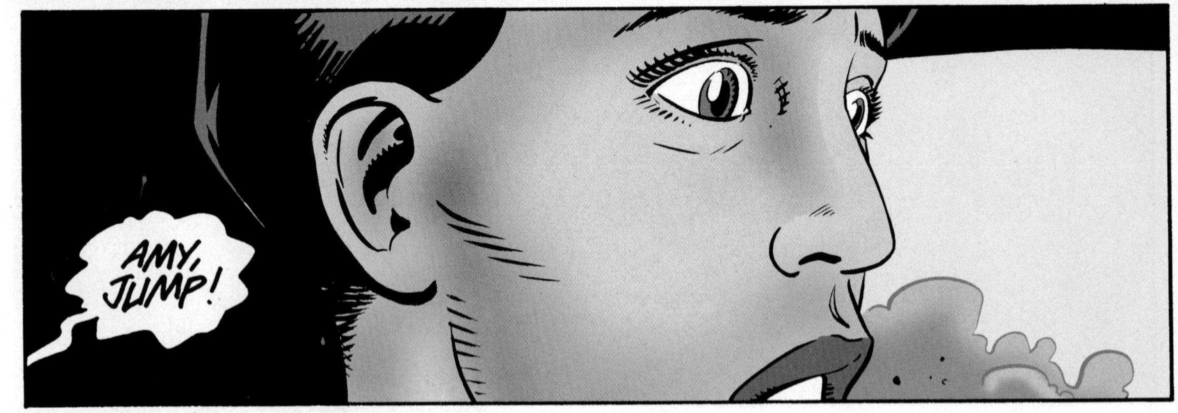
AMY, JUMP!

YEEEOOW!
AW NO--
JESUS!

ONE
MILLION
DOLLARS...

HOW COULD YOU HAVE MADE A LOSS ON THE CARS, LANGTRY? WE NEVER EVEN GOT TO SELL THEM TO YOU.
AIN'T DISPUTIN' THAT. TALKIN' 'BOUT MY OUTLAY ON THE TRANSPORTER. EXPENSES AN' SUCH.
OFFERIN' YOU A WAY TO SQUARE THE DEBT.

AN' THAT'S FAIR. GONNA HAVE TO FIND A DIFFERENT WAY TO SQUARE IT, IS ALL I'M SAYIN'.
PLACE I COME FROM, THE WHORES GENERALLY KNOW TO KEEP THEIR MOUTHS SHUT WHEN MEN'RE DOIN' BUSINESS...

HEY, GODDAMMIT!

WE'RE THROUGH, LANGTRY. BE SMART AN' LET IT GO.

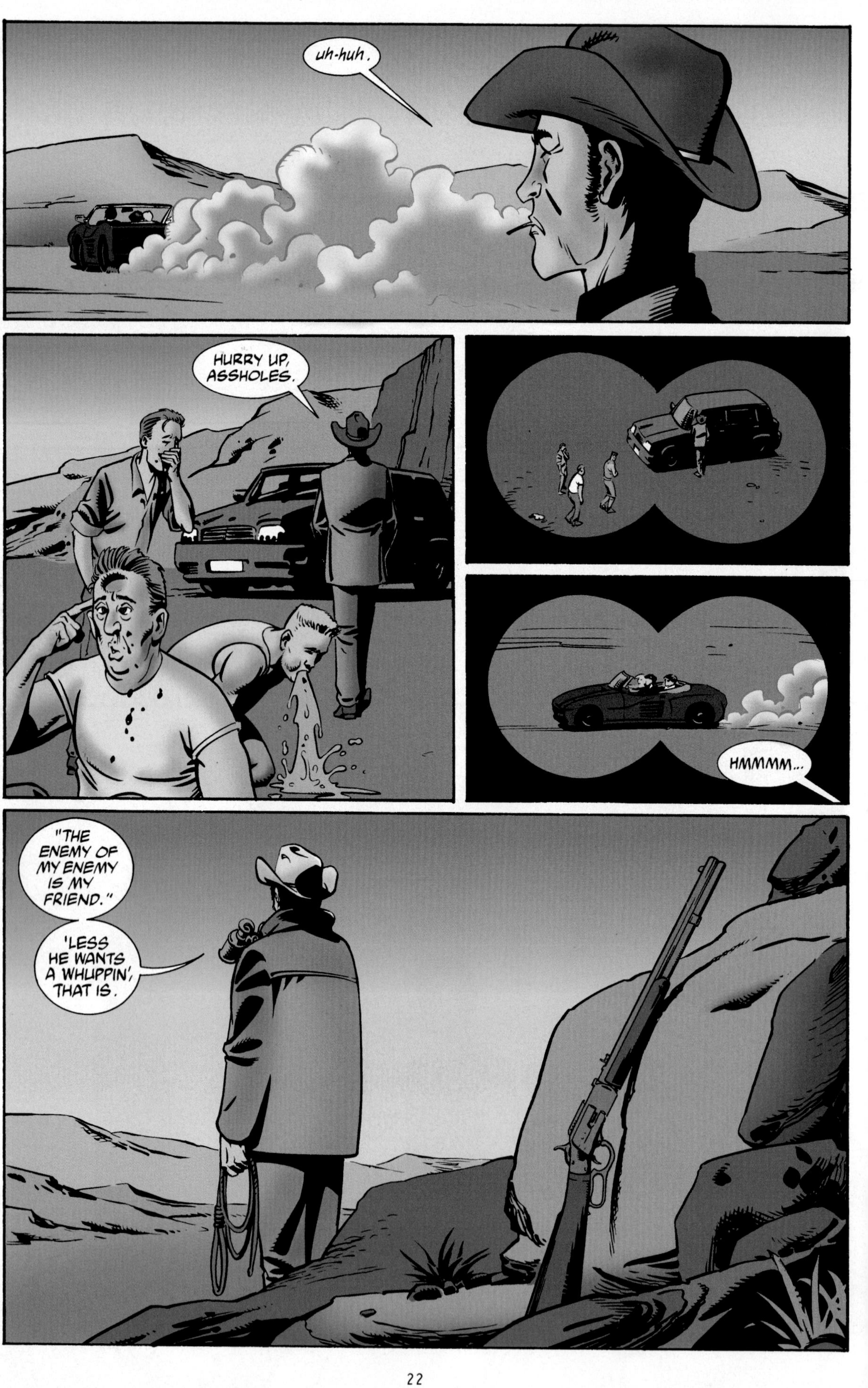

"THE ENEMY OF MY ENEMY IS MY FRIEND."

'LESS HE WANTS A WHUPPIN', THAT IS.

I AM SO SORRY...
Joe's Bar
MOTEL

WHAT HAVE YOU GOT TO APOLOGIZE FOR?
I MESSED UP. I'M THE ONE HIRED THAT LITTLE CREEP TO DRIVE FOR US.

HEY, YOU DIDN'T KNOW BOBBY WAS SUCH AN ASSHOLE...
NO, BUT ALL THE SAME. YOU GUYS DID YOUR PART, BUT HE FREAKED OUT AND NOW OUR MILLION BUCKS IS AT THE BOTTOM OF A CANYON.

YEAH, BUT YOU AIN'T.
MM?
HELL, ME AN' TULIP'D RATHER HAVE OUR BEST FRIEND ALIVE THAN A LOUSY MILLION DOLLARS ANYDAY, RIGHT?

RIGHT.

THANKS, YOU GUYS.

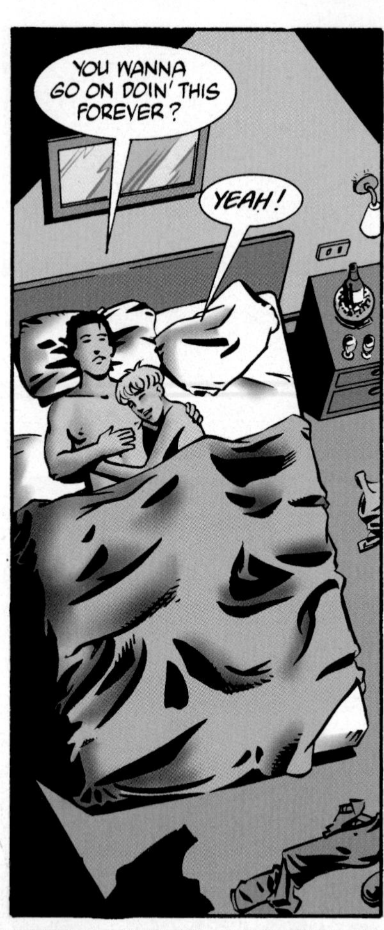
YOU WANNA GO ON DOIN' THIS FOREVER?
YEAH!

I MEANT THE CARS...
OH.

WAY I SEE IT, WE KEEP ON STEALIN' TO MAKE A LIVIN' AN' MIXIN' WITH TRASH LIKE LANGTRY--WELL, SOONER OR LATER SOMEONE'S GONNA GET HURT THAT DON'T DESERVE IT...
MAYBE A FELLA CROSSIN' THE STREET, SOME OL' JOHNNY COP THROWS DOWN ON US...GONNA STOP BEIN' FUN REAL FAST AFTER THAT, BABY.

SUCH A WISE HEAD ON THOSE NOT EVEN TWENTY-YEAR-OLD SHOULDERS...!
JUST THINKIN'.
I KNOW. I'M GLAD. I DON'T WANT TO HURT ANYONE EITHER.

SHALL WE HAVE A DRINK TO GOING LEGIT?
YOU FINISH IT. DAMN STUFF GIVES ME GAS.

ALL THE MORE FOR ME!
EEEAAAGHH!

MOTE
YOU OKAY, AME?
HEY...
CAN'T SLEEP. SAW YOU STANDIN' OUT HERE ALL ON YOUR LONESOME.
YOU AIN'T STILL UPSET OVER THIS MORNIN', ARE YOU?
OH, IT ISN'T JUST THAT, IT... THANKS...
IT'S ME, JESSE. I JUST FEEL LIKE I'M SUCH A LOSER.
BULLSHIT...!
OH YEAH?
I PICKED THE BIGGEST WASTE OF SPACE SINCE GODZOOKY TO BE OUR GETAWAY DRIVER. I LET A MILLION DOLLARS ROLL OFF A MOUNTAIN. JESUS, I INHERITED EIGHT MILLION, AND I INVESTED IT IN A COMPANY WITH PLANS TO RELAUNCH BETAMAX...
I MEAN I'M THE ONE WHOSE FATHER WAS THE ONLY UNITED STATES SENATOR TO DIE PERFORMING CUNNILINGUS ON A TEN-DOLLAR CRACK WHORE! ELL-OH-ESS-EE-ARE!

COME AGAIN...?
OH, IT GOT COVERED UP...

HE LIKED TO PICK UP THESE SKINNY HOOKERS IN HIS LIMO, AND THIS ONE TIME HE HAD ONE LIKE BLOWING HIM AND ANOTHER ON HIS FACE, AND HE WAS PARKED IN FRONT OF THE CAPITOL BUILDING--
AND HE SUFFOCATED.

THEY WERE SO HIGH THEY DIDN'T EVEN NOTICE, I MEAN ISN'T THAT PATHETIC?
WELL, uh...er...
I'M THE WEAK LINK AROUND HERE, JESSE. IT'S IN MY BLOOD.

HEY, I DON'T WANNA HEAR NO MORE NONSENSE LIKE THAT...
YOU KNOW WHAT'S FUNNY? I USED TO THINK TULIP WAS THE WEAK ONE.

WHEN I FIRST MET HER I THOUGHT I'D HAVE TO LOOK AFTER HER. BUT NO, SHE'S STRONG AND FAST AND SHE ALWAYS KNOWS EXACTLY WHAT TO DO...
YOU AIN'T WEAK. YOU'RE SMART AN' FUNNY AN' PRETTY AS HELL--

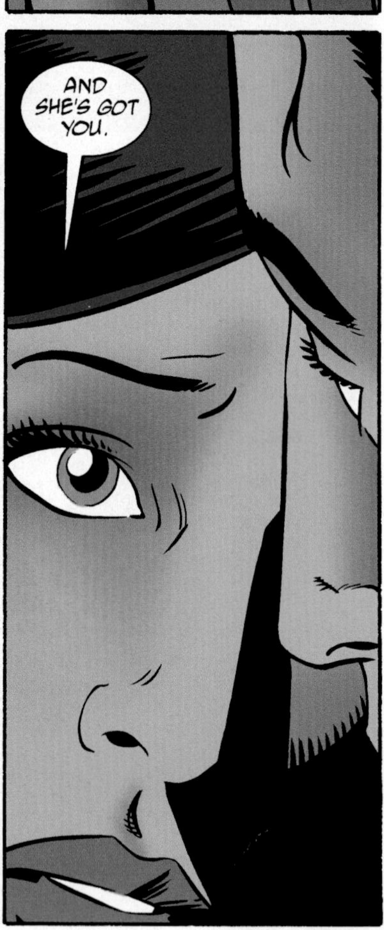
AND SHE'S GOT YOU.

WE CAN'T.
I KNOW.
WE REALLY CAN'T.

WE LOVE HER WAY TOO MUCH.

MOMENT OF MADNESS. SORRY.
DON'T BE. TAKES TWO.
C'MON, I'LL BUY YOU ONE OF THEM STUPID UMBRELLA DRINKS THE TWO OF YOU LIKE SO MUCH...

MORNIN'. HOW BAD Y'ALL WANNA STAY OUTTA JAIL?

SAY WHAT?
'SCUSE ME THERE, YOUNG LADY... THANK YOU KINDLY...
IT'S A SIMPLE QUESTION, SON.
I AIN'T YOUR GOD-DAMN SON, MISTER.

NO YOU AIN'T. WHAT YOU ARE, BOY, IS BEHIND ENOUGH COUNTS OF GRAND THEFT AUTO TO PUT YOU AWAY 'TIL THE HAIR ON YORE BALLS TURNS WHITE.
BEGGIN' YOU LADIES' PARDON.

SO... MISTER...
CAP'N TOM PICKETT, MA'AM.
TEXAS RANGERS.
OH GOD, OH GOD, THIS IS *REAL*...
AN' HOW LONG THE RANGERS BEEN RECRUITIN' IN NURSIN' HOMES, EXACTLY?
RETIRED, BOY. OR RETIRED AS I WANNA BE...
NOW I CAN SEE YOU'RE PLUMB FULLA SALT AN' THAT AIN'T NO BAD THING IN A FELLA YORE AGE. BUT YOU BETTER DAMPEN IT DOWN SOME, BOY, OR YOU AN' ME GONNA GO FIND OUT JUST HOW FAR I AM FROM THAT NURSIN' HOME.
AN' I DON'T THINK THAT'S SOMETHIN' YOU WANT THESE TWO PRETTY LITTLE THINGS TO SEE..
WOULDN'T DO NEITHER OF US NO GOOD, ANYHOW.
NOT WHEN WE CAN BE SO MUCH HELP TO EACH OTHER.

HOW?
MM? OH, WELL, LITTLE LADY, IT HAS TO DO WITH A MUTUAL ASSOCIATE OF OURS, A MISTER B.W. LANGTRY...

YOU KNOW THAT SON OF A BITCH?
SAD TO SAY. YOU HAPPEN TO RECALL-- 'FORE THINGS GOT UNCIVIL BETWEEN YOU AN' THAT TRASH OF HIS--HIM SAYIN' ANYTHING ABOUT HORSEFLESH?

HEY, YEAH...HE'S GOT A TRUCKLOAD OF STOLEN HORSES IN MULESHOE AND HE WANTS THEM MOVED, BUT JESSE WOULDN'T DO IT...
COMMENDABLE ATTITUDE, BOY.
WHY THANK YOU, OL' MAN.

Y'ALL DON'T MIND ME DOIN' THIS, DO YOU? HELPS ME RELAX, EVER SINCE MY DAUGHTER MADE ME QUIT THE SMOKES.
LANGTRY--AMONG A LOTTA BAD, BAD THINGS--IS WHAT THEY CALL A KILLER BUYER. HE PROCURES OLD, LAME HORSES FOR SLAUGHTER-HOUSES, WHO SHIP THE MEAT OUT TO FRANCE AN' BELGIUM AN' OTHER DENS OF SAVAGES WHERE IT'S CONSIDERED A DELICACY.

BUT THERE'S BOYS WILLIN' TO PAY EXTRA FOR YOUNG, TENDER HORSEFLESH, KIND YOU ONLY GET IF YOU'RE PREPARED TO STEAL IT. RUSTLIN', PLAIN AN' SIMPLE, JUST LIKE IN THE OL' DAYS.
THAT'S WHERE I COME IN.

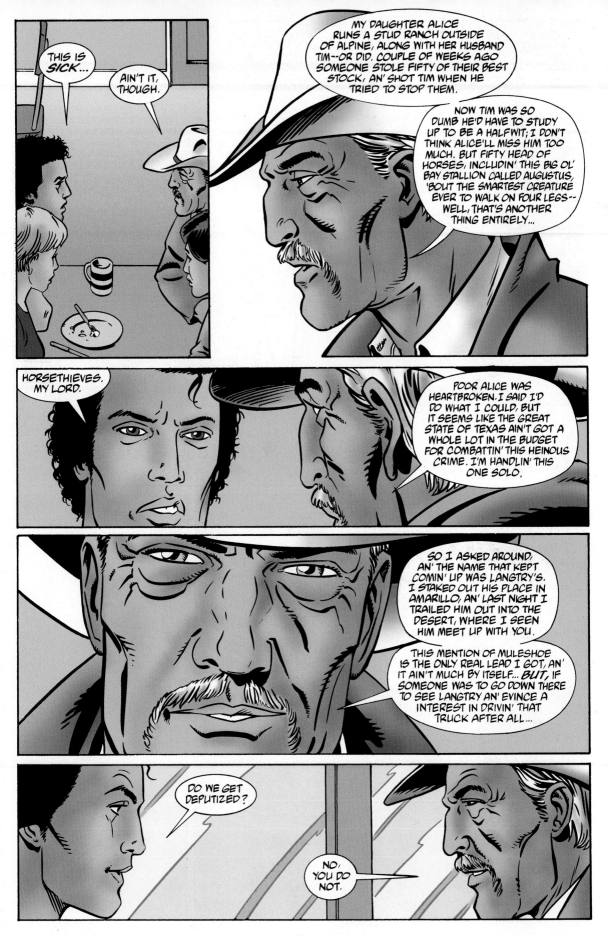

THIS IS SICK...
AIN'T IT, THOUGH.
MY DAUGHTER ALICE RUNS A STUD RANCH OUTSIDE OF ALPINE, ALONG WITH HER HUSBAND TIM--OR DID. COUPLE OF WEEKS AGO SOMEONE STOLE FIFTY OF THEIR BEST STOCK, AN' SHOT TIM WHEN HE TRIED TO STOP THEM.
NOW TIM WAS SO DUMB HE'D HAVE TO STUDY UP TO BE A HALFWIT; I DON'T THINK ALICE'LL MISS HIM TOO MUCH. BUT FIFTY HEAD OF HORSES, INCLUDIN' THIS BIG OL' BAY STALLION CALLED AUGUSTUS, 'BOUT THE SMARTEST CREATURE EVER TO WALK ON FOUR LEGS-- WELL, THAT'S ANOTHER THING ENTIRELY...

HORSETHIEVES. MY LORD.
POOR ALICE WAS HEARTBROKEN. I SAID I'D DO WHAT I COULD, BUT IT SEEMS LIKE THE GREAT STATE OF TEXAS AIN'T GOT A WHOLE LOT IN THE BUDGET FOR COMBATTIN' THIS HEINOUS CRIME. I'M HANDLIN' THIS ONE SOLO.

SO I ASKED AROUND, AN' THE NAME THAT KEPT COMIN' UP WAS LANGTRY'S. I STAKED OUT HIS PLACE IN AMARILLO, AN' LAST NIGHT I TRAILED HIM OUT INTO THE DESERT, WHERE I SEEN HIM MEET UP WITH YOU.
THIS MENTION OF MULESHOE IS THE ONLY REAL LEAD I GOT, AN' IT AIN'T MUCH BY ITSELF... BUT, IF SOMEONE WAS TO GO DOWN THERE TO SEE LANGTRY AN' EVINCE A INTEREST IN DRIVIN' THAT TRUCK AFTER ALL...

DO WE GET DEPUTIZED?
NO, YOU DO NOT.

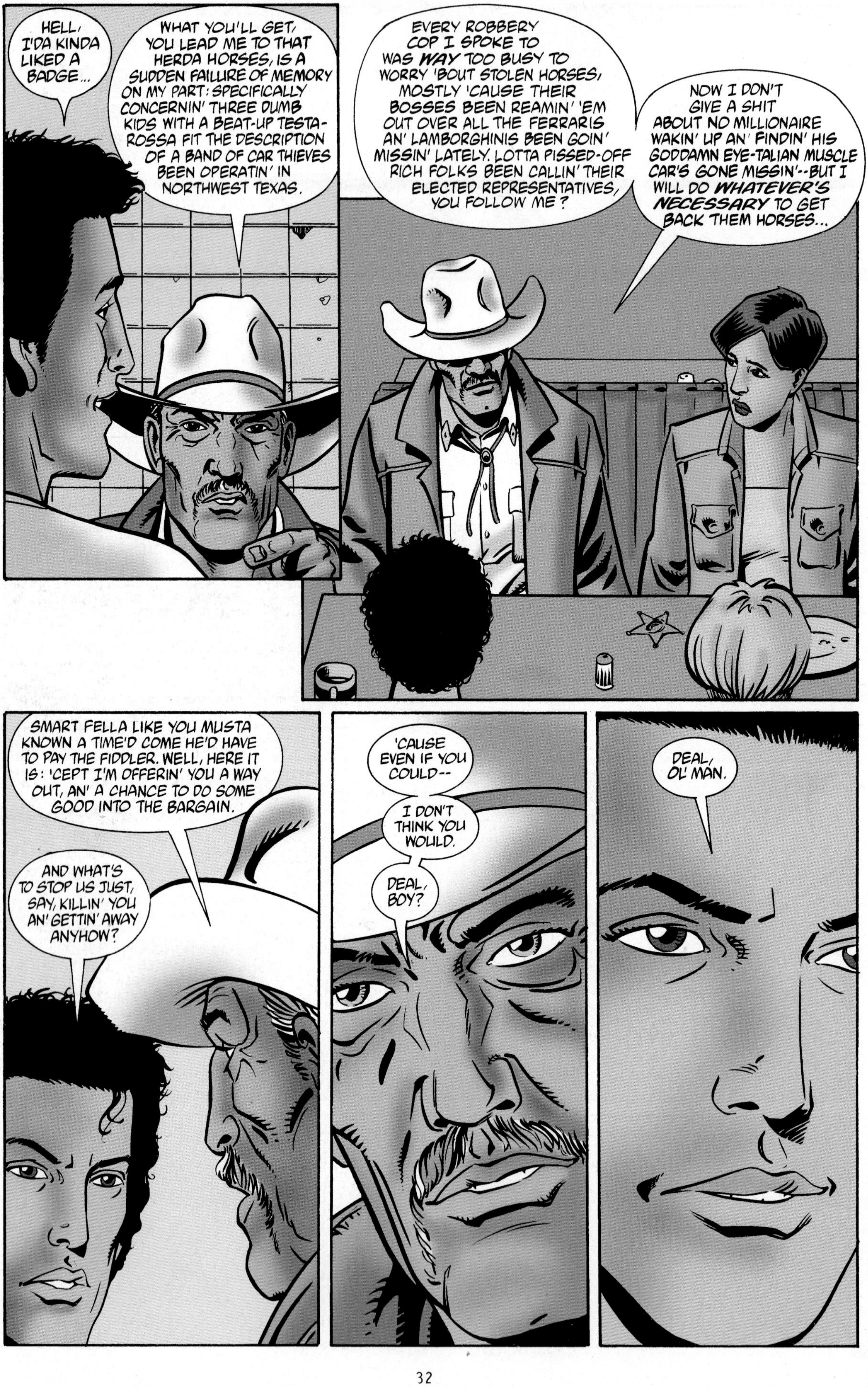

HELL, I'DA KINDA LIKED A BADGE...
WHAT YOU'LL GET, YOU LEAD ME TO THAT HERDA HORSES, IS A SUDDEN FAILURE OF MEMORY ON MY PART: SPECIFICALLY CONCERNIN' THREE DUMB KIDS WITH A BEAT-UP TESTA-ROSSA FIT THE DESCRIPTION OF A BAND OF CAR THIEVES BEEN OPERATIN' IN NORTHWEST TEXAS.

EVERY ROBBERY COP I SPOKE TO WAS ***WAY*** TOO BUSY TO WORRY 'BOUT STOLEN HORSES, MOSTLY 'CAUSE THEIR BOSSES BEEN REAMIN' 'EM OUT OVER ALL THE FERRARIS AN' LAMBORGHINIS BEEN GOIN' MISSIN' LATELY. LOTTA PISSED-OFF RICH FOLKS BEEN CALLIN' THEIR ELECTED REPRESENTATIVES, YOU FOLLOW ME?
NOW I DON'T GIVE A SHIT ABOUT NO MILLIONAIRE WAKIN' UP AN' FINDIN' HIS GODDAMN EYE-TALIAN MUSCLE CAR'S GONE MISSIN'--BUT I WILL DO ***WHATEVER'S NECESSARY*** TO GET BACK THEM HORSES...

SMART FELLA LIKE YOU MUSTA KNOWN A TIME'D COME HE'D HAVE TO PAY THE FIDDLER. WELL, HERE IT IS: 'CEPT I'M OFFERIN' YOU A WAY OUT, AN' A CHANCE TO DO SOME GOOD INTO THE BARGAIN.
AND WHAT'S TO STOP US JUST, SAY, KILLIN' YOU AN' GETTIN' AWAY ANYHOW?

'CAUSE EVEN IF YOU COULD--
I DON'T THINK YOU WOULD.
DEAL, BOY?

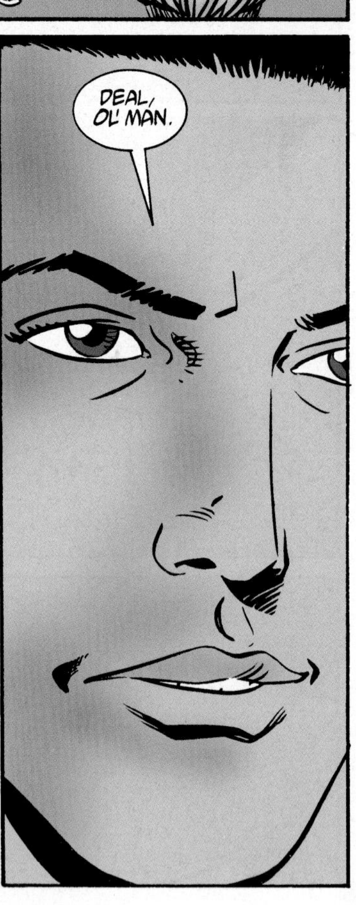

DEAL, OL' MAN.

♪
I THINK HE'S SWEET...

YEAH, ME TOO... HE'S GOT THAT KIND OF FAVORITE UNCLE THING GOING ON, EXCEPT SEXY...
MM...
WHAT?

PICKETT? HELL, THAT OL' BUZZARD AIN'T EVEN GONNA LAST ANOTHER WINTER! AN' DON'T LET THAT SMILIN', SPARKLIN'-EYED GOOD OL' BOY ACT FOOL YOU, 'CAUSE THAT SON OF A BITCH WAS READY TO COOK OUR GOOSE!
HE'S JUST LUCKY I'M PLAYIN' ALONG WITH HIS DAMN PLAN, THAT'S ALL. HE KNOWS I GOT HIM BUFFALOED...

THAT'S FUNNY, BECAUSE HE STRIKES ME AS THE KIND OF GUY YOU'D LIKE TO BE WHEN YOU GROW UP...
HOW YOU FIGURE THAT?

STRAIGHT OUT OF A MOVIE, MAN O' MINE.
ONE HUNDRED PERCENT COWBOY.

BULLSHIT...
SO WHY ARE YOU PLAYING ALONG WITH HIM, THEN? APART FROM TO KEEP US OUT OF PRISON?
IT'S...KINDA HARD TO EXPLAIN. IT'S THIS THING WITH THE HORSES.
IT JUST AIN'T RIGHT.
WHY MISS TOOLIP, AH DO DECLARE! DO Y'ALL THINK THIS MIGHT BE SOME SUTHAN THANG...?
WHY, AH DO BELIEVE YOU'RE RIGHT, MISS AMY...
YEAH, YEAH, LAUGH IT UP. YOU JUST DON'T WORRY YOUR PRETTY LITTLE HEADS ABOUT IT; I GOT EVERYTHING UNDER CONTROL...
SEE?
YOU ARE JUST LIKE THAT GUY...!
WELCOME TO MULESHOE
YOU SINNED IN A PREVIOUS LIFE

LANGTRY MENTION HOW YOU WERE S'POSED TO CONTACT HIM?
I GOT THE NUMBER OF HIS OFFICE HERE. EXCEPT... UH...

I'M GETTIN' THE FEELIN' I AIN'T GONNA NEED IT...

I'M GETTIN' THE SAME FEELIN'.

HOW'D YOU FIND US IN THE FIRST PLACE, LANGTRY?
BEEN TRAILIN' YOU ASSHOLES ALL DAY. WHO'S THE FOSSIL?
THIS HERE'S MR. METHUSELAH. I AIN'T THE FIRST CUSTER HE'S FOUGHT BESIDE, BUT THAT DON'T MAKE HIM NO FOSSIL.

REMEMBER THIS SHITBIRD?

WELL, YOU CAN FORGET HIM.

BOBBY--!

READY, BOY?

READY, OL' MAN.

JESUS!

THIS TIME, PUNK--

TULIP! GO! GO NOW!

GO, TULIP!
BUT--
THAT'S A MACHINE-GUN, AMY.

SKEDADDLE, BOY!
YEEEOW!

YOU OTHER ASSHOLES?
THEY'RE ON THEIR WAY.

THEM GIRLS BE WAITIN' FOR US?
OUT FRONT, YOU THINK YOU CAN MAKE IT THAT FAR...

LONG AS I DON'T DIE LAUGHIN'-- SHIT!
SHIT!

SHIT, SHIT, SHIT.
LATER

PLAIN TO SEE WHY YOU COME LOOKIN' FOR ME, RANGER.

ONE-MAN TASK FORCE, HUH?
CAME LOOKIN' FOR HORSETHIEVES, LANGTRY. YOU SURE SEEM TO FIT THE BILL.

MURDERIN' HORSETHIEVES, AFTER WHAT YOU DONE TO THAT BOY THIS AFTERNOON.
NO END TO MY AWFUL CRIMES.
WELL, I GUESS I OUGHTTA LET YOU TWO HEROES IN ON WHAT'S IN STORE FOR YOU.

THITH THON OF A BITTH ITH *MINE*, FOR THTARTERTH. AN' THITH TIME IN A *FAIR FIGHT*, HEAR?
I WAS YOU I'D CHEAT LIKE HELL, DONNY.
AN' SHUT UP.

AH...! OUR GUESTS HAVE ARRIVED, YES?
YES THEY HAVE, MR. VITCHY.

VICHY, M'SIEUR. VICHY.

NAPOLEON VICHY.

SO THESE ARE THE BIG, TOUGH COWBOYS WHO WOULD STAND AGAINST US, YES? FOOLS!

THE DINING TABLES OF BRUSSELS AND PARREE-- AH, PARREE! ARE CRYING OUT FOR FRESH, SUCCULENT YOUNG HORSEFLESH! M'SIEUR LANGTRY AND I HAVE A--HOW YOU SAY-- GOOD THING GOING HERE! WE ARE NOT ABOUT TO LET A PAIR OF MEDDLERS LIKE YOU DESTROY IT ALL!

ANYONE ELSE SMELL GARLIC...?
THIS GOOD THINGA YORES IS AGAINST THE LAW ROUND HERE, FAT BOY. MEANIN' I'M GONNA MEDDLE WHETHER YOU LIKE IT OR NOT.

YOU AMERICANS! WITH YOUR STUPID SENTIMENTALITY ABOUT HORSES! HOW WOULD YOU LIKE IT IF YOU SAT DOWN TO ONE OF YOUR BIG, JUICY STEAKS--AND IT WAS OLD AND TOUGH AND STRINGY, BECAUSE THE RESTAURANT WAS NOT ALLOWED TO BUY YOUNG COWS?
POO-POO ON YOUR LAW!

STUPID YANKEE COWBOY GUN... FEH...
WELL IF YOU FRENCH BOYS LIKE HORSE-MEAT SO MUCH, HOW COME YOU DON'T JUST RAISE YOUR OWN? IN PARIS OR WHATEVER?

PARREE! PAARRRCCH-RREEEEE!! NOT THIS PARISS!
YOU AMERICANS! WITH YOUR AWFUL, HARSH, GRATING ACCENTS! WHEN, OH WHEN WILL YOU LEARN TO SPEAK AS WE DO-- THE LANGUAGE OF LOVE!
YOU SPEAK GERMAN, MISTER?
UH? NO...
NO.
WE'RE WHY.
COCHON!
SON OF A BITCH--
YOU WANT SOME TOO, YOU PUNK? COME ON! FAISEZ MON JOUR!
WHOA THERE, MONSEWER.
I WAS JUST ABOUT TO TELL THESE BOYS WHAT THEY GOT COMIN'.

'KAY, CLOSE IT DOWN FOR THE NIGHT...
AN' ONCE WE CATCH THEM TWO BITCHES OF YORES? Y'ALL ARE GOIN' IN THERE TOO, BOYS.
JUST FOR LAUGHS AS MUCH AS ANYTHING ELSE.

UHHNNHH...
SHOT...SHOT A DOZEN SONS OF BITCHES WITH THAT DAMN PEACEMAKER. NEVER FIGURED ON IT ENDIN' UP KILLIN' ME.

YOU AIN'T KILLED.
HEH.
I'M GUTSHOT. MY OWN SHIT'S GONNA POISON ME TO DEATH.
GODDAMN, I WAS SO SURE I WAS GONNA BRING ALICE BACK HER HORSES...

AN' THAT BIG OL' FELLA WITH THE ONE WHITE EAR THERE? THAT'S AUGUSTUS.

RECKON I CAN TAKE CARE OF IT.

DON'T YOU MEAN, "I CAN TAKE CARE OF IT-- OL' MAN"?

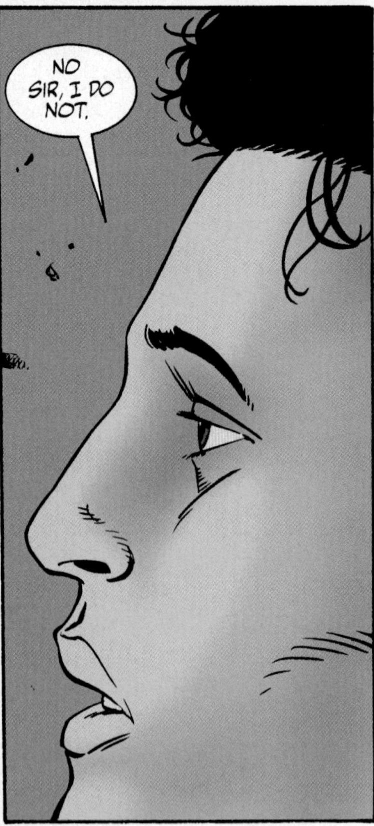
NO SIR, I DO NOT.

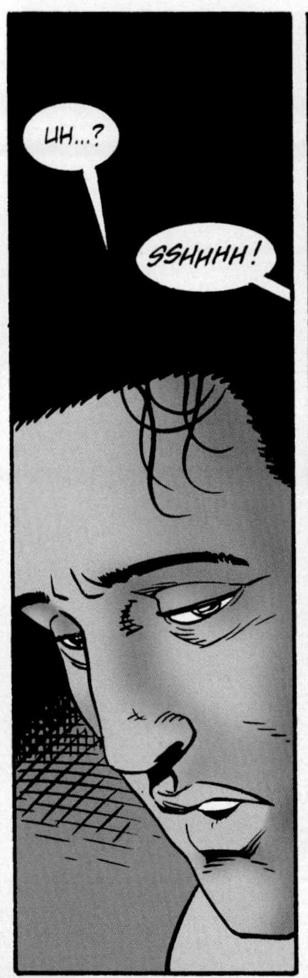
UH...?
SSHHHH!

MY LORD...
WE'VE BEEN WAITING OUTSIDE ALL NIGHT. THE DICKHEAD ON GUARD ONLY JUST FELL ASLEEP.
HURRY, TULIP!

YEAH, YOU HURRY UP, BITTH. UNTIE THAT BATHTARD.

ME AN' HIM THTILL GOT THOME BUITHNETH TO FINITH.

Y'ALL GIMME A MINUTE?

GUH--
GUH
GUH--
Y'KNOW...THAT BOY BOBBY, HE WAS DUMB AN' COWARDLY AN' KINDA WORTHLESS...

BUT ALL THE SAME, I GUESS THIS IS FOR HIM.

UNK--!
YEECH.
BOILK

CAN WE GO NOW? PLEASE?
IT'S TIME, CAP'N.
I SWEAR...

I WISH I COULD WAIT LONG ENOUGH TO SEE IT.
GIVE 'EM HELL.
MISTER CUSTER.

I WILL, SIR.

IS HE--?
NO...!
YES HE IS.

Y'ALL WANNA HELP ME SET THINGS RIGHT?

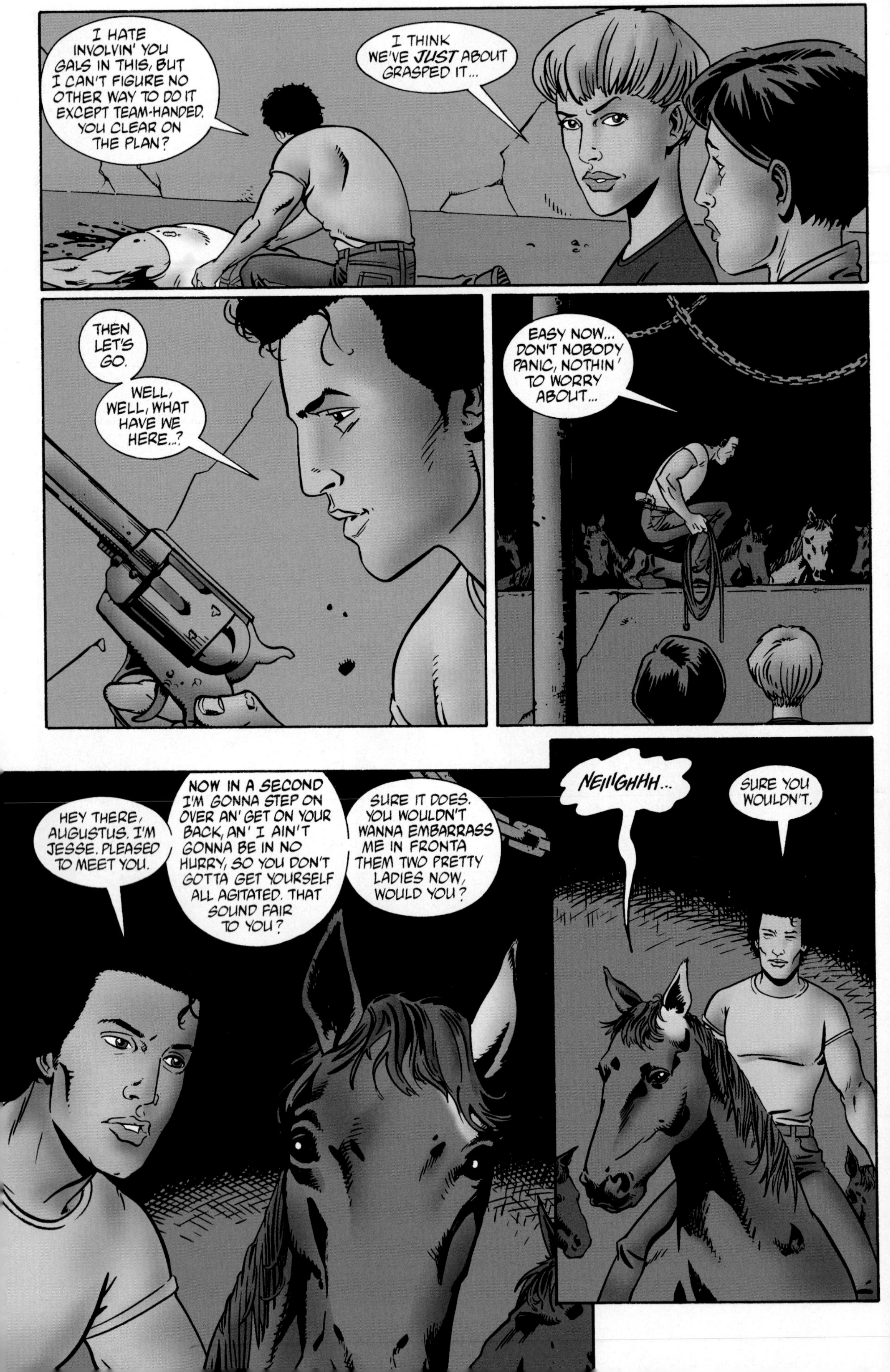

HEY THERE, AUGUSTUS. I'M JESSE. PLEASED TO MEET YOU.

NOW IN A *SECOND* I'M GONNA STEP ON OVER AN' GET ON YOUR BACK, AN' I AIN'T GONNA BE IN NO HURRY, SO YOU DON'T GOTTA GET YOURSELF ALL AGITATED. THAT SOUND FAIR TO YOU?

SURE IT DOES. YOU WOULDN'T WANNA EMBARRASS ME IN FRONTA THEM TWO PRETTY LADIES NOW, WOULD YOU?

NEIIIGHHH...

SURE YOU WOULDN'T.

THERE WE GO...
'KAY, BIG FELLA, THERE'S GONNA BE SOME SHOOTIN' NOW, BUT THAT AIN'T GONNA WORRY YOU, AM I RIGHT?
NEEIIIGHHH...
WHY ARE YOU TALKING TO A HORSE?
SOUTHERN THING.
HERE COMES ANOTHER'N.
LANGTRY! VICHY! COME OUT HERE, YOU SONS OF WHORES!!
YOU HEAR ME, ASSHOLES? IT'S TIME TO MEET YOUR MAKER!
WHAT IN THE NAME OF ALL THAT'S GALLIC--?
CUSTER?

NOW!
HYAH! HYAH!
HYAHH!!

... SHIT.

S-SACRE BLEU--!

YOU DO SOMETHIN' FOR ME, HONEY? YOU FIND A PHONE AN' CALL THE COPS, LET 'EM KNOW THERE'S A HERDA STOLEN HORSES OUT HERE NEED RETURNIN' TO THEIR OWNERS?
YOU GOT IT.
YOU BETTER HIGHTAIL IT 'FORE THEY SHOW UP. MEET ME IN FRONTA THE TOWN HALL IN ALPINE, THE DAY AFTER TOMORROW, SAY.

WHAT ABOUT YOU?
GONNA TAKE OL' GUS BACK TO THE CAP'N'S DAUGHTER. 'FORE I DO THAT, THOUGH...

THERE'S THREE HUNDRED POUNDSA GARLIC-SCENTED LARD OVER HERE THAT I STILL GOTTA HAVE WORDS WITH.

HE IS CRAZY...
HE'S MY COWBOY.

SO HERE'S HOW IT IS, MONSEWER...

HUNDRED YEARS OR MORE AGO HERE IN TEXAS, YOU STOLE A FELLA'S HORSE AN' YOU DID MORE'N JUST TAKE AWAY HIS TRANSPORT OR HIS LIVELIHOOD. YOU ALL BUT CONDEMNED HIM TO DEATH.
YOU LIKE AS NOT STRANDED HIM IN THE DESERT, SEE, ALL ALONE IN A HOSTILE WILDERNESS FULLA SNAKES AN' SPIKES AN' VICIOUS CRITTERS AN' INJUNS READY TO SCALP HIM...
WH-WH-WHAT ARE YOU GOING TO DO TO ME?

HEY, NOW DON'T INTERRUPT.
WITHOUT HIS HORSE HE WAS GOOD AS DEAD. WASN'T NO BREAKDOWN SERVICE HE COULD CALL--HELL, WASN'T EVEN NO HIGHWAY. AN' THERE SURE AS SHIT WASN'T NO GODDAMN INSURANCE, NEITHER...
SO STEALIN' HORSES WAS TAKEN PRETTY DAMN SERIOUSLY BACK IN THEM DAYS.

AN' HORSE-THIEVES...
WELL, THE OUTLOOK FOR THEM WAS GENERALLY KINDA BLEAK.

OH MY GOD.
YOU WOULDN'T.

I CANNOT BELIEVE YOU ARE GOING TO DO THIS...!
♪
JESUS CHRIST, YOU ARE! WAIT! I'LL MAKE AMENDS! I'LL DO ANYTHING!
PLEASE! I DON'T WANT TO DIE LIKE THIS! I'LL BE LESS FRENCH! ANYTHING! PLEASE!
AUGUSTUS--
HYAHH!!
AAK--!
AAAAH-- UUUHH--
HHHHHHHHH...

RRTCCCHHH!
PSSSS

ARRSSHH...!
PSSQUU
PSSSSSHHH!

PSSSS
QQQUAARRSSH..!
BBLLP

DAMNED IF THAT DON'T LOOK LIKE JUSTICE TO ME.

SO AUGUSTUS, I GOT KIND OF A QUESTION I BEEN WONDERIN' ABOUT, COULD USE A LITTLE ADVICE.

IF YOU WERE WITH THIS GAL--WELL, THIS MARE IN YOUR CASE, BUT YOU GET THE IDEA--AN' YOU LOVED HER MORE DEARLY'N ANYTHING IN THE WORLD... AN' YET SHE HAD THIS FRIEND WHO WAS REAL CUTE, AN' THEY WERE REAL CLOSE, AN' EVERYTHING WAS REAL FRIENDLY BETWEEN THE THREE OF YOU...
WOULD YOU--SEEIN' AS IT'S BEEN A FANTASY YOU HAD EVER SINCE YOU WERE OLD ENOUGH TO JERK OFF, AN' YOU TRY YOUR BEST TO BE A REAL STAND-UP GUY BUT JESUS, YOU'RE ONLY HUMAN--WOULD YOU JEOPARDIZE EVERYTHING YOU'VE GOT WITH THE FIRST GAL, WHO YOU ARE TRULY IN LOVE WITH, AS OPPOSED TO THE SECOND GAL, WHO YOU JUST THINK IS REAL SWEET--

BY TRYIN' TO GET 'EM BOTH IN THE SACK WITH YOU AT THE SAME TIME?

NEEIIIGHHH...

NOPE.

NEITHER WOULD I.

GLENN FABRY
·99·

"Funny thing 'bout Cassidy.
All ya ever gotta say's the bastard's name."

TWO MILLION, NINE HUNDRED AND NINETY-NINE THOUSAND, NINE HUNDRED AND NINETY-*SEVEN*...
TWO MILLION, NINE HUNDRED AND NINETY-NINE THOUSAND, NINE HUNDRED AND NINETY-*EIGHT*...

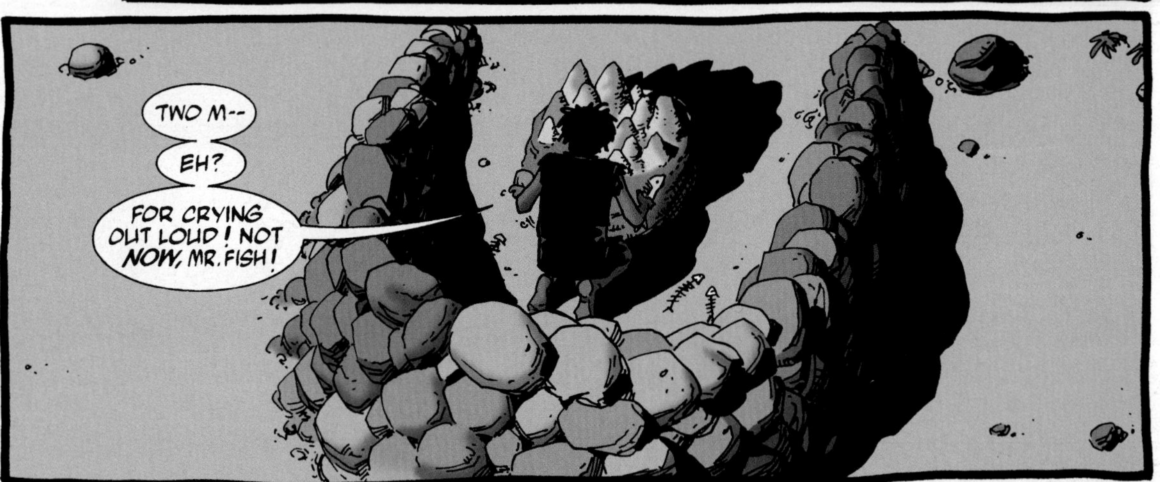
TWO M--
EH?
FOR CRYING OUT LOUD! NOT *NOW*, MR. FISH!

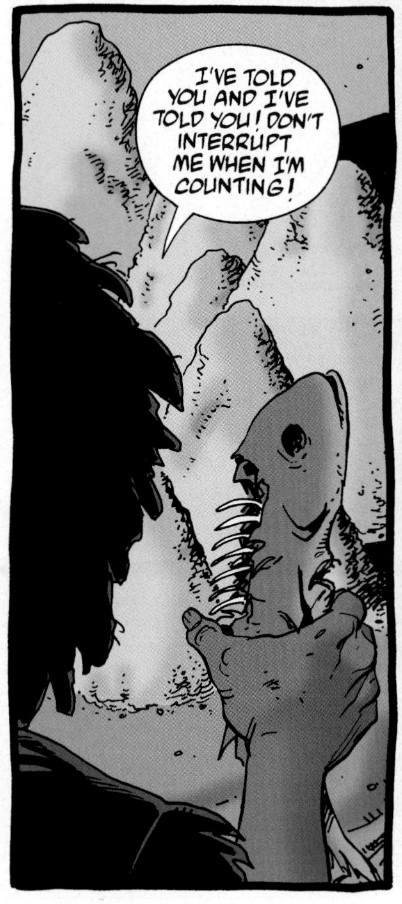
I'VE TOLD YOU AND I'VE TOLD YOU! DON'T INTERRUPT ME WHEN I'M COUNTING!

AND THE SAME GOES FOR YOU, MR. ROCK! DON'T BOTHER ME, NOT WHEN I'M SO CLOSE!

OKAY... EASY NOW...
TWO MILLION, NINE HUNDRED AND NINETY-NINE THOUSAND, NINE HUNDRED AND NINETY-*NINE*...
OH MY GOD--

HARBINGER

GARTH ENNIS - Writer STEVE DILLON - Artist
PAMELA RAMBO - Colorist CLEM ROBINS - Letterer AXEL ALONSO - Editor
PREACHER created by GARTH ENNIS and STEVE DILLON

NEW YORK CITY:
McSORLEY'S OLD ALE HOUSE
ESTABLISHED 1854

I CAN NEVER SAY GOODBYE, JESSE.

FATHER?
CLOSE. I'LL TAKE A BEER.
SOME KIND OF, uh, BAPTIST OR SOMETHIN'?
OR SOME-THIN'. HELL OF A PLACE YOU GOT HERE.
IT USED TO BE. TIME WAS ANYONE WAS ANYONE DRANK HERE. NOW IT'S MOSTLY TOURISTS OR KIDS FROM N.Y.U.
BUT THERE WAS A TIME WHEN THIS PLACE WAS SOMETHIN', ALL RIGHT.
MUCH OBLIGED... YOU WORKED HERE A WHILE, HUH?
AH, ABOUT TEN YEARS. USED TO COME IN HERE AS A KID, TOO.
THAT A FACT.
SAY, MAYBE YOU CAN HELP ME OUT, OR MAYBE YOU KNOW SOMEONE CAN. YOU EVER HEARD OF A GUY USED TO DRINK IN HERE A LONG TIME AGO...
A GUY BY THE NAME OF CASSIDY?

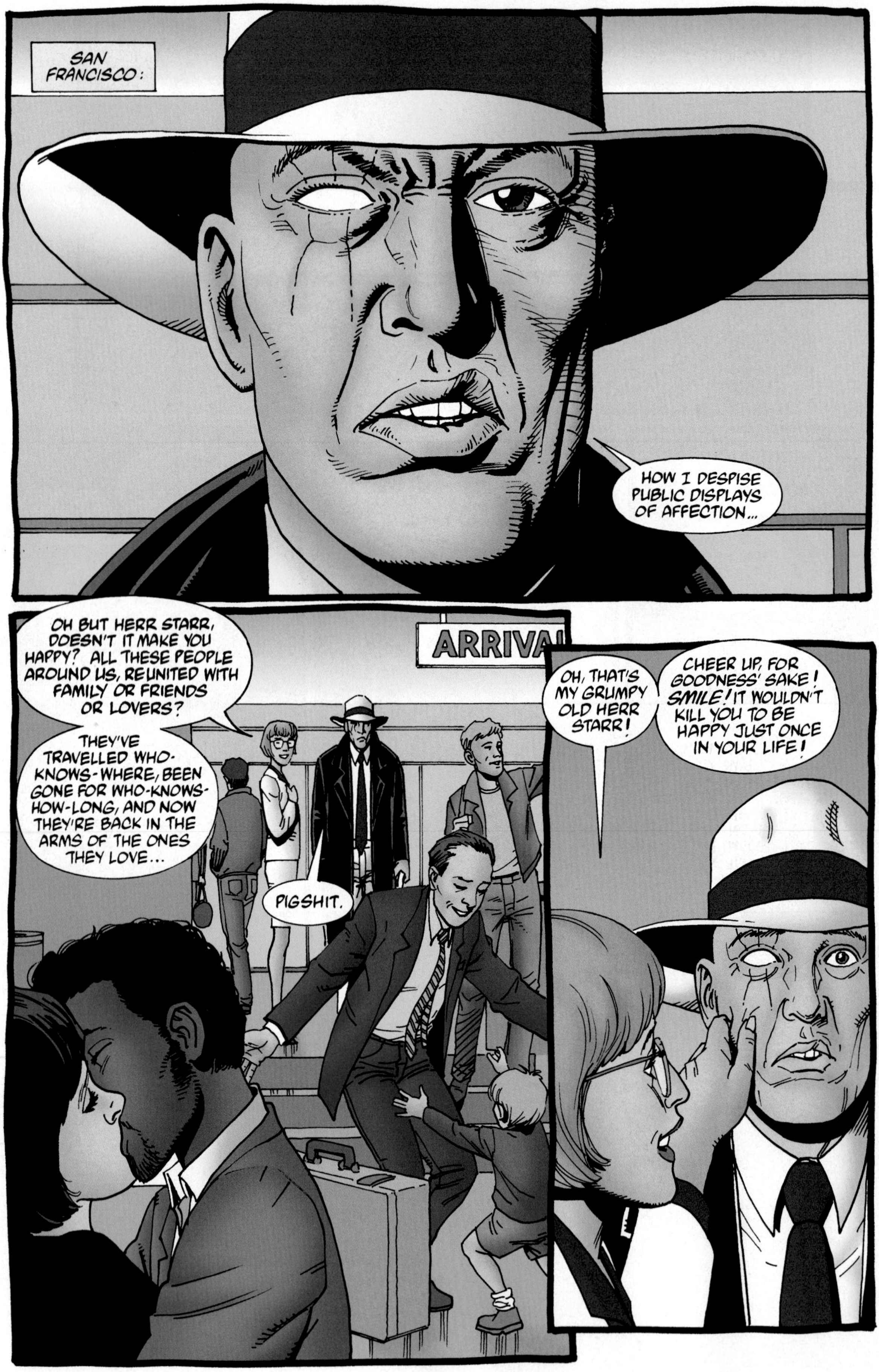

SAN FRANCISCO:

HOW I DESPISE PUBLIC DISPLAYS OF AFFECTION...

ARRIVA

OH BUT HERR STARR, DOESN'T IT MAKE YOU HAPPY? ALL THESE PEOPLE AROUND US, REUNITED WITH FAMILY OR FRIENDS OR LOVERS?

THEY'VE TRAVELLED WHO-KNOWS-WHERE, BEEN GONE FOR WHO-KNOWS-HOW-LONG, AND NOW THEY'RE BACK IN THE ARMS OF THE ONES THEY LOVE...

PIGSHIT.

OH, THAT'S MY GRUMPY OLD HERR STARR!

CHEER UP, FOR GOODNESS' SAKE! *SMILE!* IT WOULDN'T KILL YOU TO BE HAPPY JUST ONCE IN YOUR LIFE!

FEATHERSTONE, DON'T TELL ME WHAT TO DO--
LET ME SEE, AIR FRANCE PASSENGERS HAVE TO PASS THROUGH IMMIGRATION FIRST... I THINK WE NEED TO BE AT THE OTHER END OF THE TERMINAL...
FEATHERSTONE--!
OOPS! I'M SORRY, I FORGOT ABOUT YOUR POOR LEG!
NEVER MIND MY FUCKING LEG! WHAT'S GOT INTO YOU?
WHO IS THIS WE'RE HERE TO MEET AGAIN?
IT'S SOME WORTH-LESS CRUMB OF DICKCHEESE Le SAINT MARIE HAVE SENT TO LOOK INTO THE MONUMENT VALLEY THING, AND IF THOSE CLOWNS THINK THEY CAN QUESTION THE ACTIONS OF THEIR OWN ALLFATHER THEY CAN FUCK-ING THINK AGAIN.
"WE ARE PERTURBED AT SUCH UNUSUALLY OVERT ACTION INVOLVING THE SACRIFICE OF IRREPLACEABLE MUNITIONS AND MANPOWER FOR NO APPRECIABLE GAIN"--I'LL SEND THEIR FUCKING ERRAND BOY BACK WITH TWO FEET OF WOODEN LEG JAMMED UP HIS ARSEHOLE; WE'LL SEE HOW FUCK-ING PERTURBED THEY ARE THEN...
I DIDN'T THINK THERE WAS ENOUGH OF THE GRAIL HIERARCHY LEFT TO CAUSE YOU ANY REAL TROUBLE.
THERE ISN'T. AS ONE VERY JETLAGGED CATAMITE IS ABOUT TO DISCOVER.

JESUS, NOT AGAIN! OUT!
GIMME A BEER, FUCK YA!

YOU KNOW YOU AIN'T ALLOWED IN HERE, GODDAMMIT! OUT! GET OUT NOW!
I AIN'T SUCKIN' YA DICK! HEHHHN!

WANTS ME TO SUCK HIS DICK! KEEP YA FUCKIN' BEER!
I'M GONNA CALL THE COPS AN' HAVE 'EM BUST YOUR ASS! I'M GONNA HAVE 'EM SHOOT YOU!
HEHHHN! HEHHHN!

...NO, SORRY, I DUNNO ANYONE COULD HELP YOU. IT'S LIKE I SAID, WE MOSTLY GET KIDS IN HERE NOW.
GUYS USED TO DRINK IN HERE'RE SCATTERED TO HELL AN' GONE.

LOOKIN' FER CASSIDY?

LOOKIN' FOR SOMEONE MIGHT KNOW HIM.
UH-HUH. UH-HUH.
SAYIN' YOU DO, HUH?

CASSIDY USETA DRINK INNA PLACE HERE, UH-HUH. GIMME FIVE BUCKS.
'FRAID YOU NEED TO NARROW IT DOWN SOME.
SO LONG.

CASSIDY CAME ONNA BOAT FROM IRELAND 'BOUT A HUNNERD YEAZ AGO, USETA DRINK INNA PLACE HERE WITH MICK McCANN ANNA CREW. CASSIDY THE FUCKIN' CRAZY MAN, AWAYZ *LOOKIT ME, LOOKIT ME...*
CASSIDY CAN'T GO OUT INNA SUN.

HEHHHN.
FUNNY THING 'BOUT CASSIDY.

ALL YA EVER GOTTA SAY'S THE BASTARD'S NAME.

YOU ARE APPROACHING THE END OF THE MOVING WALKWAY. PLEASE BE READY TO PUSH YOUR TROLLEY, OVER THE RAMP.
YOU ARE APPROACHING THE END OF THE MOVING WALKWAY. PLEASE BE READY TO PUSH YOUR TROLLEY, OVER THE RAMP.
YOU ARE APPROACHING THE END OF THE MOVING WALKWAY. PLEASE BE READY TO PUSH YOUR TROLLEY, OVER THE RAMP.
YOU ARE APPROACHING THE END OF THE MOVING WALKWAY. PLEASE BE READY TO PUSH YOUR TROLLEY, OVER THE RAMP.
YOU ARE APPROACHING THE END OF THE MOVING WALKWAY. PLEASE BE READY TO PUSH YOUR TROLLEY, OVER THE RAMP.
MOVING WALKWAY, GRANNY FUCK! NOT MOVING FUCKING STANDWAY!!

IT'S OKAY, EVERYONE! DON'T BE ALARMED! WE'RE SHOOTING A MOVIE!

THAT'S PATRICK STEWART AND BRAD PITT! EVERYTHING'S FINE!

YOU ARE APPROACHING THE END OF THE MOVING WALKWAY. PLEASE BE READY TO **PUSH** YOUR TROLLEY, **OVER** THE RAMP.

GATES 11 TO 20

YOU ARE APPROACHING THE END OF THE MOVING WALKWAY. PLEASE BE READY TO **PUSH** YOUR TROLLEY, **OVER** THE RAMP.

YOU ARE APPROACHING THE END OF THE KKRRRRZZZZZZTTTT

ARE YOU INSANE? YOU CAN'T GO AROUND DOING THINGS LIKE THAT!
I CAN DO ANYTHING, FEATHER-STONE.

I'M THE MOST POWERFUL MAN IN THE WORLD.

YES... TRUE...
AND THE GRAIL IS THE BEST-KEPT SECRET IN THE WORLD, ISN'T IT? BUT IT WON'T BE FOR MUCH LONGER IF YOU START TERRORIZING INTERNATIONAL AIRPORTS...

BOLLOCKS. I COULD DRIVE A BIG RED-AND-WHITE TRUCK THROUGH HERE WITH OFFICIAL SPONSORS: ARMAGEDDON 2000 PAINTED ON IT, AND THESE SHEEP WOULDN'T BAT A BLOODY EYELID. THE ONLY CONSPIRACIES THEY TAKE SERIOUSLY THEY SEE ON THE FUCKING X-FILES.
RIGHT, WHERE IS THIS ARSEHOLE?

AH.
GATE 11

THIS WON'T TAKE A SECOND. A QUICK BOLLOCKING TO PUT THE FEAR OF HOLY FUCK IN HIM, AND ONCE HE'S PISSED OFF BACK TO HIS PLANE WE CAN GO AND HAVE A BITE TO--

EISENSTEIN

WHAT IS IT WITH THIS DOG? LOOK AT HIM, HE'S GOT A FACE LIKE A TEDDY BEAR...!
WUFF!
A BIG, DOPEY TEDDY BEAR, *YES*...
TYPICAL MALE. GETTING BY ON HIS LOOKS.

LITTLE EARLY FOR SEARING INSIGHT, ISN'T IT?
KINDLY LEAVE ME TO MY WRETCHED ENNUI. YOU'RE JUST SMUG BECAUSE YOU HAVEN'T TOUCHED CIGARETTES OR ALCOHOL IN OVER A MONTH.

LET'S NOT FORGET ALL THE GREAT SEX I'M HAVING...
LET'S *NOT*...

MEANWHILE THE NICEST GUY *I'VE* MET IN ABOUT FIVE YEARS HAS HAD HIS SCROTUM CHEMICALLY DISINTEGRATED. THERE'S FUCKING IRONY FOR YOU.

THE HELL WITH IT. I SHALL BECOME A BITTER, TWISTED HAG WITH NOTHING BUT ROUGE AND ONE-LINERS TO DISGUISE THE EMPTINESS OF MY EXISTENCE, AND I SHALL DROWN THE MEMORY OF NUMEROUS LOVELESS AFFAIRS IN A TSUNAMI OF VODKA.
I THINK GIN'S MORE TRADITIONAL.
IT REALLY IS GREAT OF YOU TO LET US STAY HERE, AMY. DON'T THINK WE DON'T APPRECIATE IT.
AH, YOU GUYS PULL YOUR WEIGHT. AND YOU'RE GOOD COMPANY FOR THIS PATHETIC OLD MAID.
WHERE IS JESSE, ANYWAY? I THOUGHT THE TWO OF YOU WOULD'VE BEEN ON THE ROAD AGAIN BY NOW.
ME TOO. BUT I MEAN WE NEVER THOUGHT WE'D SEE EACH OTHER AGAIN; MOST OF THE TIME WE CAN'T EVEN GET OUT OF BED--
RIGHT...
JESSE TALKS ABOUT GETTING ON WITH THE JOB, BUT... IT'S CASSIDY.
TO ME THE WHOLE THING IS JUST THIS HORROR THAT I WANT TO PUT BEHIND ME. TO JESSE IT'S MORE LIKE A MYSTERY--YOU KNOW, HOW COULD HE HAVE LET SOMEONE THAT BAD GET SO CLOSE TO HIM?
AND NOW HE CAN'T GO ON UNTIL HE'S GOTTEN TO THE BOTTOM OF IT.
HONEY, HE SAID--
THAT SON OF A BITCH IS UNDER MY SKIN LIKE A CHIGGER.

BLESSED ARE WE.
ALLFATHER STARR.

...
RIGHT.

IT HAS BEEN A LONG TIME. MANY THINGS HAVE CHANGED. MY VISIT HERE CONCERNS THEM ALL.
I HAVE SOME RESEARCH TO CONDUCT.
THEN WE SHOULD TALK.

WE PROBABLY SHOULD.
GOOD.

MY AIDE AND I HAVE SOMETHING TO COLLECT BEFORE PROCEEDING TO OUR LODGINGS. I WOULD BE GRATEFUL FOR YOUR COMPANY ON THE JOURNEY, ALLFATHER STARR.
VERY WELL.

THE FEMALE TOO.

HOW THE FUCK CAN HE STILL BE ALIVE? HE LOOKED ABOUT A HUNDRED WHEN I MET HIM!
WHO IS HE?
NO ADMITTANCE

HE'S THE MAN WHO INITIATED ME INTO THE GRAIL.
HALF OF EVERYTHING I KNOW I LEARNED FROM HIM.

I WAS SACRED EXECUTIONER. I WAS SUPPOSED TO BE THE ALLFATHER'S RIGHT-HAND MAN, BUT ALL I EVER REALLY DID WAS BUMP PEOPLE OFF.
IT WAS EISENSTEIN WHO SET THEM UP FOR ME. HE GATHERED THE DATA. HE KNEW EVERYTHING. IT WAS THANKS TO HIM THAT D'ARONIQUE'S GRIP ON THE GRAIL WAS ABSOLUTE.
I HADN'T HEARD FROM HIM IN YEARS; I ASSUMED HE'D POPPED HIS CLOGS. THAT'S WHY I FELT CONFIDENT ENOUGH TO MAKE THE MOVES I DID...

BUT YOU'RE ALLFATHER NOW. YOU CAN JUST TELL HIM TO GO HOME.
USE YOUR HEAD, FEATHERSTONE. IF I DO THAT TO HIM THE WANKERS IN LeSAINT MARIE WILL KNOW SOMETHING'S UP.
MASADA, THE VALLEY, SEIZING CONTROL--ONE MORE FOOT WRONG AND I CAN KISS GOODBYE TO THE GRAIL'S FUNDS AND RESOURCES. AND THEN I'LL BE ALLFATHER OF SWEET FUCK ALL.

THAT'S HOW THE LITTLE TURD WORKS, MANIPULATING POWER TO--
JESUS FUCKING CHRIST.

HHRRRR
HRRRRR
HHRRRR
TANCE

HER NAME IS *JEZEBEL*.
MY AIDE IS ALSO HER KEEPER. BEFORE HE JOINED THE GRAIL HE WAS A CAPTAIN IN SOVIET SPECIAL FORCES.

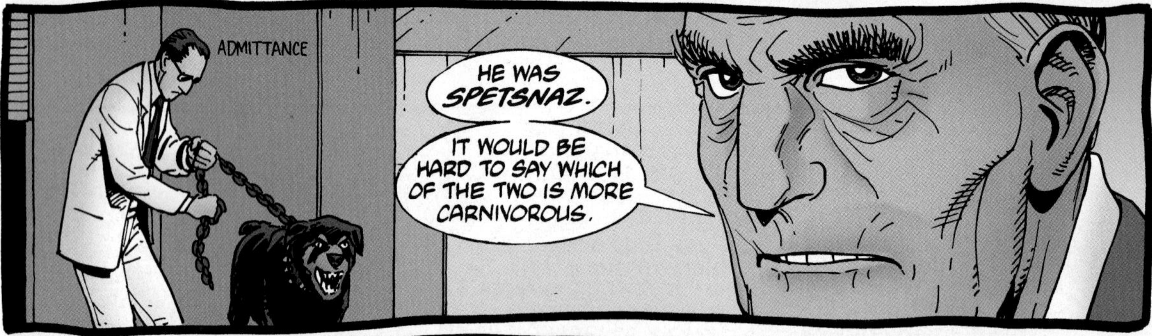
ADMITTANCE
HE WAS *SPETSNAZ*.
IT WOULD BE HARD TO SAY WHICH OF THE TWO IS MORE CARNIVOROUS.

I HAVE LOOKED LIKE THIS SINCE I WAS TWELVE.

ALLFATHER STARR.

NAME'S SALLY. AIN'T GONNA SHAKE HANDS, JUST WIPED MY ASS WITH MINE.

HHEHHN!
HOW D'YOU KNOW HIM?

KNEW 'EM ALL. BEEN GOIN' IN THERE ALL MY LIFE.
BEEN EATIN' OUTTA THE TRASH OUT-SIDE IT LAST TEN YEAZ, BUT YA KNOW WHADDA MEAN.
McSORLEY'S
ESTABLISHED

HOW DO YOU KNOW HIM?
...

MESSED YA UP, HUH? MONEY OR WOMAN?
HHEHHN!

NOW: YA SAID YA WANNADA FIND SOMEONE KNOWS HIM, NOT FIND *HIM*. SO WHAT YA REALLY WANNIZ TO KNOW *'BOUT HIM*.

HE TOL' YA A BUNCHA STUFF 'BOUT HIMSELF AN' THEN YA FOUND OUT WHADDA SONUVABITCH HE IS, AN' NOW YA WANNA KNOW THE TRUTH.
RIGHT?

RIGHT.

THAT'S CASSIDY. THAT'S HIS FUCKIN' TRICK.
WHAT YOU GONNA DO TO HIM YA EVER SEE HIM AGAIN?

...
HHEHHN!
THAT'S HIS OTHER FUCKIN' TRICK.

GETS YA TO FUCKIN' LOVE HIM AN' THEN STABZ YA INNA BACK. LOVE HIM SO MUCH YA DON'T BELIEVE HE DID IT. BLOOD ALL OVER YA, BIG FUCKIN' KNIFE IN YA BACK, AN' YA DON'T BELIEVE HE DID IT.
MAYBE HEZ SICK. MAYBE IT WASN'T HIM, JUST LOOKED LIKE HIM. MAYBE HE MADE A MISTAKE.
GIMME FIVE BUCKS AN' MEET ME HERE LUNCHTIME TOMORRA.

CAN'T WE TALK NOW?
TIRED. GONNA GET A BEER AN' GO TO SLEEP.
GIMME FIVE BUCKS.
LISTEN, TAKE THIS. GET A ROOM, STAY OUTTA THE COLD...
PROTECTIN' YER INVESTMENT? HHEHHN!
JUST GONNA GET MORE BEER. SLEEP INNA SUBWAY, SAME AS AWAYZ.
BUT I'M GONNA BE HERE TOMORRA. AIN'T GONNA CROAK ON YA.
GONNA TELL YA 'BOUT HIM.
'BOUT THE PEOPLE HE LOVED AN' THE PEOPLE LOVED HIM, AN' ALLA THE HAPPY, HAPPY NIGHTS, AN' THE SMACK AN' THE HELL 'ROUND THE BACKA THE BARS...
ALLA THE STUFF HE LEFT OUT.
HHEHHN!

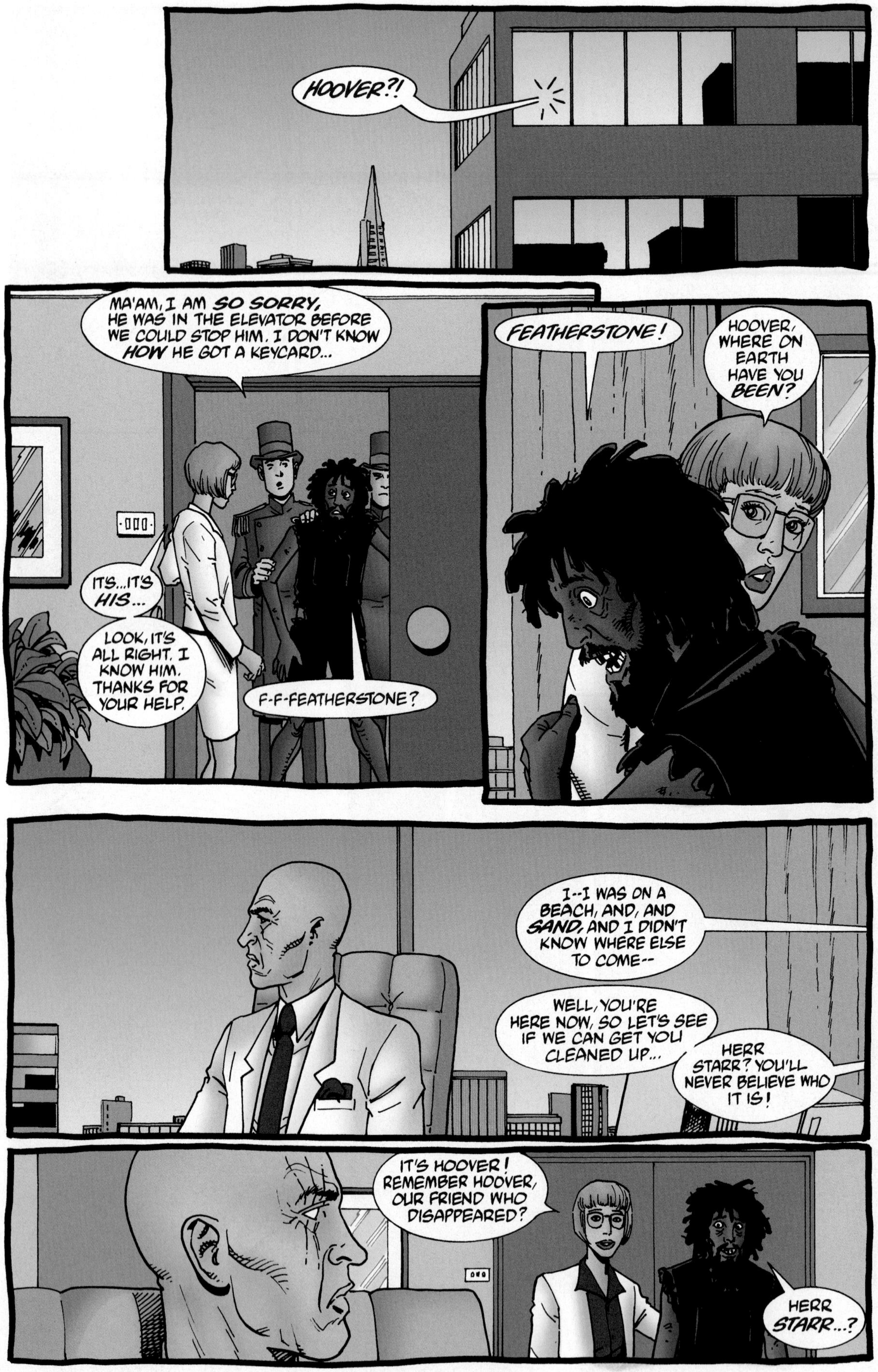

HOOVER?!

MA'AM, I AM SO SORRY, HE WAS IN THE ELEVATOR BEFORE WE COULD STOP HIM. I DON'T KNOW HOW HE GOT A KEYCARD...
IT'S...IT'S HIS...
LOOK, IT'S ALL RIGHT. I KNOW HIM. THANKS FOR YOUR HELP.
F-F-FEATHERSTONE?
FEATHERSTONE!
HOOVER, WHERE ON EARTH HAVE YOU BEEN?

I--I WAS ON A BEACH, AND, AND SAND, AND I DIDN'T KNOW WHERE ELSE TO COME--
WELL, YOU'RE HERE NOW, SO LET'S SEE IF WE CAN GET YOU CLEANED UP...
HERR STARR? YOU'LL NEVER BELIEVE WHO IT IS!
IT'S HOOVER! REMEMBER HOOVER, OUR FRIEND WHO DISAPPEARED?
HERR STARR...?

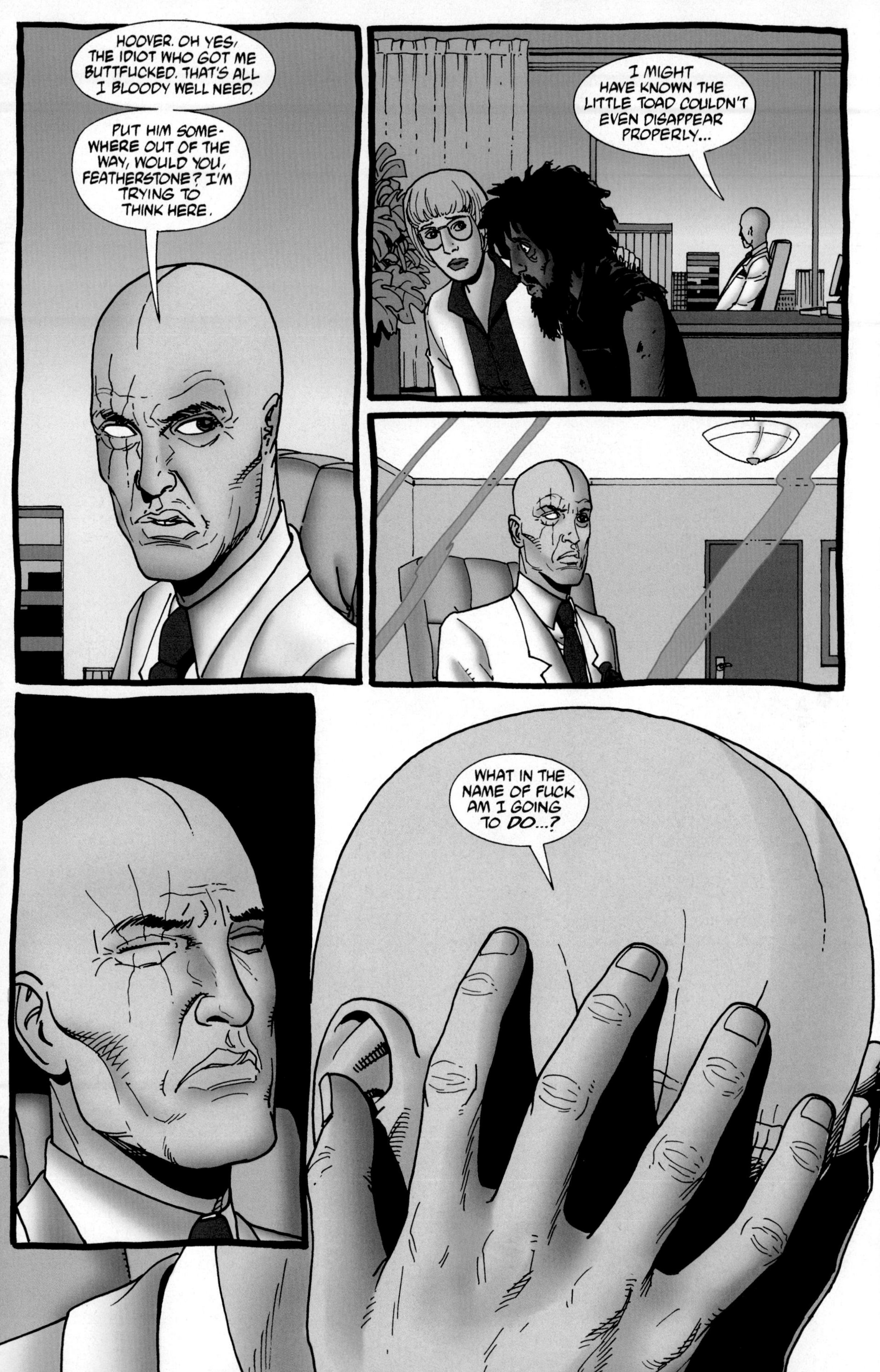
HOOVER. OH YES, THE IDIOT WHO GOT ME BUTTFUCKED. THAT'S ALL I BLOODY WELL NEED.
PUT HIM SOME-WHERE OUT OF THE WAY, WOULD YOU, FEATHERSTONE? I'M TRYING TO THINK HERE.
I MIGHT HAVE KNOWN THE LITTLE TOAD COULDN'T EVEN DISAPPEAR PROPERLY...
WHAT IN THE NAME OF FUCK AM I GOING TO *DO*...?

GLENN
FABRY
·99·

"You should have had him killed, Featherstone.
You should have had his throat cut from ear to ear."

SECURITY
MAH CONSIDERED OPINION IS FUCK YOU...
AN' FUCK YOUR MEDIA WATCHDAWG GROUP TOO, MA'AM. ARSEFACE'S RESPONSIBILITY TO THE PUBLIC BEGINS AN' ENDS WITH THE TIMELY RELEASE OF HIS MATERIAL, NOTHIN' MORE.
F.A.O. GENE
tone
ARSEFACE ON THE COPY-CATS
'DARWIN HAD A POINT'
CERTAINLY AH'LL ELABORATE: ANYONE BLAMIN' THEIR ILLS ON THE BOY--FROM EXPLOSIVE FACIAL SHREDDIN' TO CLINICAL DEPRESSION--CAN SHOVE THEIR LAWSUIT UP THEIR ASS.
WE AT GEORGIA RECORDS SHIT FROM A GREAT HEIGHT ON THE SUGGESTION HE CAN BE HELD LIABLE FOR ANYTHIN', WHETHER THROUGH HIS LYRICS, APPEARANCE OR ACTIONS...
HUH, GEUHN!
ONE MOMENT, MA'AM.

AH'LL BE RIGHT WITH YOU, SON. YOU AMUSE YOUR-SELF FOR A SECOND.
SHUH THUHNG!

NOW WHERE WERE WE...YES, OF COURSE AH'M SPEAKIN' FOR THE BOY. AH'M HIS MANAGER; AH MERELY PASS ON HIS OPINIONS DUE TO HIS, HA-HA, LITTLE PROBLEM WITH SELF-EXPRESSION.
WHATEVER AH SAY COMES STRAIGHT FROM THE ARSE'S MOUTH...

GLAD AH COULD CLEAH THAT UP FOR YOU, MA'AM. AN' MAY AH SAY WHAT A PLEASURE IT HAS BEEN TALKIN' TO YOU, AS USUAL.
BE THAT AS IT MAY, MA'AM, IT WAS A PLEASURE FOR ***ME***.
YOU TAKE CARE NOW.

NOW, MAH YOUNG FRIEND, WHAT CAN AH DO FOR YOU ON THIS FINE MAWNIN'?
WUHL... UH GUHD THUZ ***BUHLZ*** IN THUH MUHL...

BILLS, HMMM?
FUNUHL DUMUHNZ, UGSHULLUH.
THE HOUSE, THE CARS, THE POOL...THE ESCAWT AGENCY...

WELL, THIS IS CLEAHLY JUST AN OVAHSIGHT. AH'LL LOOK INTO IT DIRECTLY.
BUB--HUHZ THUH BUZZUZT? HUH THUHT UHT MUHT BUH TUH DUH WUTH UH RUHYULTUHZ. THUH HUVUND BUHN PUHD YUHD UTHUH.
IS THAT A FACT.
MAH BOY, PLEASE DON'T CONCERN YOURSELF ABOUT YOUR ROYALTIES. AH ASSURE YOU THEY--AN' THESE BILLS--WILL BE PAID AT ONCE.
GRUHD!
OH, AN' NEXT TIME YOU SEE BOB, WOULD YOU TELL HIM AH'D LIKE A LITTLE WORD? IT'S ABOUT HIS BASS-PLAYIN'.
AMONG OTHAH THINGS.
MEANWHILE, HEAH'S A YOUNG LADY WITH ENAWMOUS BREASTS.
ANY OTHAH PROBLEMS, BE SURE AN' LET ME KNOW.

"HE WUZ FUNNY AN' CRAZY AN' CHARMIN' AN' LUCKY, AN' HE AWAYZ KNEW JUST WHATTA SAY.
"NICEST PIECE A' SHIT I EVER DID MEET."

SMILE LIKE THE GATES OF HELL

GARTH ENNIS - Writer STEVE DILLON - Artist

PAMELA RAMBO - Colorist CLEM ROBINS - Letterer AXEL ALONSO - Editor

PREACHER created by GARTH ENNIS and STEVE DILLON

OH, LORD...
OH LORDZ RIGHT.
HEHHN!

HEHHN! HEHH-- CCCCHH--
TOOF

GODDAMN, SALLY--!
OH, RELAX. HAPPENZ ALLA TIME.
RELAX HELL, WE GOTTA GET YOU SOME HELP!

WORKIN' ON IT MYSEFF. SLEP' TWENNY HOURZ STRAIGHT LAS' NIGHT. TRYNNA FIX IT SOZ I DON' WAKE UP ATALL.
WHERE WUZ I?

JESUS...
OH YEAH.
YEAH, FRUM WHAT YOU SEZ, IT SOUNZ LIKE HE PRETTY MUCH TOL' YOU THE TRUTH 'BOUT HIMSEFF. ITZA BITZ IN BETWEEN ALLA THAT WHERE THE INNEREZIN' STUFF HAPPENZ.

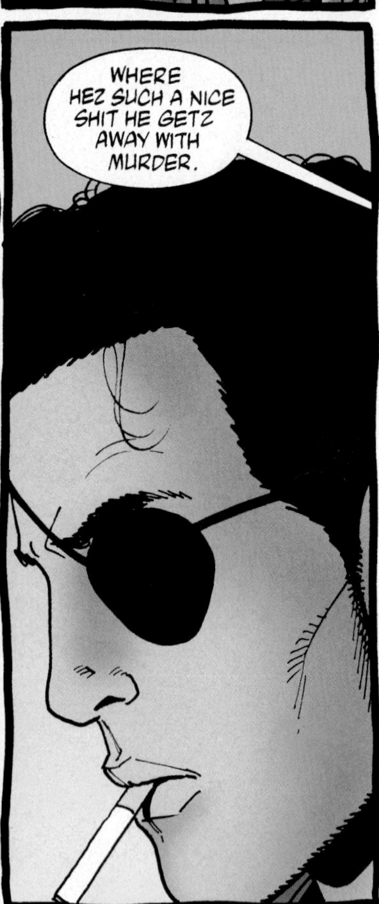
WHERE HEZ SUCH A NICE SHIT HE GETZ AWAY WITH MURDER.

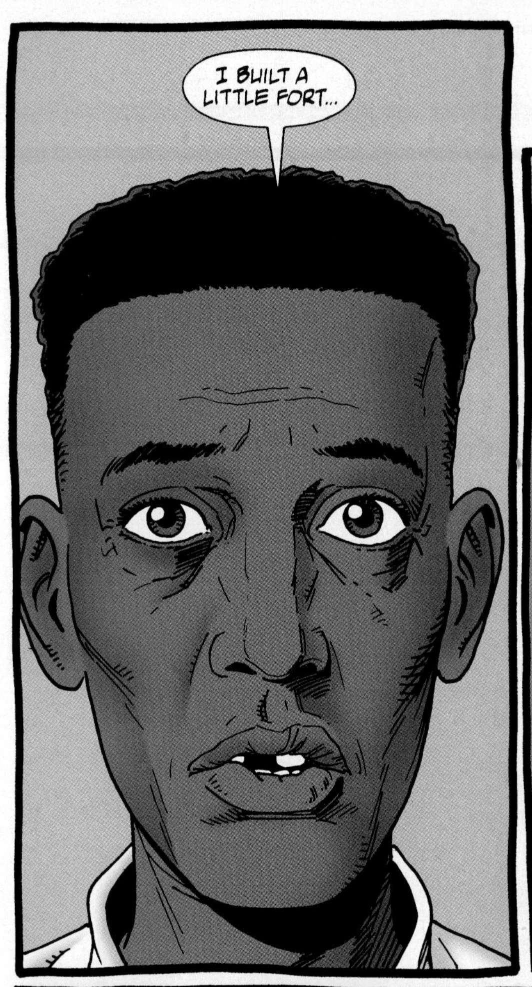
I BUILT A LITTLE FORT...

WAIT, LET ME GET THIS STRAIGHT: YOU'VE BEEN STUCK ON A BEACH THIS ENTIRE TIME?
I BUILT A LITTLE FORT, YOU SEE, BECAUSE AFTER A COUPLE OF MONTHS I FIGURED IT OUT...
I COULD LIVE IN IT, AND FISH WOULD GET CAUGHT IN IT AT LOW TIDE AND I WOULDN'T HAVE TO EAT QUITE SO MUCH SEAWEED, AND THE WIND COULDN'T BLOW THE SAND AWAY AND I COULD COUNT...!

OH, HOOVER.

POOR, POOR HOOVER.

HOW HAVE YOU BEEN, FEATHERSTONE?
OH, I'VE... I'VE BEEN FINE...

I'VE BEEN DOING ALL KINDS OF STRANGE THINGS, ACTUALLY. I DON'T SUPPOSE YOU KNOW ABOUT MONUMENT VALLEY, BUT... WELL.
HERR STARR'S BEEN KEEPING ME BUSY, ANYWAY. HE'S... HAD A COUPLE OF ODD MOMENTS RECENTLY, BUT NOTHING *THAT* IRRATIONAL...

NO, HE'S JUST THE SAME OLD HERR STARR.

FUCKING COMPUTERS!!

FUCKING STUPID BASTARD COMPUTERS! FUCKING INFORMATION SUPER-HIGHWAY HORSESHIT! MAKE LIFE EASIER MY HAIRY FAT COCK!
HERR STARR--!
BRING ME THE HEAD OF BILL FUCKING GATES!

BUT WHAT'S WRONG WITH THE COMPUTERS?
YOU CAN FUCKING HACK INTO THEM, THAT'S WHAT! AND THAT LITTLE BASTARD EISENSTEIN *HAS!*

YOU CAN'T BE SURE HE'S-- HERR STARR--!
OF COURSE HE FUCKING HAS! IT'S PROBABLY THE FIRST THING HE FUCKING DID!
MR. STARR, DON'T BE MEAN TO HER--
CRAWL AWAY AND DIE, FUCKWIT. FEATHERSTONE, DID YOU HAVE ANYTHING ON THOSE FILES THAT EISENSTEIN COULD USE TO FUCK ME? ANY-THING THE GRAIL SHOULDN'T KNOW ABOUT?
I--I--
ANY-THING AT ALL, FEATHER-STONE...
WELL I--I'M NOT SURE IF--
FEATHERSTONE.
YOU ARE A HIGHLY INTELLIGENT WOMAN. AN EXCELLENT ADMINISTRATOR. YOU HAVE NEVER FAILED ME.
TELL ME YOU WEREN'T STUPID ENOUGH TO KEEP DATA THAT SENSITIVE ON A GODDAMNED COMPUTER...
NO...NO, I...I WOULDN'T HAVE.
GOOD--
EXCEPT...
EXCEPT?
OH GOD.
EXCEPT FOR EDDIE PECK.

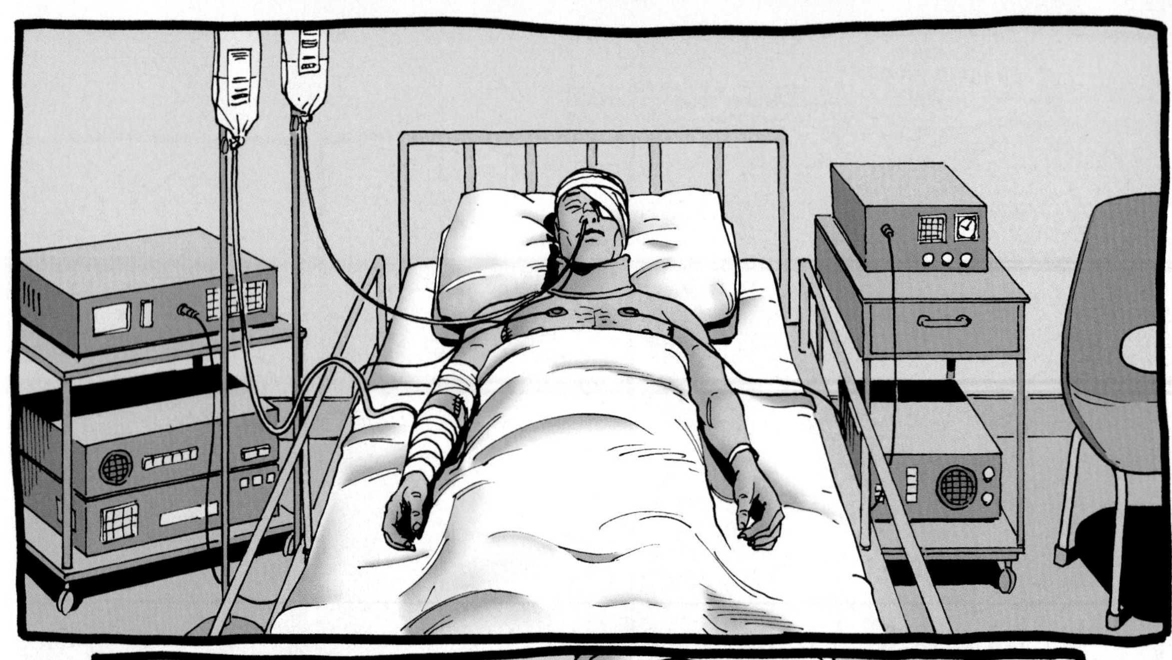

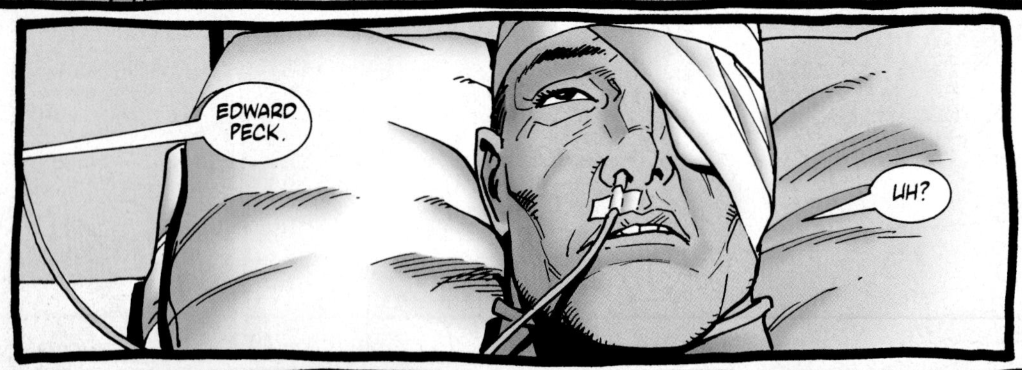
EDWARD PECK.
UH?

MY NAME IS EISENSTEIN.

WHO?
MR. PECK.
WAIT, WHO THE FUCK--
MR. PECK.
WHATEVER YOU DO.

DON'T LOOK ROUND.

HE WUZ A LOTTA FUN WHEN I FIRST MET HIM, AN' BY THE TIME I'M TALKIN' ABOUT HE WUZ MORE FUN'N A BODY COULD STAND...

HE LOST TOUCH WITH McCANN. M'SORTA GLAD 'BOUT THAT.
McCANN KNEW CASSIDY AT IZ BEST. BEEN A FUCKIN' SHAME HE SEEN WHAT HAPPENED LATER.
MICK McCANNZA GOOD OL' GUY.

"WUZ HIM INNERDUCED US ALL. ME AN' MY FRENZ JOAN AN'... GILLY OR HILDY, CAND 'MEMBER...US AN' CASSIDY.
"WAR WUZ ON AN' THE GIRLS WORKED INNA FACTORY, AN' THEY MADE A LOTTA MONEY, AN' HE BORROWED A LOTTA MONEY--

"AN' HE WUZ LIVIN' WITH... IT WUZ GILLY OR HILDY ATTA TIME, IT WUZN'T JOAN, AN' AFTER A WHILE SHE FOUN' OUT WHY HE WUZN'T PAYIN' IT BACK:
MMH--!

MM-HMM-HMMM...

WHAT YOU DOIN', SWEETIE?
MM? OH...
WHAT'S THAT?

FUN.

YEAH?

DIN' KNOW HE DID IT?
I KNEW.
DIN' KNOW WUZ LIKE THIS?
NOPE.

WHY NOT, HUH? HE KIN TRY EVERYTHIN' THERE IS TO TRY. HEZ GOT LIFETIMEZ.
'CEPT GILLY OR HILDY'D ONLY ONE.

HE TOLD YOU WHAT HE IS?
FUCKIN' LEECH YA MEAN?
HEHHHN!

EDDIE PECK WAS ONE OF THE FREELANCERS WE HIRED FOR THE DeSADE RAID.
HE CAUGHT A STRAY BULLET IN THE FACE AND LOST AN EYE. A SECOND ONE BLEW OUT HIS SPINE. HE ENDED UP A PARAPLEGIC, HIS KIDNEYS FAILED...

AND I THOUGHT IT WAS ONLY FAIR THAT WE PAID FOR HIS TREATMENT--
OH MY GOD.

YOU SHOULD HAVE HAD HIM KILLED, FEATHERSTONE.
HERR STARR, THE MAN WAS CRIPPLED IN OUR SERVICE! AND HE WOULDN'T TELL THE POLICE ANYTHING! HE KEPT HIS END OF THE DEAL!
YOU SHOULD HAVE HAD HIS THROAT CUT FROM EAR TO EAR.

WELL...I...
I GOT HIM A PRIVATE ROOM AND THE BEST CARE AFFORDABLE. I'VE BEEN MONITORING HIS PROGRESS VIA THE HOSPITAL'S RECORDS, CORRESPONDING WITH HIS SPECIALISTS ON THE NET, THAT KIND OF THING...

APPARENTLY HE'S DOING VERY WELL INDEED--
HE'S DOING REMARKABLY. HE'S GOING TO GET ME KILLED.

ONCE EISENSTEIN GETS TO PECK HE'S GOING TO DISCOVER THAT I LED A TEAM OF ARMED THUGS, ALL UNAFFILIATED WITH THE GRAIL. INTO A PRIVATE RESIDENCE PACKED WITH SEVERAL HUNDRED WITNESSES.
LOOKING FOR SOMEONE CALLED JESSE CUSTER.

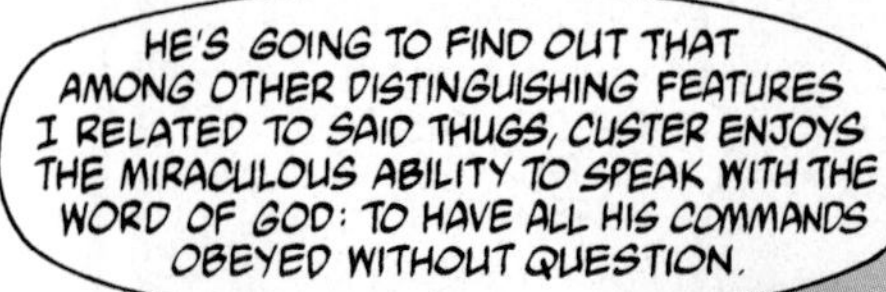
HE'S GOING TO FIND OUT THAT AMONG OTHER DISTINGUISHING FEATURES I RELATED TO SAID THUGS, CUSTER ENJOYS THE MIRACULOUS ABILITY TO SPEAK WITH THE WORD OF GOD: TO HAVE ALL HIS COMMANDS OBEYED WITHOUT QUESTION.

ARMED WITH THIS NUGGET, EISENSTEIN WILL RECALL THE DEATH OF OUR OWN MIRACLE WORKER-- THAT FUCKING CHIMP'S AFTERBIRTH THE GRAIL SOMEHOW RAISED AS A CHILD-- IN THE DESTRUCTION OF MASADA, THE CONFLAGRATION THAT I ALONE SURVIVED.
HE WILL CONSIDER HOW THE CHILD WAS INTENDED TO BE REVEALED AS THE MESSIAH DURING ARMAGEDDON, THE WORLD-SHATTERING EVENT THAT I AM SUPPOSED TO BE ORCHESTRATING--

AND HE WILL THEN PUT TWO AND TWO TOGETHER AND COME UP WITH MY BALLS ON A STICK.

MIGHT HAVE DIED IN THE VALLEY...
CUSTER SURVIVED. WHO D'YOU THINK SHERIFF JESSE CUSTER WAS ON THAT NAMESEARCH YOU DID ON YOUR STUPID FUCKING COMPUTER?
CUSTER SURVIVED, PECK WILL TALK, EISENSTEIN WILL KNOW...

ANY OTHER ACTS OF KINDNESS YOU WANT TO TELL ME ABOUT, FEATHERSTONE? SET UP A RELIEF FUND FOR THE POOR IRRADIATED NAVAJO WITH MY FUCKING NAME ON IT, ANYTHING LIKE THAT?
NO?

GOOD.
WELL, I'M GOING TO SPEND SOME TIME WITH MY SCROTUM. WE MAY AS WELL ENJOY OUR LAST COUPLE OF HOURS TOGETHER.

CAN'T... FEEL...
LOCAL ANESTHETIC.
DON'T LOOK ROUND.

YOU MUSTN'T LOOK ROUND.
YOU ARE A STRONG MAN, MR. PECK. EX-MILITARY. YOU DO NOT BREAK EASILY.

FOR MY PART, I AM OLD. I HAVE SEEN A THOUSAND TORTURES.
I HAVE NEITHER TIME NOR INCLINATION FOR EXTRACTING INFORMATION, UNDER AGONIZING DURESS, WORD BY PAINFUL WORD. I SIMPLY WANT MY QUESTIONS ANSWERED WITHOUT HESITATION. WITH-OUT EVEN THE HOPE OF RESISTANCE.
THESE ARE MY TWILIGHT YEARS.

SO: A CONVERSATION, THEN MY QUESTIONS.
WHAT DOES THE TERM SPETSNAZ MEAN TO YOU?
IT'S...RUSSKI COMMANDOS, RIGHT? LIKE GREEN BERETS?

NOT LIKE THEM, NO.
DON'T LOOK ROUND.

THE SOVIETS TRAINED MEN WHO WOULD SURVIVE NO MATTER WHAT.
DEATH MEANS FAILURE IN THE MISSION, AFTER ALL. SO IN SELECTING MY CURRENT BODYGUARD, I HAD BUT ONE PREREQUISITE: THAT HE BE RUSSIAN.
LOOK, FUCK THIS, OKAY? I--
NO, NO. DON'T LOOK ROUND.
YOU CAN'T LOOK ROUND.
WITH THE END OF THE COLD WAR CAME AN ERA OF COOPERATION.
A SPETSNAZ UNIT WAS INVITED ON A N.A.T.O. SPECIAL FORCES EXERCISE IN NORTHERN NORWAY. BUT THE WEATHER CLOSED IN FASTER THAN EXPECTED. THE TEAM WAS CUT OFF.
IN THEIR PATRONIZING WAY, THE WESTERN MILITARY BELIEVED THEY HAD A LOT TO TEACH THE RUSSIANS. THEY THOUGHT IN TERMS OF METHOD...
WHEN IN FACT IT WAS A MATTER OF PHILOSOPHY.
DON'T LOOK ROUND.
IT WAS FORTY DEGREES BELOW ZERO.
THE FOUR-MAN UNIT STUMBLED ON AN ELDERLY COUPLE STRANDED IN THEIR MOUNTAIN CABIN. THEY HAD FOOD IN THEIR LARDER FOR ANOTHER WEEK.
THE BLIZZARD LASTED TWO.
YOU CAN LOOK NOW.

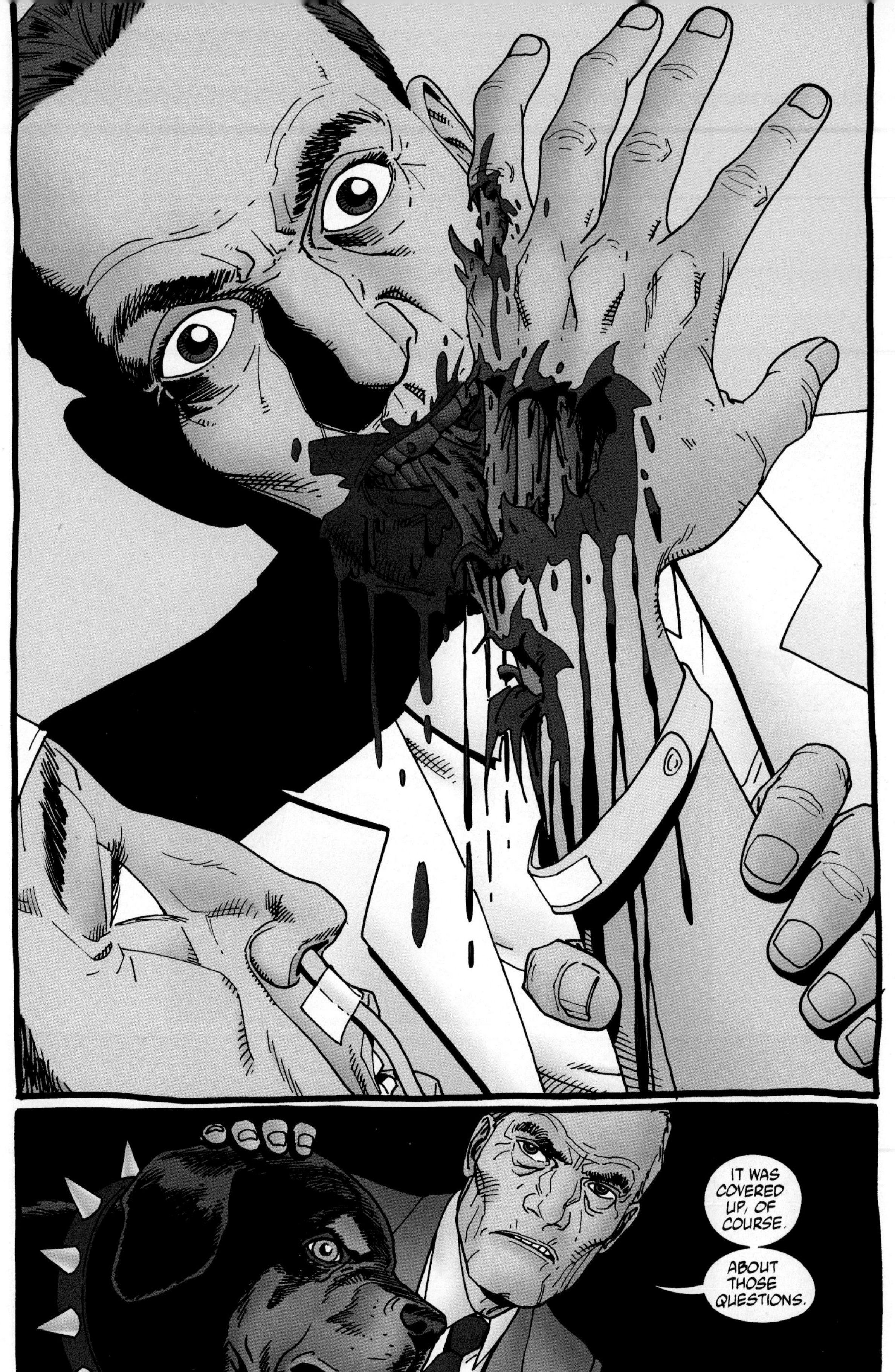
IT WAS COVERED UP, OF COURSE.
ABOUT THOSE QUESTIONS.

WUHG THUH SHUVD...
WUHG THUH SHUVD...

KISS MY FACE
An Insult to All?
NO

STORM OF CONTROVERSY
Falwell Told To Eat S**t and Die

ERTAINMENT NE
TOP 40 SINGLES
1. "Line Up Them Bitches"
Da Brown Dogg
2. "Dyslexic Fro Loev"
Analis Sorrimette
3. "My Heart Will Go On"
Arseface
"I Wonder What You Hear"
...?

THAT WILL NEVAH DO.

GET ME THE VATICAN, PLEASE...

ME AN' JOAN'D SEE IT BUT WE DIDN'T UNNERSTAN' IT...

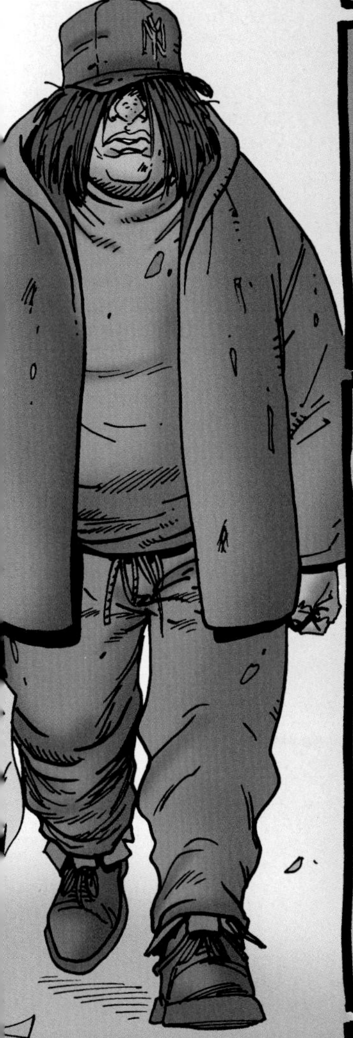

I THOUGHT YEH GOT PAID YESTERDAY?
THAT WAS LAST WEEK. LAST FRIDAY OF THE MONTH, REMEMBER?

OH, AYE... WELL GIVE US WHATEVER YEH'VE GOT ON YEH, THEN.
CASS, YOU GOT A SAWSKI OFF ME TUESDAY. I AIN'T GOT A DIME TO MY NAME.

NOTHIN'? ABSOLUTELY NOTHIN', YEH'RE COMPLETELY CLEANED OUT?
WELL... I MEAN THERE'S MY SAVINGS, BUT--
THERE YEH ARE THEN. YEH CAN GO AN' GET YER SAVIN'S OUT TOMORROW MORNIN', SOON AS THE BANK OPENS.

BUT...BABY, I WANTED NEW SHOES, AND THERE'S THE RENT...
I AIN'T TOO SURE ABOUT THIS, YOU KNOW?

BE A GOOD GIRL, NOW.

...YEH STUPID FUCKIN' HOOER, HOW'RE WE MEANT TO SCORE WI' NOTHIN'? WHAT THE FUCK IS NOTHIN' GONNA BUY?

B-B-BUT THE RENT--

FUCK THE RENT!

WELL MAYBE WE CAN GO WITHOUT FOR A WHILE...

GO WITHOUT?

HAVE YEH EVER FUCKIN' TRIED TO GO WITHOUT? HAVE YEH?

NO! OF COURSE YEH FUCKIN' HAVEN'T!

YEH HAVEN'T A FUCKIN' CLUE WHAT YEH'RE TALKIN' ABOUT, 'CAUSE I'M THE ONE DOES ALL THE THINKIN' ROUND HERE! I ALWAYS FUCKIN' HAVE BEEN!

OH HOLY FUCKIN' JESUS, ARE WE GONNA HAVE SOME FUN NOW!!

I DO NOT APPRECIATE BEING HAULED OUT OF MY CARD GAME, CASSIDY. ESPECIALLY NOT BY A LOWLIFE LIKE YOU.
AW BILL, C'MON NOW...!

IT'S LIKE I SAID ON THE 'PHONE, I'M ONLY AFTER A FEW CAPS. JUST TO SEE ME AN' YER ONE THERE ALL RIGHT 'TIL TOMORROW.
I MEAN YEH CAN SEE SHE'S NOT DOIN' SO WELL...
LIKE *I* SAID ON THE PHONE, GO FUCK YOURSELF. NO CASH, NO JUNK, AND IF YOU THINK BRINGING THIS COOZE DOWN HERE'S GOING TO TUG ON MY HEART-STRINGS THEN YOU'RE A BIGGER MORON THAN I THOUGHT.

YEH LITTLE *BOLLICKS*...!
I DON'T HAVE IT ON ME, CASSIDY.
YEH TALK TO ME LIKE THAT I'LL RIP YER--
I SAID I DON'T HAVE IT ON ME.

IT DOESN'T MATTER WHAT YOU DO TO ME, YOU WON'T GET WHAT YOU NEED. AND IN A DAY OR TWO, WHEN YOU'RE REALLY GOOD AND SICK, MY BROTHERS'LL FIND YOU AND PAY YOU BACK DOUBLE.
NOW: I'M A GOOD GUY. I'LL FORGET THIS HAPPENED.

YOUR GIRLFRIEND CAN SUCK MY DICK FOR A COUPLE OF CAPS.

SO CAN YOU.
I'M NOT PARTICULAR.

FUCKER.
LITTLE FUCKER.
SAYIN' THAT TO ME--!

I FEEL SICK...
OH NO YEH DON'T. ANOTHER HOUR OR TWO, THEN YEH'LL KNOW WHAT SICK MEANS.
I CAN'T BELIEVE THAT WEE BASTARD...

OHH--!
MAYBE I COULD GO AND SEE HIM?

I DIDN'T FUCKIN' SAY THAT, DID I?
JUST TO GET WHAT WE NEED--
DID I FUCKIN' SAY THAT?!
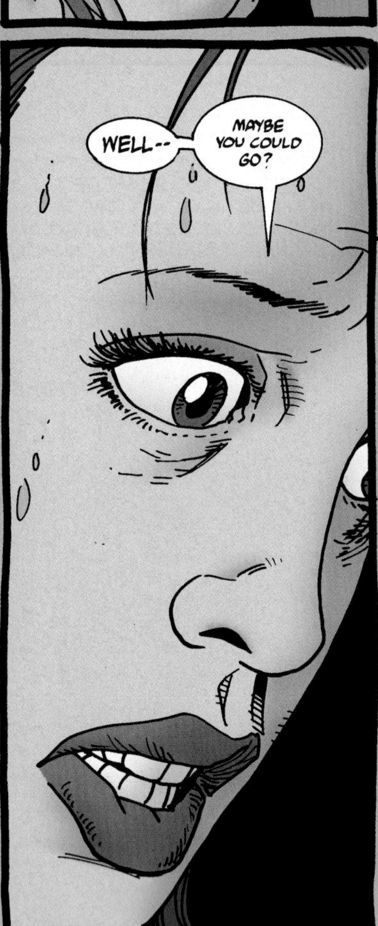
WELL--
MAYBE YOU COULD GO?

I DIDN'T MEAN--

GETS WORSE.
GIMME FIVE BUCKS AN' MEET ME HERE LUNCHTIME TOMORRA.
CASSIDY.

GLENN
FABRY
·89·

"Day we dropped the bomb onna Japs, Joanie an' Cassidy got engaged."

H + F

F+S

RIGHT, ENOUGH IS ENOUGH. GET ON THE PHONE AND HIRE SOME SCUM, FEATHERSTONE.

WE'RE GOING TO KILL THAT BASTARD.

WE'RE GOING TO WIPE HIM OFF MY ARSE LIKE A ***DINGLEBERRY***.

"GILLY OR HILDY... I NEVER DO 'MEMBER.
"SHE HEALED UP AN' CLEANED UP AN' WENT BACK TO IOWA, ALLA THEM BIG CITY DREAMS IN SHREDS."
UNI
BUT SHE TOLD ME AN' JOAN EVERY-THIN' FIRST. AN' ROUND 'BOUT THEN CASSIDY DISAPPEARED, JUST UP AN' LEFT, AN' WE DIDN'T SEE HIM AGAIN FOR A YEAR.
WENT WHEREVER HE WENT.
AN' THEN ONE NIGHT THE WAR ENDED.
AN' EVERY-ONEZ HAPPIER'N THEY'D EVER BIN IN THEIR LIVES.
AN' WE'RE IN SOME BAR AN' SOMEONE TAPS JOANIE ONNA SHOULDER AN' SEZ--
HOW'RE YEZ!!

OF THE IRISH IN AMERICA

GARTH ENNIS - Writer STEVE DILLON - Artist

PAMELA RAMBO - Colorist CLEM ROBINS - Letterer AXEL ALONSO - Editor

PREACHER created by GARTH ENNIS and STEVE DILLON

A MOMENT OF YOUR TIME, MAH BOY...?
SHUH THUNG, GEUHN!
A TRIFLIN' MATTAH, AH ASSURE YOU. A JOURNALIST LADY WOULD LIKE A BRIEF WORD FOR AN ARTICLE SHE'S PREPARIN'...
BUH RUHD WUTH YUH--

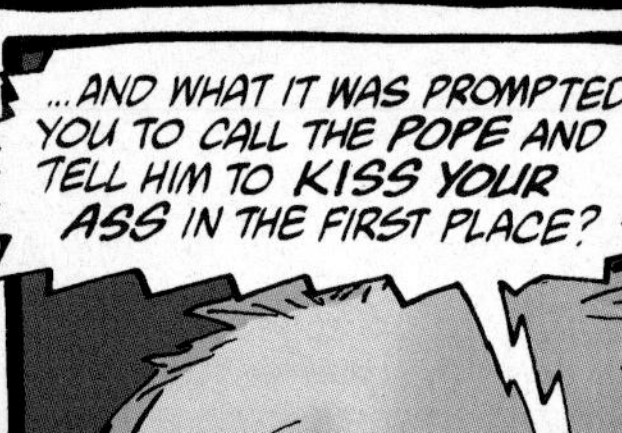

I DUNNO WHAT IT IZ KEEPS CASSIDY GOIN' BUT ITZ GOD ITZ LIMITS SAMEZ ANY-THIN' ELSE.

HEZ SMART, HEDA DRUNK NUFF BLOOD TO SEE HIM THROUGH STUFF LIKE THIZ. 'COURSE, HEZ SMART, HEDA NEVER DONE THE JUNK INNA FIRST PLACE.
HEZ STILLA SAME STOOPID KID OFFA FUGGIN' BOAT, WAITIN' FOR SOMEONE A' TELLIM WHADDA DO.

"ENDA THAT YEAR I COULDA KICKED HIS ASS.
"THINGS GOT BAD FOR JOANIE. HE KEPT SAYIN' HE WUZN'T SCORIN', HOW COULD HE WITH NO MONEY? BUT SHE KNEW HE WUZ.
"ONE NIGHT SHE WEN' OUT BY HERSELF, HADDA GET A CAP OR SHEDA FUGGIN' DIED, SHE SED.

"WENNA SEE THAT PIECE A' SHIT BILL, CASSIDY'S CONNECTION DOWNTOWN. SED SHEDA DONE ANYTHIN' SO HEDA HELPED HER.
"WOULDNA LET HER INNA DOOR SO SHE WENT ROUNNA BACK. CALL TO BILL WHEN HE WENNA THE JOHN."

AND WHAT THE FUCK ARE YOU LOOKING AT?

MM?

I GUESS YOU TWO KNOW EACH OTHER.

OH, SORRY, CASSIDY, FORGOT TO TELL YOU.

FUCK OFF! FUCK OFF!
AAAAH--!
FUCKIN' LEAVE ME ALONE!
WHAT THE FUCK'RE YEH DOIN', I FUCKIN' TOLD YEH NOT TO COME AFTER ME! YEH STUPID FUCKIN' HOOER, YEH'VE WRECKED EVERYTHING!!
I SAID I'D FUCKIN' SCORE, DIDN'T I? I FUCKIN' SAID I WOULD! I WAS--I WAS SCORIN' FOR BOTH OF US--
B-B-BUT CASSIDY...!
AW, FUCK OFF, JOANIE.
JUST FUCK OFF AN' LEAVE ME ALONE.
...HELP ME.

AN' SHE DID.

"DRAGGED HIS ASS HOME, GOTTIM BACK JUSTAFORE SUNRISE.
"HE KNEW SHE WOULD, SEE."

CASSIDY AWAYZ KNOWS, CUZ CASSIDY FUGGIN' *PREYZ* ON PEOPLE.

JUST NEED...A WEE BIT, LOVE...

WE BOTH DO, HONEY.
NO.
NO.
JUST A WEE BIT.
JUST TO MAKE ME STRONG--

WHATAAAAAAAHHH!!

JOANIE IT'S JUST A DROP, JUST A FUCKIN' DROP!
NO--GET OFF--NO, YOU'RE NOT DOING THAT TO ME--
I CAN SCORE, FOR FUCK'S SAKE! I'LL BE STRONG ENOUGH TO GO OUT, I CAN GET US ALL THE JUNK WE NEED!

NO! NOOOOOOO!!
YEH SELFISH FUCKIN' BITCH--

EEAAAAGH!

SHE RAN. HE HID.
SHE NEVER SEEN HIM AGAIN.

I MADE FUGGIN' SURE'VE IT; SHEZ SICK FOR A LONG TIME AN' THEN I PUT HER ONNA BUS MYSELF.
BUT I WENNA SEE HIM.

JUS'...
WANNADA KNOW HEZ OKAY.

HOW'RE YEH, SALLY.

JUST GIVE'S A MINUTE.
BE RIGHT WITH YEH.

?
SHIT.

27
25
HEL-LO! I HAVE A BEAUTIFUL BOUQUET ARRANGEMENT FOR A MISTER EISENSTEIN, IF YOU'D JUST LIKE TO SIGN FOR IT--
20
27
15
OH NO--
OH GOD--
10
5
SHIT.

HAAAAAIIIIEE!!

UNK

NO--
JESUS--

NNOOOOAAARRGGHHH!!

GO AND FUCK YOURSELF, CASSIDY.

S'WHAT I SAID.

DUNNO'F WUZ BOSTON OR CHICAGO, BUT IT MUSTA BIN TEN YEARS SINCE I SEEN HIM. JUS' RUN INTO HIM BY ACCIDENT, HIM ALL HOW ARE YA SALLY DARLIN', S'IF NOTHIN'D HAPPENED.

YOU'RE SO FULL OF FUCKING SHIT, YOU WITH YOUR SMILE AND YOUR JOKES AND YOUR STUPID MICK ACCENT--YOU THINK THAT MAKES YOU ROMANTIC? YOU THINK YOU'RE THIS CHARMING ROGUE OR SOMETHING?
WHO THE FUCK DO YOU THINK YOU ARE EVEN TALKING TO ME? YOU LET LOOSE FUCKING HELL ON EARTH AND NOW YOU'RE GOING TO PAT THE WORLD ON THE BACK AND BUY IT A DRINK AND EVERYTHING'LL BE ALL RIGHT?!!

SAWD ON HIS FACE. NOBODY'D EVER TALKED LIKE THAT TO HIM. NOBODY'D CALLED HIM ON ALLAT FUCKIN' BULLSHIT, HE DIDN' EVEN KNOW IT WAS BULLSHIT...
HE SED SOMETHIN' BUT I JUZ WALKED OUT AN' THATSA LAST I SEEN'VE HIM, EVER EVER EVER.

CRIED MY FUGGIN' HEART OUT THAT NIGHT.

YOU RECALL WHAT IT WAS HE SAID?
MIGHTA BIN SORRY.
AN' I NEED YA.
HEY, GOT A PICTURE. ONLY THING I DO GOT, 'CEPT FORRA CLAP.
HEHHN!
NEW YEARZ I THINK. DUNNO WHICH.
THEREZ McCANN SO IT WUZ EARLY ON. THATZ GILLY OR HILDY WITHIM, AN' THEREZ LI'L JOANIE.
AN' THAZ CASSIDY.
SO WHO'S THIS RIGHT HERE?

SALLY?

...AW, HELL...!

YOU REST, GIRL.

SO WHAT EXACTLY HAPPENED TO HER?
AH, WAY THESE OLD BUMS LIVE THE BODY EVENTUALLY QUITS ON 'EM. JUST UP AN' SHITS ITS GUTS OUT, OR WHAT-EVER.

WHO KNOWS *HOOOWW!*
LISTEN, ASSHOLE--

WH-WH-WHOA, REVEREND! TAKE IT EASY!
I MEAN-- C'MON, MAN--

...JESUS.
I AIN'T PISSED AT YOU, PARDNER.

I'M JUST PISSED.

DIRTY MOTHER-FUCKER!
HANG HIM!
BURN IN HELL!
KILL THE ARSE!
WE'RE CHRISTIANS, YOU FUCKIN' SICK FUCK!
HANG HIM HIGH!
WIPE HIM OUT!
WIPE THE ARSE!
ARSE OF SHAME
BAN THE ARSE
FUCK WITH THE POPE YOU FUCK WITH ME
YOU KISS HIS ASS

WIPE THE ARSE WIPE THE ARSE WIPE THE AR

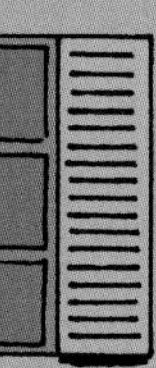

UH DUHN UHNUHSTUHN...

UHVRUHWUHN HUHDS MUH... BUHD UH NUVUH CUHLD THUH PUHP, UH NUVUH SUHD UHNY UHV UD...!

OF COURSE NOT, MAH YOUNG FRIEND. THERE MUST'VE BEEN SOME KIND'VE AWFUL MISUNDAHSTANDIN'.
OH, BAH THE WAY, GOOD NEWS.

YOUR SINGLE'S BACK AT NUMBAH ONE.
WIPE THE ARSE
WIPE THE ARSE
WIPE THE ARSE

HERR STARR?
IT'S... AH... IT'S...
THIS IS ALL YOUR FAULT, FEATHERSTONE.
YES?
ALLFATHER STARR?
YOU WILL BE PLEASED TO HEAR I HAVE COMPLETED MY RESEARCH.
I WOULD LIKE TO DISCUSS MY CONCLUSIONS WITH YOU. OVER BREAK-FAST. IN MY SUITE.
EIGHT O'CLOCK SHARP, ALLFATHER STARR.

WHAT YOU LOOKIN' AT?
ONLY GOOD THING THERE IS.
HMH.
YOU LOOK TIRED, BABY.
ARE YOU GOING TO BE DONE WITH THIS SOON, JESSE? WILL IT ALL BE FINISHED, SO WE CAN GO AWAY AND BE TOGETHER AND HAVE REGULAR LIVES?
SURE, HONEY.
ALL BE OVER SOON.

WHERE'S AMY GOT TO, ANYHOW?
P.T.A. NIGHT AT HER SCHOOL. SHE HAS TO EXPLAIN TO MR. AND MRS. FLUTTERMAN WHY LITTLE JOHNNY CAN'T HAVE HIS UZI BACK.
SO WHAT'VE YOU BEEN UP TO FOR THE LAST COUPLE OF DAYS? I'VE HARDLY EVEN SEEN YOU...
BEEN TURNIN' OVER STONES, I GUESS.
FIND ANYTHING INTERESTING?
JUST THE KINDA THINGS LIVE UNDER 'EM.
JESSE... WHAT ARE WE TALKING ABOUT?
NOK NOK
MUST BE OUR GIRL.
PROBABLY FORGOT HER DOOR KEY, THE DITZ.
PROBABLY DID.

BANNED
GLENN FABRY 99

"I wish I was one of you. Either one."

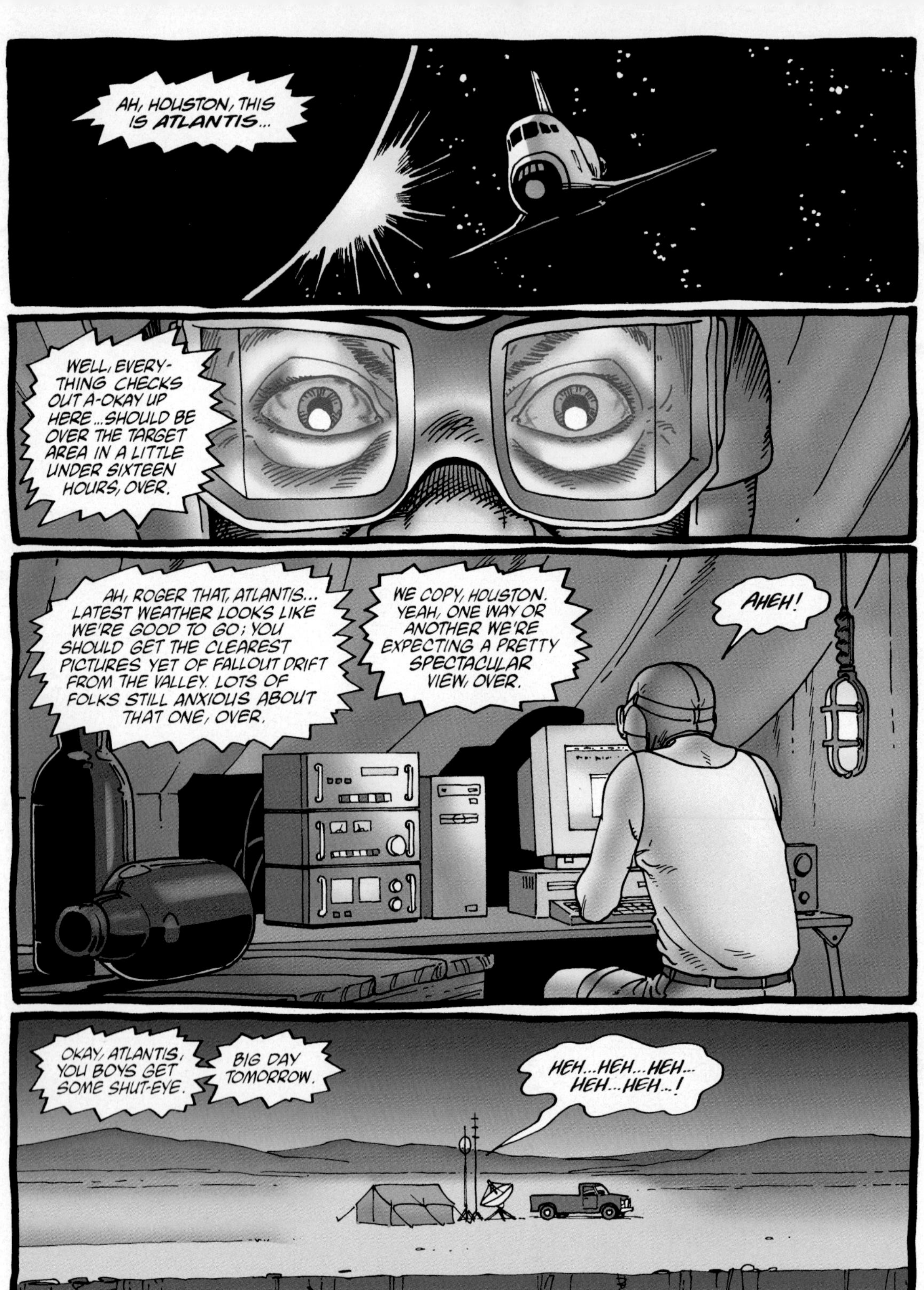
AH, HOUSTON, THIS IS ATLANTIS...
WELL, EVERY-THING CHECKS OUT A-OKAY UP HERE...SHOULD BE OVER THE TARGET AREA IN A LITTLE UNDER SIXTEEN HOURS, OVER.
AH, ROGER THAT, ATLANTIS... LATEST WEATHER LOOKS LIKE WE'RE GOOD TO GO; YOU SHOULD GET THE CLEAREST PICTURES YET OF FALLOUT DRIFT FROM THE VALLEY. LOTS OF FOLKS STILL ANXIOUS ABOUT THAT ONE, OVER.
WE COPY, HOUSTON. YEAH, ONE WAY OR ANOTHER WE'RE EXPECTING A PRETTY SPECTACULAR VIEW, OVER.
AHEH!
OKAY, ATLANTIS, YOU BOYS GET SOME SHUT-EYE.
BIG DAY TOMORROW.
HEH...HEH...HEH... HEH...HEH...!

...I THOUGHT YEH WERE...

DID YEH... WHAT HAPPENED TO YEH, DID YEH LAND IN A RIVER OR SOME-THIN'?

I CAME TO SEE IF, *uh*, TULIP WAS STAYIN' HERE. WITH HER MATE AMY, I MEAN.

SHE WASN'T DOIN' SO WELL THE LAST TIME I SAW HER, YEH KNOW, AN' I DUNNO IF SHE'S SAID ANYTHING BUT SHE WAS IN A BIT'VE A STATE...

GET THE FUCK AWAY FROM HERE!!
JAYSIS, HOUL' ON--
FUCK YOU, YOU PIECE OF SHIT! GET OUT OF HERE! NOW!
FOR FUCK'S SAKE, TULIP--!

I JUST WANTED TO SEE YEH WERE ALL RIGHT! I WAS WORRIED ABOUT YEH, THE LAST TIME I SAW YEH YEH DIDN'T KNOW WHAT YEH WERE DOIN'!

THE LAST TIME YOU SAW ME I KNEW EXACTLY WHAT I WAS DOING. I PUT A BULLET THROUGH YOUR WORTHLESS ASS AND I'LL FUCKING PUT ANOTHER ONE THROUGH YOU RIGHT NOW.
YOU FUCKING SEE IF I DON'T...

LOOK, THIS IS FUCKIN' CRAZY...
FUCKING CRAZY IS WHAT YOU MUST BE IF YOU THINK I DON'T KNOW WHAT YOU'RE HERE FOR: ME.
HOLY SHIT!

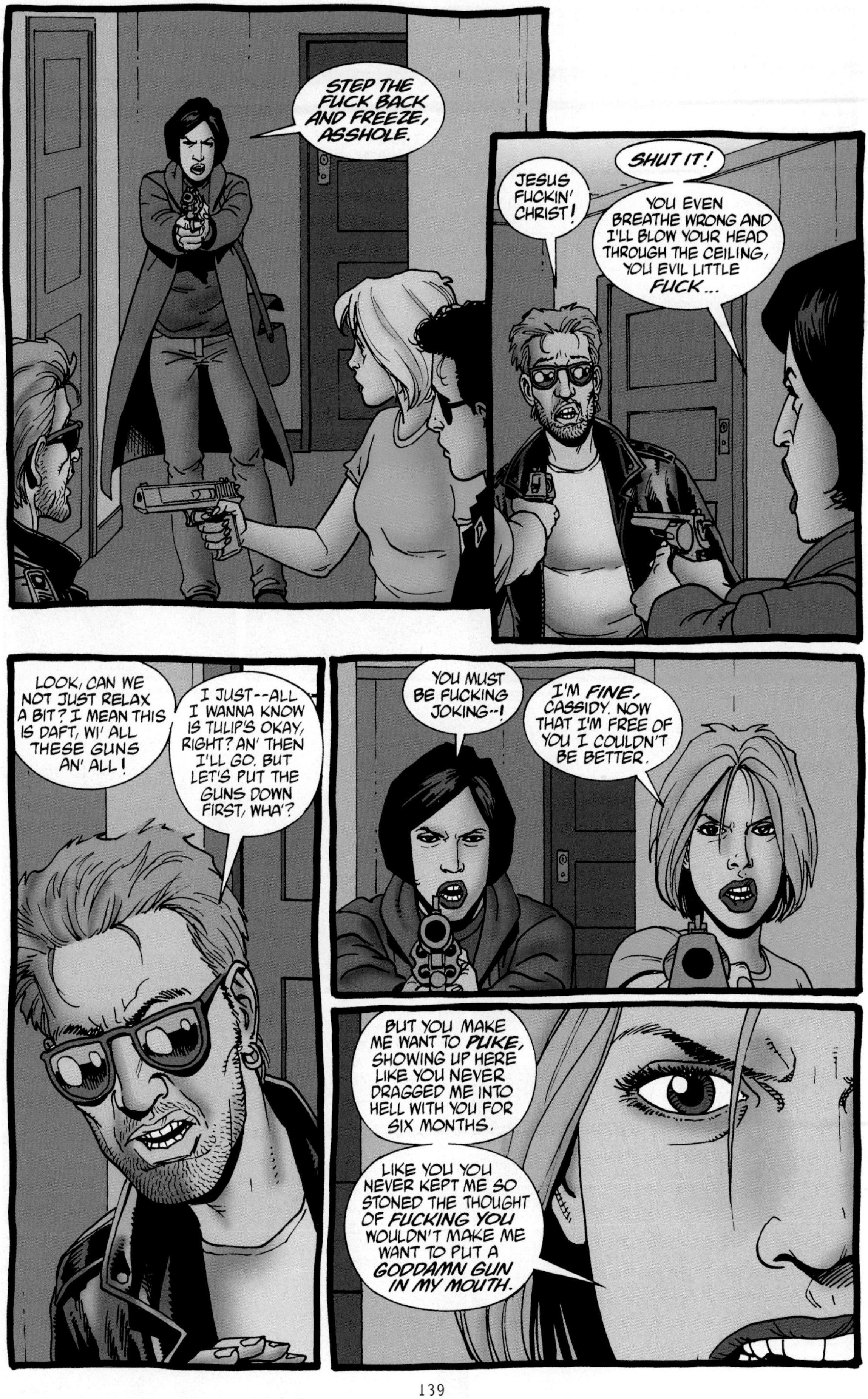

STEP THE FUCK BACK AND FREEZE, ASSHOLE.
SHUT IT!
JESUS FUCKIN' CHRIST!
YOU EVEN BREATHE WRONG AND I'LL BLOW YOUR HEAD THROUGH THE CEILING, YOU EVIL LITTLE FUCK...

LOOK, CAN WE NOT JUST RELAX A BIT? I MEAN THIS IS DAFT, WI' ALL THESE GUNS AN' ALL!
I JUST--ALL I WANNA KNOW IS TULIP'S OKAY, RIGHT? AN' THEN I'LL GO. BUT LET'S PUT THE GUNS DOWN FIRST, WHA'?

YOU MUST BE FUCKING JOKING--!
I'M FINE, CASSIDY. NOW THAT I'M FREE OF YOU I COULDN'T BE BETTER.

BUT YOU MAKE ME WANT TO PUKE, SHOWING UP HERE LIKE YOU NEVER DRAGGED ME INTO HELL WITH YOU FOR SIX MONTHS.
LIKE YOU YOU NEVER KEPT ME SO STONED THE THOUGHT OF FUCKING YOU WOULDN'T MAKE ME WANT TO PUT A GODDAMN GUN IN MY MOUTH.

WHAT--WHAT D'YEH MEAN? LOOK, BACK OFF--
YOU KNOW WHAT I MEAN, ASSHOLE.
WILL YEH STOP POINTIN' THEM FUCKIN' GUNS AT ME, FOR JAYSIS' SAKE--
NOT 'TIL YOU'RE GONE OR THEY'RE EMPTY.

I FUCKIN' MEAN IT!
SO DO WE. GO.
I DON'T LIKE HAVIN' GUNS POINTED AT ME, RIGHT?
POOR BABY. GO.
I'M FUCKIN' WARNIN' YEZ HERE!

WELL I GUESS THAT'S MORE'N GILLY GOT.

WHAT?

GILLY FROM IOWA. YOU REMEMBER.
YOU SMASHED HER FACE AN' WRECKED HER LIFE.
YOU NEVER GAVE HER NO WARNIN'.

UHH.

HOW...DID YEH...
IT DON'T MATTER.

LOOK--I DUNNO WHAT YEH'VE HEARD, OR--
IT WASN'T THAT SIMPLE, RIGHT? I MEAN I KNOW THIS ALL SEEMS A BIT WEIRD WI' TULIP AN' EVERYTHING, BUT...JAYSIS, I WOULDN'T DO THAT TO HER, I'M STILL ME...

YOU'RE A ANIMAL THINKS IT'S A MAN.

WELL FUCK YEH--
JESSE!!

THIS AIN'T THE TIME OR THE PLACE.
WHAT IS IT YOU WANT, EXACTLY?

I JUST...
AW, CAN WE NOT GO SOMEWHERE AN' TALK? HAVE A DRINK OR SOMETHIN', LIKE WE USED TO?

WELL I AIN'T TOO INCLINED TO TALK TO YOU RIGHT NOW.

AN' I GOT SOME THINGS I GOTTA DO. SO.
THERE'S A BAR IN SAN ANTONE CALLED HONDO'S, COUPLE BLOCKS FROM THE ALAMO. I'LL BE THERE TWO MONTHS FROM TONIGHT.
WE'LL TALK THEN.

HOUL' ON...

I THOUGHT YOU GUYS SAID HE WAS SOME KIND OF MONSTER, JESUS, HOW THE HELL DID YOU *DO THAT*...?
JESSE, ARE YOU OKAY?

MM? OH.
COULD ONE'VE YOU DRIVE ME TO THE HOSPITAL, PLEASE? I THINK I JUST BROKE EVERY BONE IN MY HAND.

HERR STARR, PLEASE LET US COME WITH YOU...!
DON'T BE STUPID, FEATHERSTONE, THAT RUSSIAN BASTARD WOULDN'T EVEN LET YOU IN THE DOOR. AND WHAT FUCKING USE WOULD YOU BE, ANYWAY?

I'M ON MY WAY TO MEET MY DOOM HERE; THE LAST THING I NEED IS YOU TWO CLOWNS COMING ALONG TO TURN A TRAGEDY INTO A FARCE...

WAIT HERE.
OR FUCK OFF, FOR THAT MATTER. WHAT THE HELL DO I CARE?
HERR STARR...

HE'S HORRIBLE TO YOU...!
NO...
NO, HOOVER.

IT'S JUST HIS FUNNY LITTLE WAY.

WIPE THE ARSE
WIPE THE ARSE
WIPE THE ARSE
GEUHN!
GEUHN! HULB!

THUH *RUHPUZUSSUHN UHVRUTHUHNG!* THUH SUH UH HUHVUH GUHD UHD UHVA *HUHZ!*

THUH SUH THUH *BUHLZ* NUVUH GUHD PUHD! *GEUHN!*

GEUHN...?
ARSEFACE

YOU HYPOCRITICAL LITTLE SHIT.
YOU EXPECT ME TO HAND OVER MY FILES ON CUSTER SO YOU CAN USE MY PLAN AND MY MESSIAH-- CHRIST, MY FUCKING STAND-IN MESSIAH!
YOU DON'T BUY THAT SACRED BLOODLINE CRAP THE GRAIL HAVE BEEN PEDDLING ANY MORE THAN I DO...!
YOU ARE WRONG, STARR.
YOUR LACK OF FAITH IS YOUR WEAKNESS. YOU DO NOT BELIEVE-- THEREFORE NO ONE BELIEVES.
SO VERY, VERY WRONG.
YOU DESTROYED MASADA. YOU KILLED THE CHILD. AN IMBECILE COULD SEE IT.
BUT ARMAGEDDON MUST AND SHALL BE BROUGHT ABOUT, THAT THIS WORLD SHALL SEE SALVATION.

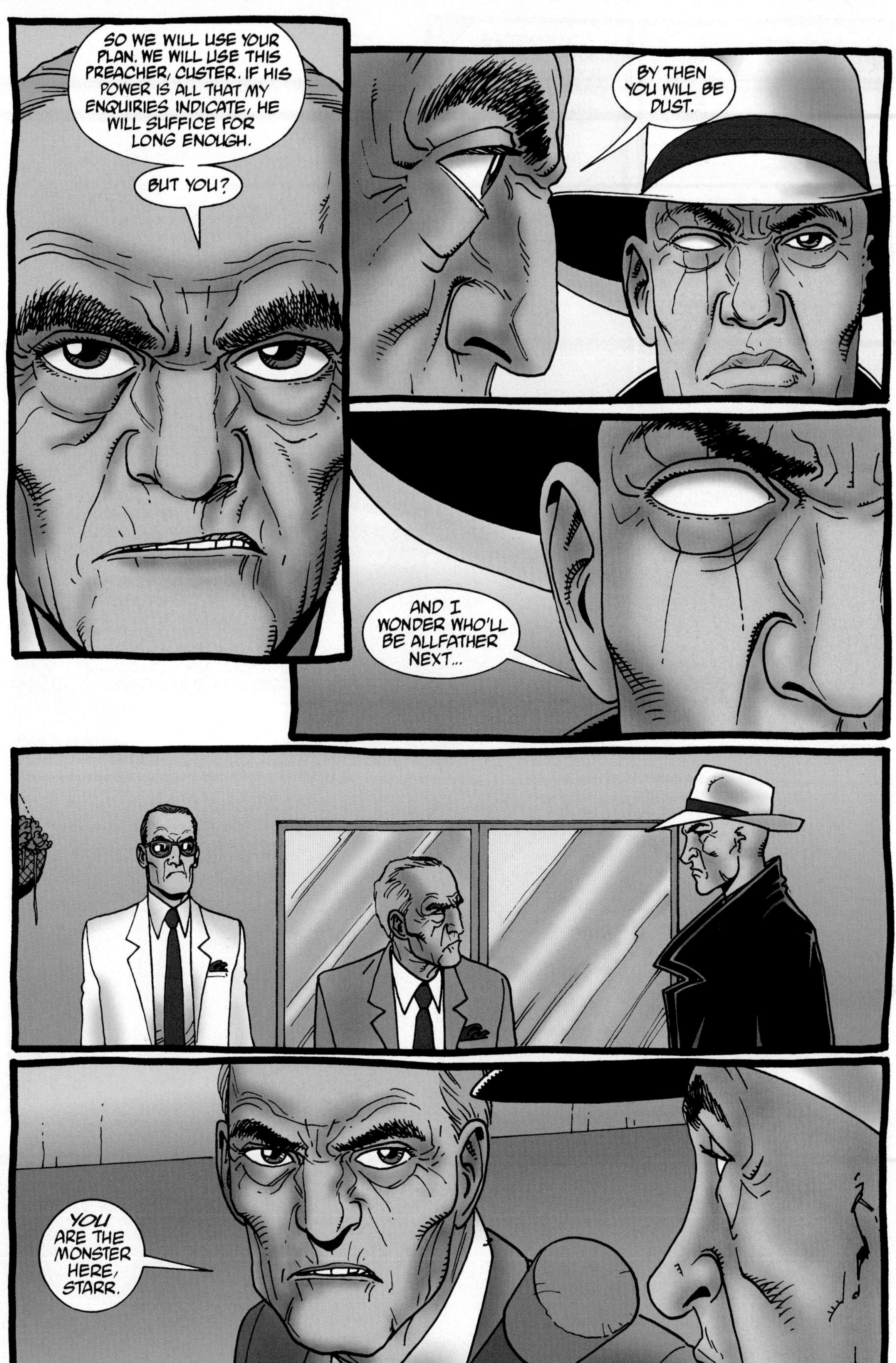
SO WE WILL USE YOUR PLAN. WE WILL USE THIS PREACHER, CUSTER. IF HIS POWER IS ALL THAT MY ENQUIRIES INDICATE, HE WILL SUFFICE FOR LONG ENOUGH.
BUT YOU?
BY THEN YOU WILL BE DUST.
AND I WONDER WHO'LL BE ALLFATHER NEXT...
YOU ARE THE MONSTER HERE, STARR.

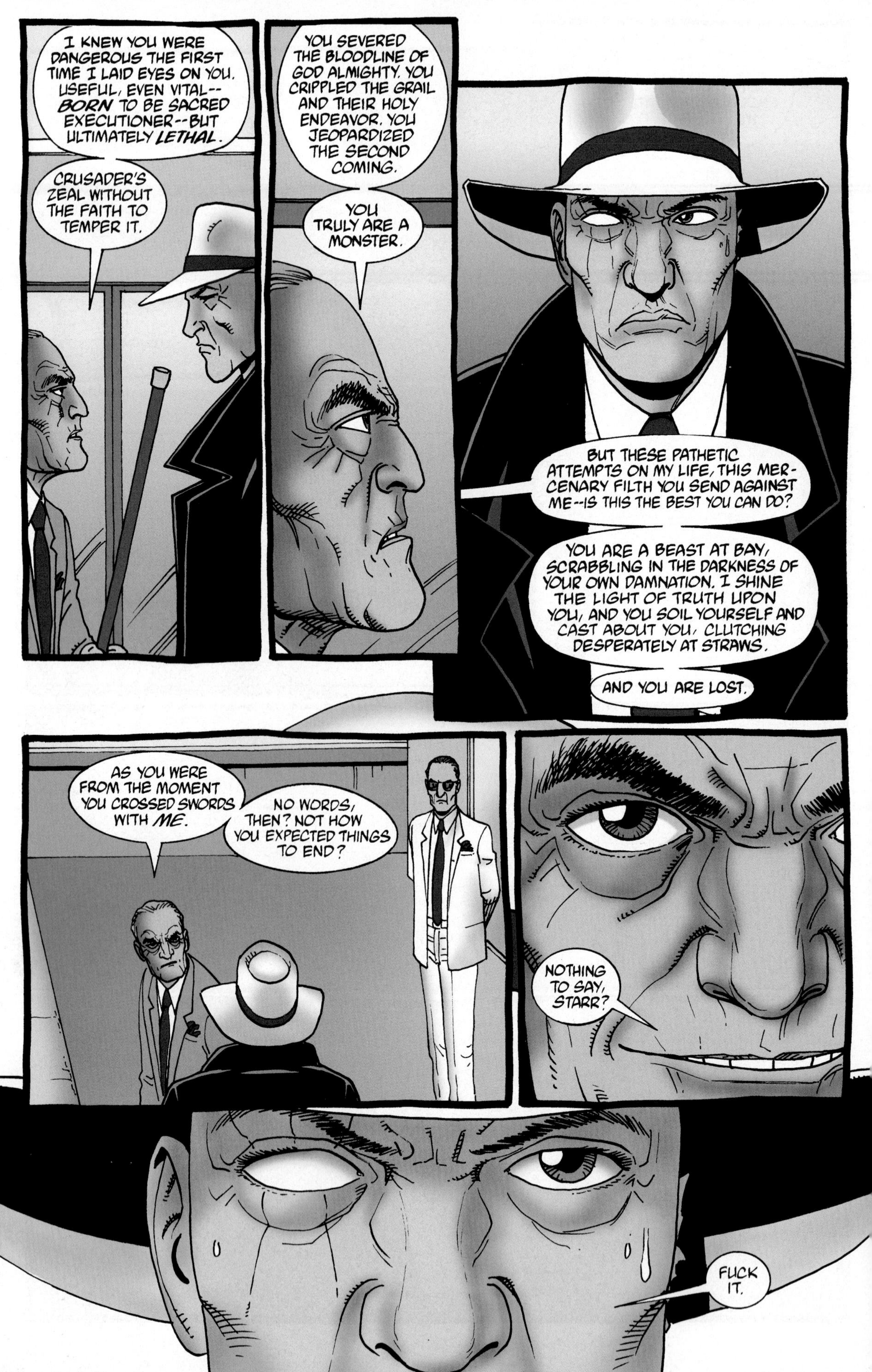
I KNEW YOU WERE DANGEROUS THE FIRST TIME I LAID EYES ON YOU. USEFUL, EVEN VITAL-- BORN TO BE SACRED EXECUTIONER--BUT ULTIMATELY LETHAL.
CRUSADER'S ZEAL WITHOUT THE FAITH TO TEMPER IT.
YOU SEVERED THE BLOODLINE OF GOD ALMIGHTY. YOU CRIPPLED THE GRAIL AND THEIR HOLY ENDEAVOR. YOU JEOPARDIZED THE SECOND COMING.
YOU TRULY ARE A MONSTER.
BUT THESE PATHETIC ATTEMPTS ON MY LIFE, THIS MERCENARY FILTH YOU SEND AGAINST ME--IS THIS THE BEST YOU CAN DO?
YOU ARE A BEAST AT BAY, SCRABBLING IN THE DARKNESS OF YOUR OWN DAMNATION. I SHINE THE LIGHT OF TRUTH UPON YOU, AND YOU SOIL YOURSELF AND CAST ABOUT YOU, CLUTCHING DESPERATELY AT STRAWS.
AND YOU ARE LOST.
AS YOU WERE FROM THE MOMENT YOU CROSSED SWORDS WITH ME.
NO WORDS, THEN? NOT HOW YOU EXPECTED THINGS TO END?
NOTHING TO SAY, STARR?
FUCK IT.

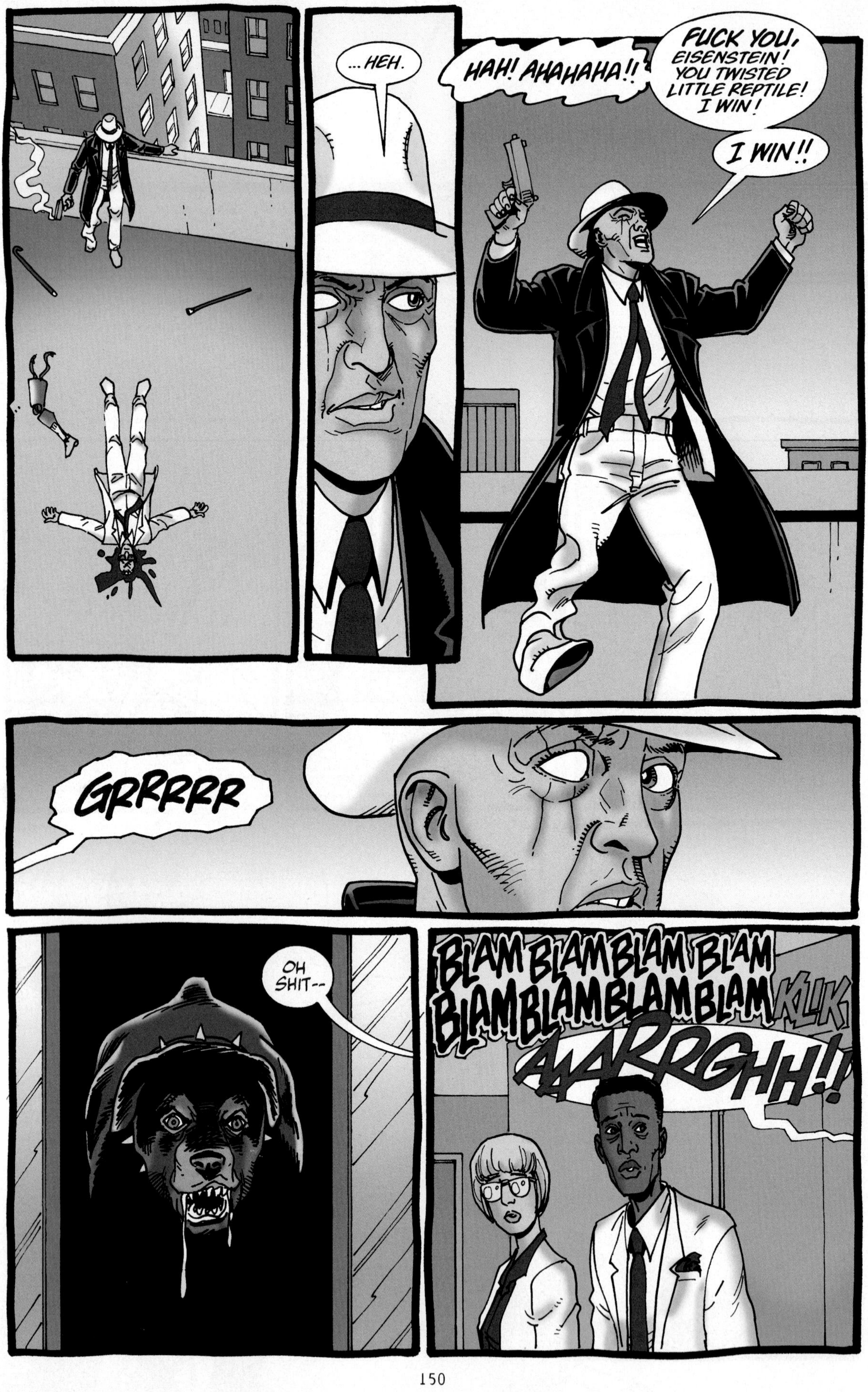

...HEH.
HAH! AHAHAHA!!
FUCK YOU, EISENSTEIN! YOU TWISTED LITTLE REPTILE! I WIN!
I WIN!!

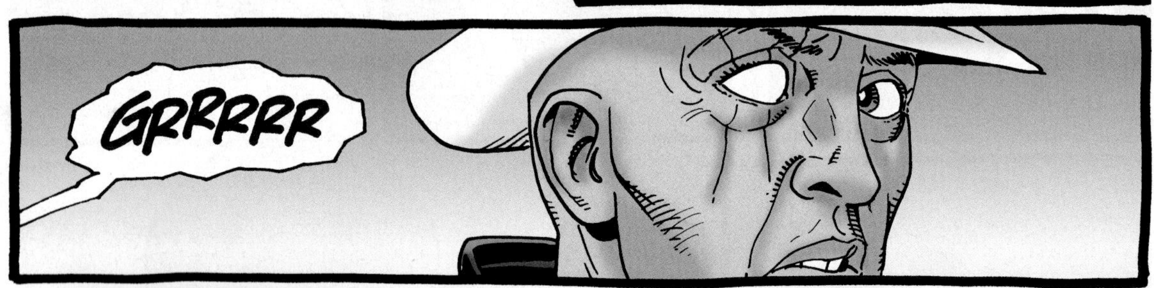

H...
HERR STARR...?
MY COCK IS IN THE BITCH'S MOUTH.
AND NOT IN A GOOD WAY.

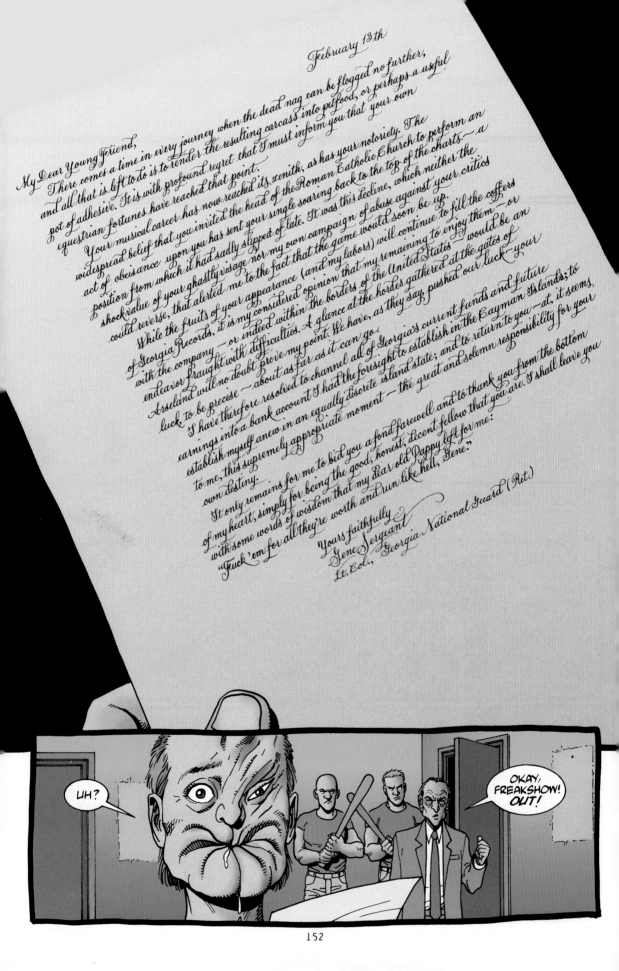

February 13th

My Dear Young Friend,

There comes a time in every journey when the dead nag can be flogged no further, and all that is left to do is to render the resulting carcass into petfood, or perhaps a useful pot of adhesive. It is with profound regret that I must inform you that your own equestrian fortunes have reached that point.

Your musical career has now reached its zenith, as has your notoriety. The widespread belief that you invited the head of the Roman Catholic Church to perform an act of obeisance upon you has sent your single soaring back to the top of the charts—a position from which it had sadly slipped of late. It was this decline, which neither the shock value of your ghastly visage nor my own campaign of abuse against your critics could reverse, that alerted me to the fact that the game would soon be up.

While the fruits of your appearance (and my labors) will continue to fill the coffers of Georgia Records, it is my considered opinion that my remaining to enjoy them—or with the company—or indeed within the borders of the United States—would be an endeavor fraught with difficulties. A glance at the hordes gathered at the gates of Arseland will no doubt prove my point. We have, as they say, pushed our luck—your luck, to be precise—about as far as it can go.

I have therefore resolved to channel all of Georgia's current funds and future earnings into a bank account I had the foresight to establish in the Cayman Islands; to establish myself anew in an equally discrete island state; and to return to you—at, it seems to me, this supremely appropriate moment—the great and solemn responsibility for your own destiny.

It only remains for me to bid you a fond farewell and to thank you from the bottom of my heart, simply for being the good, honest, decent fellow that you are. I shall leave you with some words of wisdom that my dear old Pappy left for me:

"Fuck 'em for all they're worth and run like hell, Gene."

Yours faithfully

Gene Sergeant

Lt. Col., Georgia National Guard (Ret.)

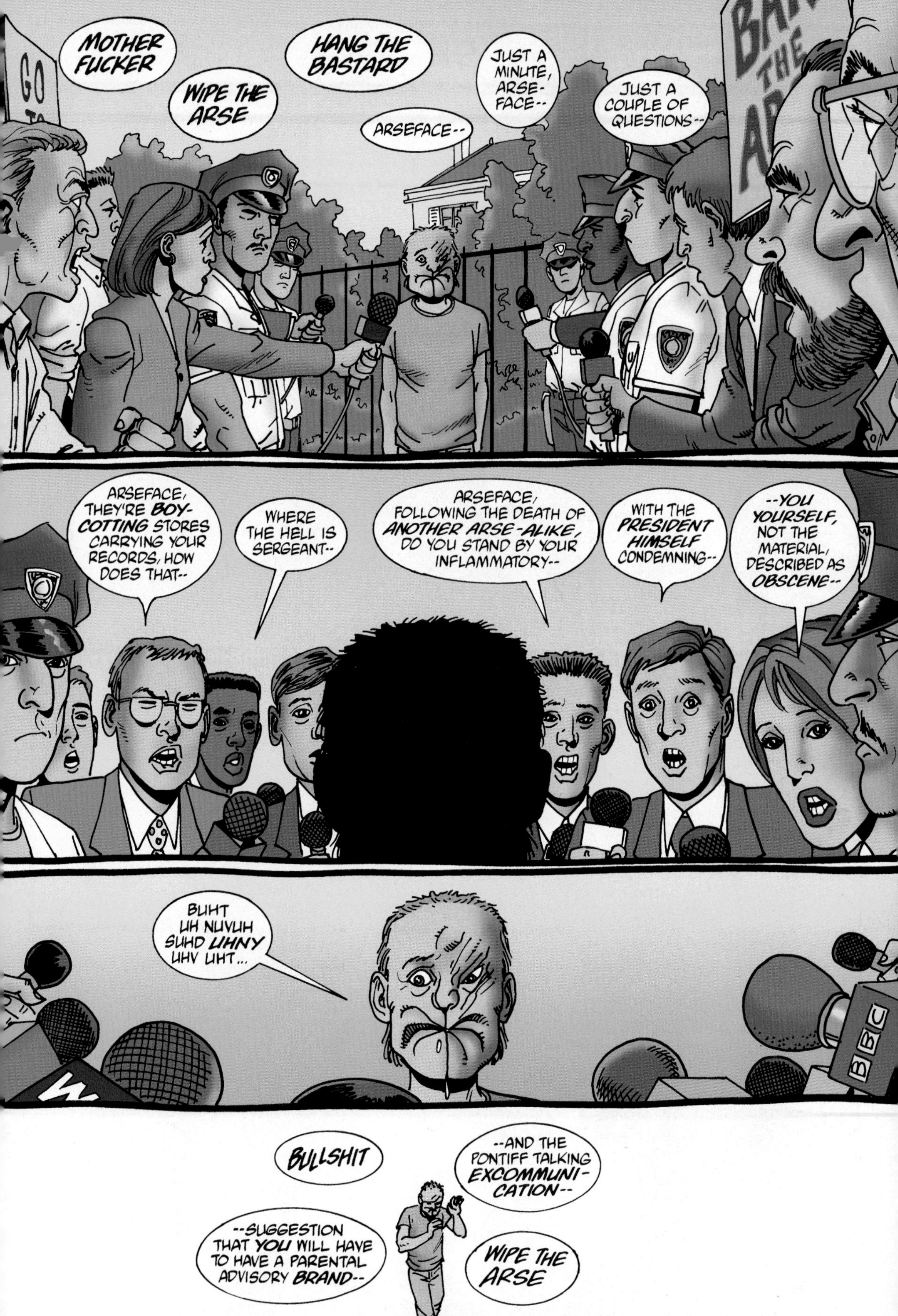

MOTHER FUCKER
WIPE THE ARSE
HANG THE BASTARD
ARSEFACE--
JUST A MINUTE, ARSE-FACE--
JUST A COUPLE OF QUESTIONS--
ARSEFACE, THEY'RE BOY-COTTING STORES CARRYING YOUR RECORDS, HOW DOES THAT--
WHERE THE HELL IS SERGEANT--
ARSEFACE, FOLLOWING THE DEATH OF ANOTHER ARSE-ALIKE, DO YOU STAND BY YOUR INFLAMMATORY--
WITH THE PRESIDENT HIMSELF CONDEMNING--
--YOU YOURSELF, NOT THE MATERIAL, DESCRIBED AS OBSCENE--
BUHT UH NUVUH SUHD UHNY UHV UHT...
BBC
BULLSHIT
--AND THE PONTIFF TALKING EXCOMMUNI-CATION--
--SUGGESTION THAT YOU WILL HAVE TO HAVE A PARENTAL ADVISORY BRAND--
WIPE THE ARSE

GUNS.
AMMO.
HUG.
HEY, GIRL-FRIEND...
THIS TIME YOU CALL ME AT THE FIRST SIGN OF TROUBLE, YOU GOT THAT?
YOU CALL AND I'LL COME RUNNING WITH AN *AIRSTRIKE*.

HELP ME.

...?
WELL, REVEREND.

WELL, AME.
YOU TAKE CARE OF HER. AND YOURSELF.
AND YOU COME BACK AND SEE THIS OLD MAID WHEN YOU'VE GOT THIS CRAZINESS BEHIND YOU, OKAY?
GOODBYE, AMY DARLIN'.

"Y'ALL DON'T MIND LOADIN' THE TRUCK YORESELVES, DO YUH?"
HUH?
"IT'S JUST THE SAWBONES TOL' ME TO REST THIS HERE SPRAINED HAND, SPEND PLENTY O' TIME SITTIN' ON MA ASS AN' SUCH..."

I WISH I WAS GOING WITH YOU.

I WISH I WAS ONE OF YOU.
EITHER ONE.

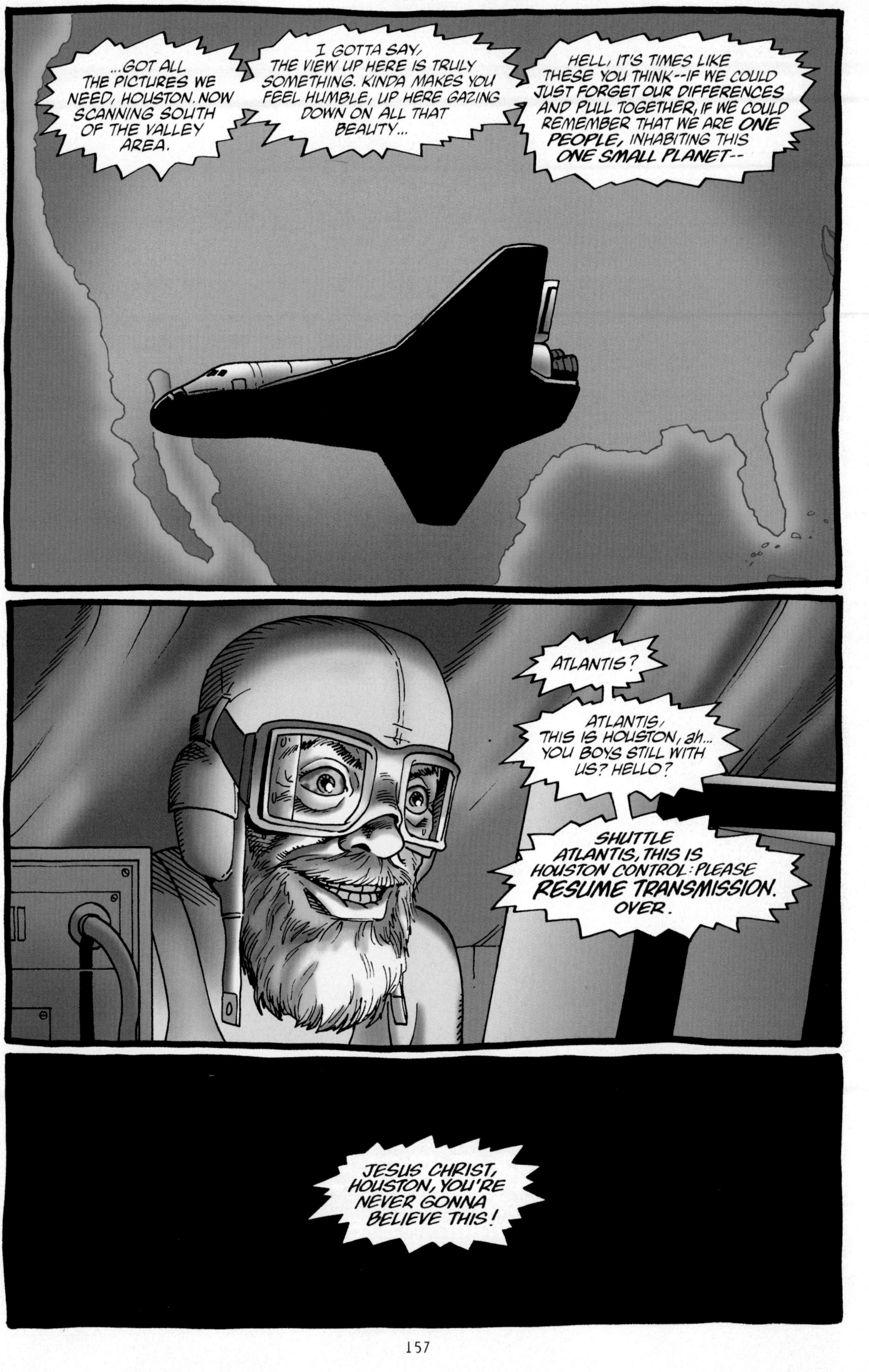

...GOT ALL THE PICTURES WE NEED, HOUSTON. NOW SCANNING SOUTH OF THE VALLEY AREA.

I GOTTA SAY, THE VIEW UP HERE IS TRULY SOMETHING. KINDA MAKES YOU FEEL HUMBLE, UP HERE GAZING DOWN ON ALL THAT BEAUTY...

HELL, IT'S TIMES LIKE THESE YOU THINK--IF WE COULD JUST FORGET OUR DIFFERENCES AND PULL TOGETHER, IF WE COULD REMEMBER THAT WE ARE **ONE PEOPLE,** INHABITING THIS **ONE SMALL PLANET**--

JESUS CHRIST, HOUSTON, YOU'RE NEVER GONNA BELIEVE THIS!

DOT THE I'S AND CROSS THE T'S

GARTH ENNIS - Writer STEVE DILLON - Artist
PAMELA RAMBO - Colorist (pages 2-8) • PATRICIA MULVILHILL - Colorist (pages 1,9-23)
CLEM ROBINS - Letter • AXEL ALONSO - Editor
PREACHER created by GARTH ENNIS and STEVE DILLON

GLENN FABRY 99

"But for Bowie and Crockett and Travis,
and a hundred and eighty men... it was the end."

IT ENDS HERE.
IT ENDS WHERE A SMALL BAND OF HEROES FOUGHT AN ARMY, WHERE THEY HELD FOR TEN LONG DAYS AND NIGHTS, WHERE THEY PERISHED IN THE DUST WHILE THE *DEGUELLO* PLAYED.
IT ENDS IN THE PLACE THAT THE LEGEND BEGAN.

TEXAS, BY GOD

GARTH ENNIS - Writer **STEVE DILLON** - Artist
PAMELA RAMBO - Colorist **CLEM ROBINS** - Letterer **AXEL ALONSO** - Editor
PREACHER created by GARTH ENNIS and STEVE DILLON

LOOK TOO CLOSE AND THE LEGEND CRACKS: BUT THEN, THAT'S LEGENDS FOR YOU.
WAS BOWIE A SLAVER, A DRUNK, A PSYCHOTIC? DID CROCKETT BEG FOR HIS LIFE BEFORE SANTA ANNA, FOR MERCY THAT COULD NEVER COME? ARE HEROES NOTHING MORE THAN DESPERATE MEN?
NO. TO DWELL ON SUCH THINGS IS TO MISS THE POINT.

THEY GAVE SAM HOUSTON TIME TO BUILD HIS ARMY. THEY GAVE THE VICTORS AT SAN JACINTO THEIR BATTLECRY. THEY GAVE THE GREATEST STATE IN THE UNION HER MYTHOLOGY.
FOR TEXAS, IT WAS THE BEGINNING.

BUT FOR BOWIE AND CROCKETT AND TRAVIS, AND A HUNDRED AND EIGHTY MEN...

IT WAS THE END.

HOW THE
HELL DID I END
UP HERE...?

WHO'S YOUR DADDY--WHO'S YOUR DADDY--OH, WHO'S YOUR MOTHERFUCKING **DADDY--**

NOK NOK NOK
FOR CHRIST'S SAKE, FIORE! ANSWER THE FUCKING DOOR, WILL YOU?
KEEPER
KEEPER - GREG
GREG RUCKA

DUUHHH...
TAKE IT, BABY, TAKE IT--
NOK NOK NOK

WHO--
FUUUUUCK!!

OH! YES! THE VINEGAR STROKES! OH! OH! OH--OH--OH-- AAAAAHH--

WHAT THE FUCK--?!

DeBLANC, IT'S GLURK
OH NO.

AN' GOOD MORNIN' TO YOU ON THIS FINE DAY.
MA'AM, WOULD YOU MIND LEAVIN' US FOR A MOMENT? ME AN' THESE FELLAS GOT SOME THINGS WE NEED TO CHEW OVER.
UM... SURE.

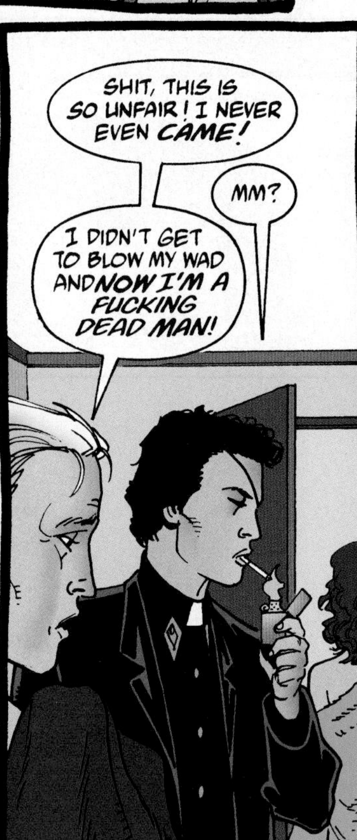
SHIT, THIS IS SO UNFAIR! I NEVER EVEN CAME!
I DIDN'T GET TO BLOW MY WAD AND NOW I'M A FUCKING DEAD MAN!
MM?

COULD BE, BOY.

HOW DO YOU LIKE IT? HOW DO YOU FUCKING WELL LIKE IT?!
BASTARDS!!
LIFE WITHOUT GENITALIA, DAY FIFTY-ONE.

HOW DID YOU FIND US?
CAUGHT YOUR COMMERCIAL. YOU BOYS BEEN HAVIN' QUITE A TIME HERE, AIN'T YOU?

HENCE THE SMACK IN THE MOUTH, I SUPPOSE.
I THINK MY HEAD'S CHANGED SHAPE...!

I BEEN HANKERIN' TO GET BACK TO KICKIN' ASS FOR A COUPLE MONTHS NOW. YOU TWO ASSHOLES FIT THE BILL JUST FINE.
YOU'RE THE ONES LET LOOSE THIS GODDAMN SPOOK I GOT IN MY HEAD.

IT WASN'T ALL OUR FAULT...
YOU MEAN GENESIS? YOU DON'T LIKE IT, ALL THAT POWER AT YOUR FINGER-TIPS?

I AIN'T DENYIN' IT'S COME IN USEFUL, AN' I AIN'T 'BOUT TO BACK DOWN FROM THIS JOB I GOTTA DO.
BUT THE ROAD THAT DAMN THING SET ME ON SURE HAS COST A LOTTA FOLKS A LOTTA BLOOD...
YES, WELL I HOPE YOU'RE USED TO IT. GENESIS' SPIRIT IS TIED TO YOUR OWN.

WHICH MEANS NOT UNTIL DEATH DO YOU PART.
REVEREND CUSTER.

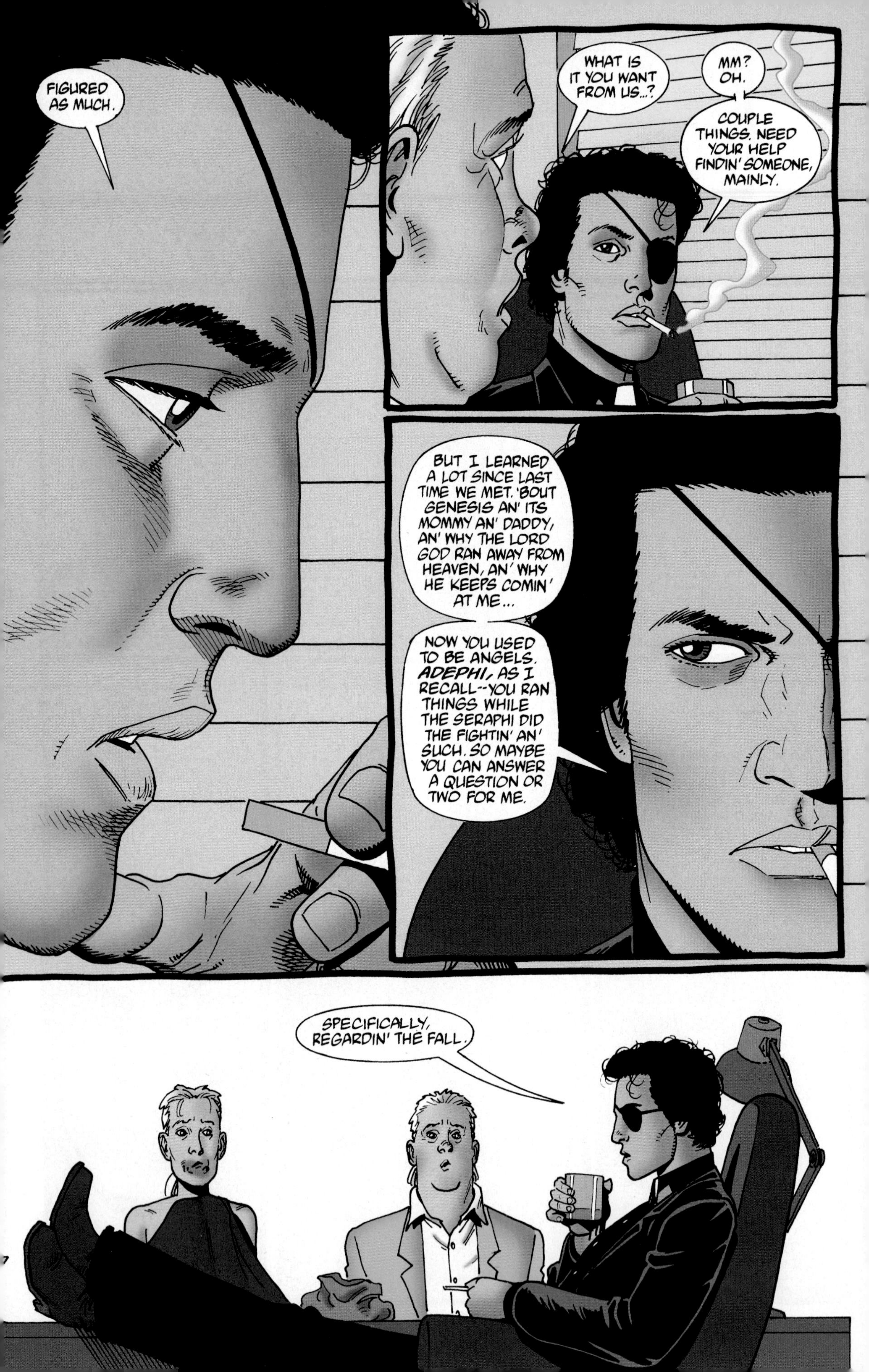

FIGURED AS MUCH.

WHAT IS IT YOU WANT FROM US...?

MM? OH.

COUPLE THINGS. NEED YOUR HELP FINDIN' SOMEONE, MAINLY.

BUT I LEARNED A LOT SINCE LAST TIME WE MET. 'BOUT GENESIS AN' ITS MOMMY AN' DADDY, AN' WHY THE LORD GOD RAN AWAY FROM HEAVEN, AN' WHY HE KEEPS COMIN' AT ME...

NOW YOU USED TO BE ANGELS. ***ADEPHI,*** AS I RECALL--YOU RAN THINGS WHILE THE SERAPHI DID THE FIGHTIN' AN' SUCH. SO MAYBE YOU CAN ANSWER A QUESTION OR TWO FOR ME.

CHRIST, WHAT DO YOU HAVE TO GO ASKING ABOUT *THAT* FOR?
REALLY DID HAPPEN, HUH? WASN'T JUST SOME POEM?
OH, IT HAPPENED, ALL RIGHT.
I'M STILL TRYING TO FORGET IT.

IT WAS A TERRIBLE TIME. ANGEL FOUGHT ANGEL. HEAVEN RANG WITH THE CLASH OF IRON, THE STREETS OF PARADISE RAN WITH BLOOD.
EVERYONE FOUGHT ON THAT AWFUL DAY. EVEN WE ADEPHI STOOD READY FOR BATTLE...
SPEAK FOR YOURSELF, CHUM. I FUCKED OFF DOWN TO THE CELLARS AND HID IN A BARREL OF BRANDY.
BUT THE LOYALIST SERAPHI TRIUMPHED WITHOUT US.
THE TRANSGRESSORS--THE FEW SURVIVORS, ANYWAY WERE ROUNDED UP. AND JUDGED. AND CAST DOWN.
THAT WAS THE LONGEST FALL OF ALL.

SO...WHY?
BECAUSE OF *YOU*.

THE LORD ANNOUNCED HIS GREAT LEAP FORWARD. LIFE ON EARTH, NOT IN HEAVEN, THAT COULD THINK FOR ITSELF AND DECIDE ITS OWN SPIRITUAL DESTINY.
MEN OF FREE WILL.
EVERY ANGEL IN PARADISE KNEW WHAT THAT WOULD MEAN. WITHOUT THE LOVE OF GOD AROUND THEM--TANGIBLE, REAL, AS IT IS IN HEAVEN--MEN ON EARTH WOULD TURN FROM GOD. GO THEIR OWN WAYS, DIVIDE INTO FACTIONS, FIGHT WAR UPON WAR UPON WAR...
HALF OF THE HOST WENT BERSERK ON THE SPOT.
WHY WOULD HE DO THAT, I WONDER.
MM?
WELL, THE LORD KNEW EVERYTHIN', RIGHT? LONG AS HE WAS IN HEAVEN, AIN'T NOTHIN' COULDA SURPRISED HIM.
SO WHY FOIST A CRAZY THING LIKE THIS ON HIS ANGELS? WHEN HE'DA KNOWN THERE'D BE SUCH GOD-AWFUL SLAUGHTER?
I AIN'T EVEN TALKIN' 'BOUT WHAT MEN'D DO ON EARTH, I'M TALKIN' 'BOUT YOU AN' YOUR KIND. HE'D A KNOWN HALFA YOU'D JUMP ONE WAY AN' HALFA YOU THE OTHER, DEPENDIN' ON YOUR NATURE.
SO WHY DO IT?

WELL--I MEAN--I--
I...
um...

FILE UNDER *MOVES IN MYSTERIOUS WAYS.*
I DON'T FUCKING KNOW.

WELL YOU LET ME KNOW, YOU EVER FIGURE IT OUT.

SO WHO'S THIS SOMEONE YOU NEED HELP FINDING, EXACTLY?

...
YOU COULD SAY IT'S ONE'VE THEM *MEN OF FREE WILL* YOU WERE TALKIN' ABOUT.

OR USED TO BE, I GUESS.

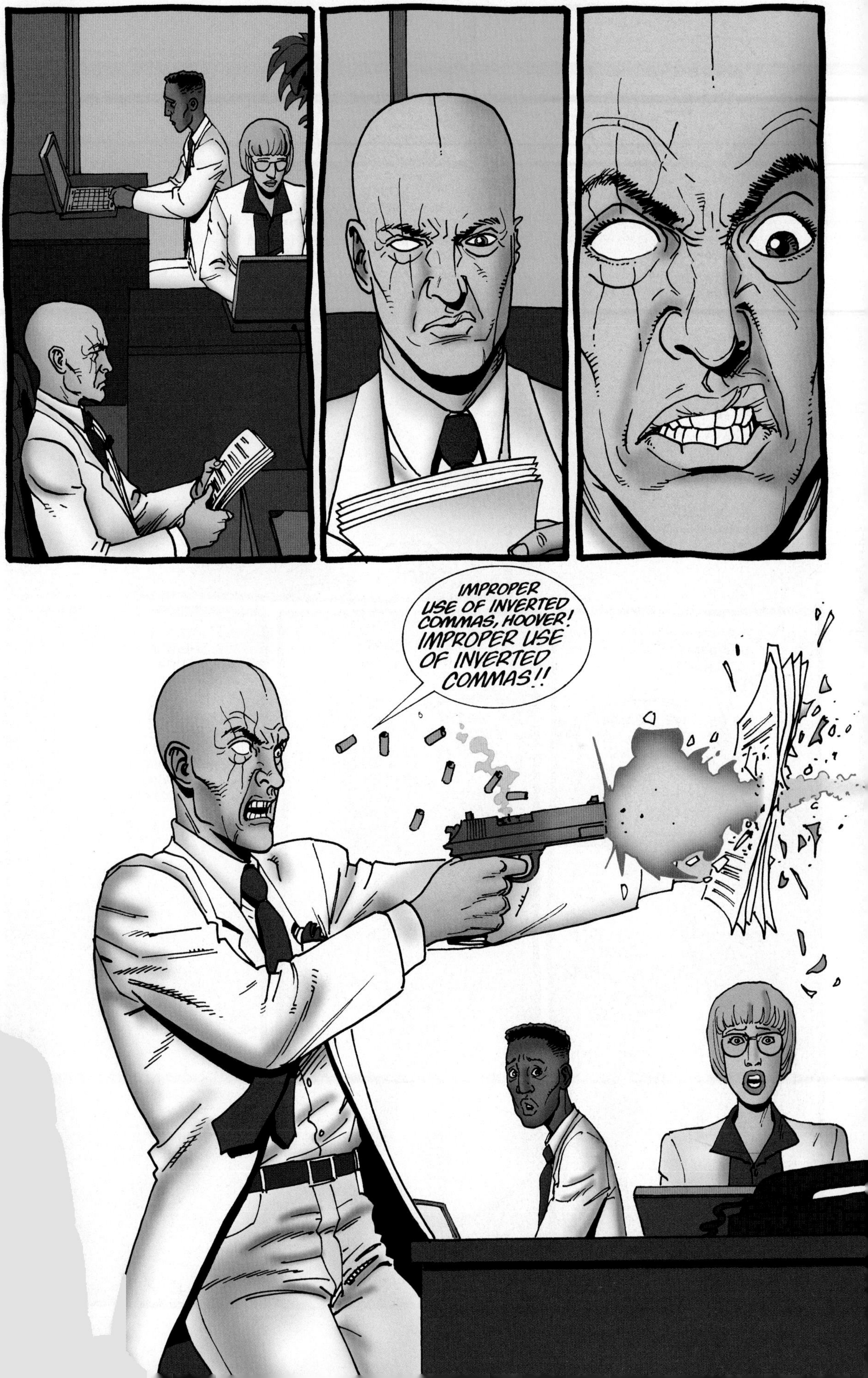

IMPROPER USE OF INVERTED COMMAS, HOOVER! IMPROPER USE OF INVERTED COMMAS!!

HERR STARR--!
WH-WH-WHAT'D I DO?
WHAT DID YOU DO? YOU DID WHAT YOU ALWAYS DO, HOOVER! YOU FUCKED UP!
THIS REPORT OF YOURS! THIS SAMSON TEAM SURVIVORS--AN EVALUATION!
YOU'VE GOT INVERTED COMMAS ROUND EACH OF THE PARAGRAPH HEADINGS! YOU'VE GOT THEM ROUND DISPOSITION, ROUND CRITICAL SHORTAGES, ROUND RECRUITMENT DIFFICULTIES-- NOW WHY HAVE YOU FUCKING DONE THAT, HOOVER?

INVERTED COMMAS?
HE MEANS QUOTES, YOU KNOW, LIKE--

DON'T DO THAT! DON'T EVER DO THAT! I HATE THAT SHIT!
LET'S FUCKING HEAR IT, HOOVER!

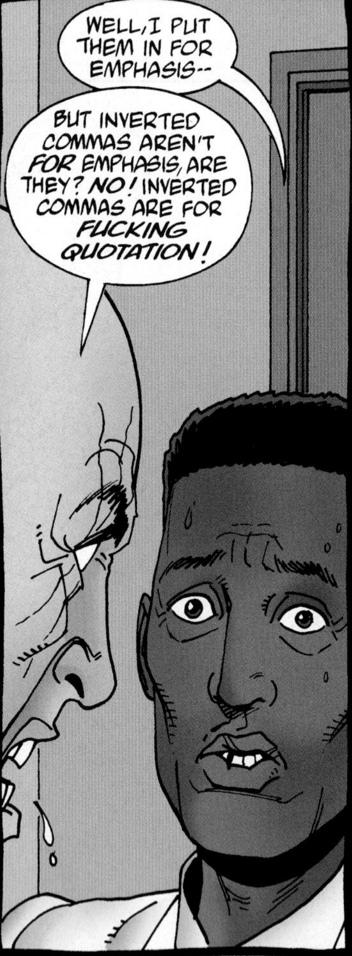
WELL, I PUT THEM IN FOR EMPHASIS--
BUT INVERTED COMMAS AREN'T FOR EMPHASIS, ARE THEY? NO! INVERTED COMMAS ARE FOR FUCKING QUOTATION!

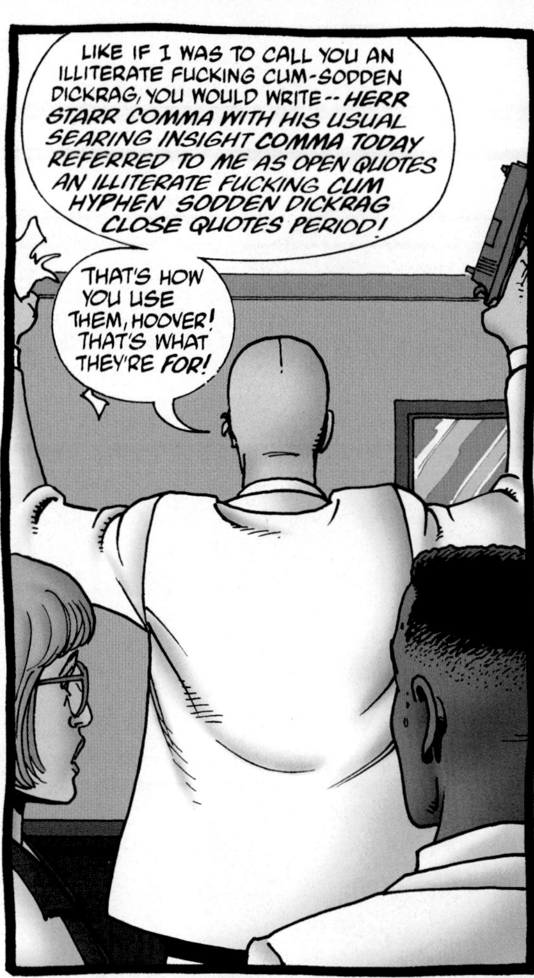

LIKE IF I WAS TO CALL YOU AN ILLITERATE FUCKING CUM-SODDEN DICKRAG, YOU WOULD WRITE-- HERR STARR COMMA WITH HIS USUAL SEARING INSIGHT COMMA TODAY REFERRED TO ME AS OPEN QUOTES AN ILLITERATE FUCKING CUM HYPHEN SODDEN DICKRAG CLOSE QUOTES PERIOD!
THAT'S HOW YOU USE THEM, HOOVER! THAT'S WHAT THEY'RE FOR!

SO I DO NOT EXPECT TO READ A REPORT BY ONE OF MY LIEUTENANTS, ONLY TO FIND PARAGRAPH HEADINGS QUOTED AT ME LIKE THEY CAME FROM SOME STUPID FUCKING THEATRE REVIEW, EVER AGAIN.
IS THAT CLEAR?

YES, MR. STARR.
I... REALLY DON'T THINK IT'S WORTH GETTING QUITE SO WORKED UP ABOUT...

OH, DON'T YOU?
IT'S JUST THAT THE MANAGEMENT HAVE MADE ONE OR TWO COMPLAINTS ABOUT FIREARMS BEING DISCHARGED IN THE SUITE, AND IT HAS BEEN HAPPENING RATHER A LOT RECENTLY...

WHAT HAVE THEY BEEN SAYING?

NOTHING. ABSOLUTELY NOTHING. THEY HAVEN'T BREATHED A WORD ON THE SUBJECT.

THIS GUN ISN'T BIG ENOUGH...
um...HERR STARR, ISN'T IT TIME YOU TOLD US WHAT OUR NEXT MOVE IS? Le SAINT MARIE ARE CALLING DAILY, DEMANDING TO KNOW ABOUT EISENSTEIN, ABOUT ALL KINDS OF THINGS...

GO OUT AND GET ME A BIGGER GUN. A MUCH BIGGER GUN. A FORTY-FOUR OR A THREE-FIFTY-SEVEN, SOMETHING ENORMOUS...
I'LL TELL YOU MY PLANS WHEN I'M GOOD AND FUCKING READY, FEATHERSTONE.

HE'S GETTING WORSE BY THE DAY. I'M BEGINNING TO WONDER JUST WHAT HE MIGHT BE CAPABLE OF...
THAT--THAT--THAT--

HOOVER...ARE YOU SERIOUSLY TRYING TO TELL ME YOU STILL CAN'T BRING YOURSELF TO SAY MOTHERFUCKER?
FEATHERSTONE--!

IN THE RIBS...
PAYDIRT.

WELL THEN, BIG MAN.
COME ON IF YOU'RE COMIN'.

RIGHT, MR. CASSIDY: ARE YEH READY TO DO THIS?

AS A MATTER OF FACT IT WAS TOO LATE A LONG TIME AGO, FATHER.
AN' I'D RATHER TALK TO THE ORGAN-GRINDER THAN THE MONKEY, SO DO US A FAVOR AN' FUCK AWAY OFF.
HOW'RE YEH.
I WANTED A WORD WITH YEH, IF YEH'VE GOT A MINUTE.

I WONDERED IF YEH'D BE INTERESTED IN MAKIN' A DEAL.

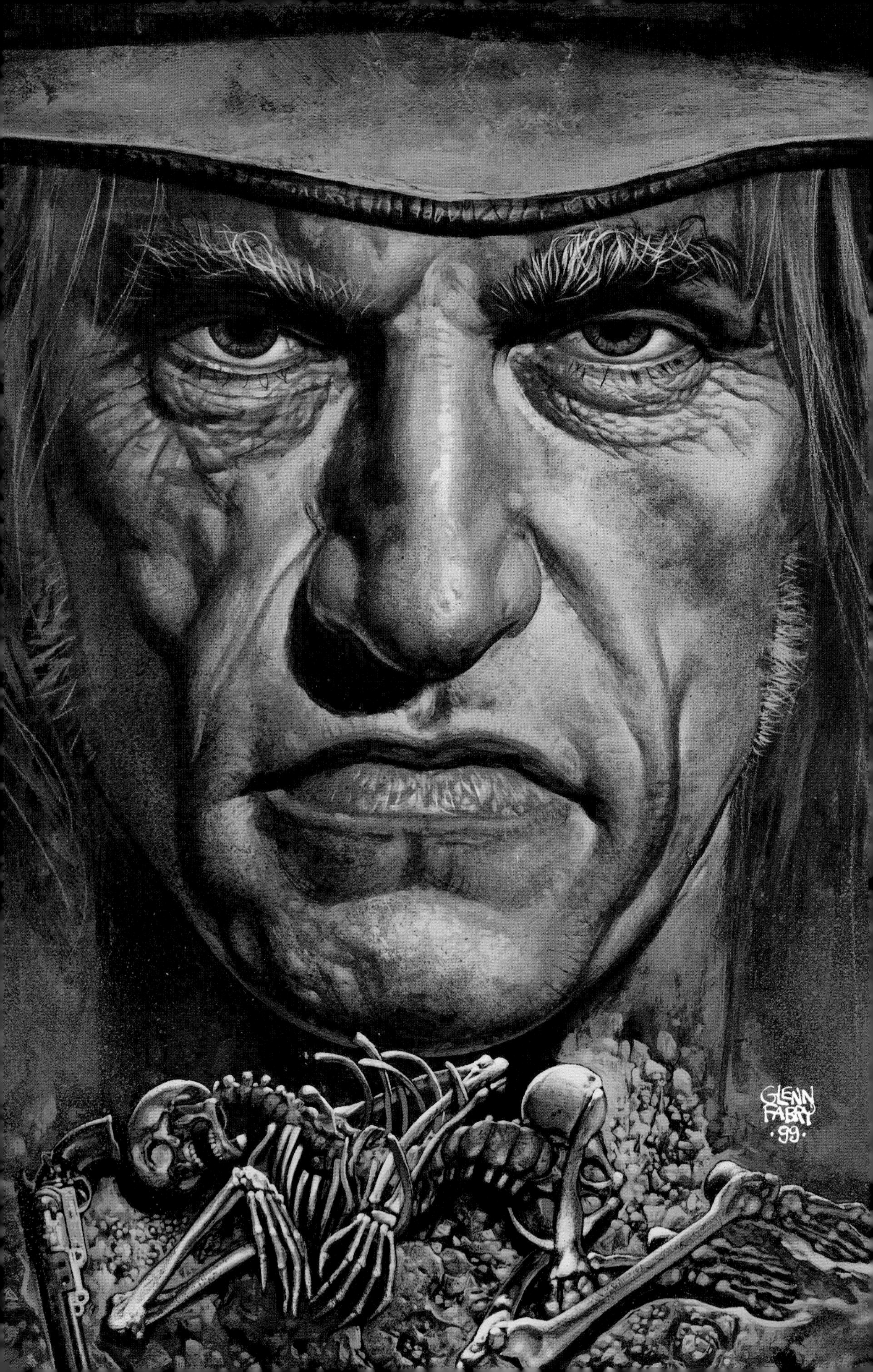
GLENN
FABRY
·99·

"I'd get the feelin' somethin' was behind me. Somethin' waitin' for me to become it."

THIS PART I NEVER CAN GET USED TO, NOT EVEN A LITTLE BIT.

THE THUNDER OF HIS GUNS

GARTH ENNIS - Writer STEVE DILLON - Artist
PAMELA RAMBO - Colorist CLEM ROBINS - Letterer AXEL ALONSO - Editor
PREACHER created by GARTH ENNIS and STEVE DILLON

DOOM
COCK...

DOOM
COCK...

DOOM
COCK...

DOOM
COCK...
H...HERR
STARR?

WHAT IS IT NOW, FEATHERSTONE?
THAT, UM...
THAT WOMAN'S HERE.
OH YES. RIGHT, GET IN HERE.
AND LE SAINT MARIE HAVE CALLED AGAIN--
WELL FUCKING STALL THEM AGAIN! JESUS!
DON'T TORMENT YOURSELF, FEATHER-STONE.
YOU'RE FAR TOO GOOD FOR HIM.

WELL I'LL GIVE YOU THIS, PREACHER.
I NEVER MET A MAN SO SET ON DYIN'.

THAT AIN'T WHAT I'M HERE FOR...
NO?

SO WHAT MIGHT THIS BE?

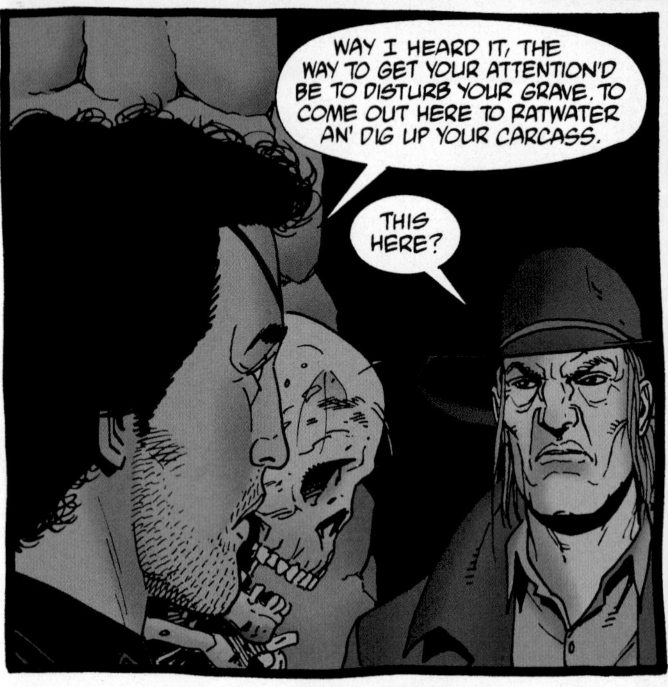
WAY I HEARD IT, THE WAY TO GET YOUR ATTENTION'D BE TO DISTURB YOUR GRAVE. TO COME OUT HERE TO RATWATER AN' DIG UP YOUR CARCASS.
THIS HERE?

THIS AIN'T BUT BONES.

THIS SHITHOLE AIN'T BEEN ON THE MAP THESE HUNDRED YEARS OR MORE. WHO WAS IT TOLD YOU ALLA THIS?
THE ANGELS. THE TWO IN VEGAS.

THEN THEY'RE NEXT, I RECKON...
HELL, THEM TWO ASSHOLES AIN'T WORTH A BULLET. YOU KNOW THAT.

DON'T GO TELLIN' ME WHAT I KNOW, BOY.

OKAY, HOW 'BOUT THIS?
I *KNOW* YOU'RE MAD AS HELL AT THE LORD GOD, FOR THE THINGS HE DID WHEN YOU WERE LIVIN'. FOR CAUSIN' THE DEATH OF YOUR WIFE AN' CHILD. FOR SETTIN' YOU ON THE ROAD TO BEIN' SAINT OF KILLERS.
AN' I'D BET MY LAST DOLLAR YOU BEEN OUT THERE LOOKIN' FOR HIM, AN' YOU AIN'T COME UP WITH ***SHIT***.

SO YOU GO RIGHT AHEAD AN' PULL THEM PISTOLS, MISTER, AN' YOU KILL THE ONLY MAN ALIVE CAN SET THAT BASTARD UP FOR YOU.
SEE WHAT YOU'RE LEFT WITH THEN.

KEEP...
TALKIN'...

WE BOTH WANT JUSTICE FROM THE LORD. YOU FOR YOUR FAMILY. ME FOR THE CRIME OF THIS FLAWED CREATION OF HIS, AN' THE SUFFERIN' IT'S BROUGHT.
NOW, HE WON'T FACE YOU, NOT WITH THEM GUNS'VE YOURS--"NO WOUND THEY GAVE WOULD BE ANYTHING BUT FATAL", AIN'T THAT HOW IT GOES?
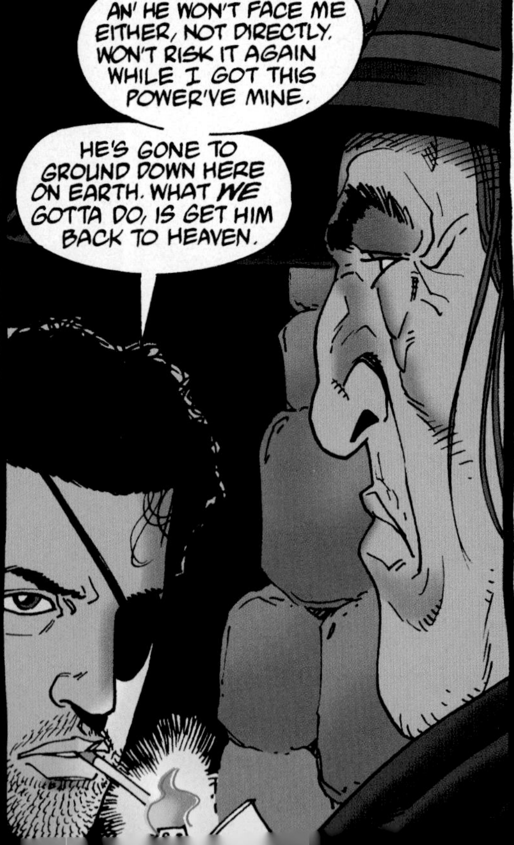
AN' HE WON'T FACE ME EITHER, NOT DIRECTLY. WON'T RISK IT AGAIN WHILE I GOT THIS POWER'VE MINE.
HE'S GONE TO GROUND DOWN HERE ON EARTH. WHAT WE GOTTA DO, IS GET HIM BACK TO HEAVEN.

HE WON'T BREAK COVER TO GET BACK THERE. NOT WHILE HE KNOWS I'M WATCHIN' OUT FOR HIM. I'D SEE HIM THE SECOND HE MADE HIS MOVE.
HOW YOU FIGURE THAT?

GENESIS. PART DEMON, PART ANGEL. A POWER LIKE THE ALMIGHTY GETS *NEAR* THE PEARLY GATES, THIS DAMN SPOOK'LL KNOW.
AN' SO WILL I.

BUT SAY GENESIS WAS GONE, AN' HE FELT SAFE ENOUGH TO TRY A RUN FOR HOME...
WON'T WORK.

TIME I GOT UP THERE AFTER HIM, HE'D BE BACK ON HIS DAMN THRONE. AN' THE LORD GOD SITS ON THE SEAT OF ETERNITY, AIN'T A GUN IN CREATION CAN SCRATCH HIS HIDE.
NOT EVEN ONE SAYS COLT ON THE BARREL.
SO HOW 'BOUT IF YOU'RE ALREADY UP THERE WAITIN'?

YOU WOULDN'T HAVE NO TROUBLE GETTIN' INTO HEAVEN NOW, WOULD YOU?
ANY FOOL TRIED TO STOP ME'D SOON KNOW WHAT TROUBLE WAS. AN' I COULD DROP THAT SON OF A BITCH 'FORE HE TOOK TWO STEPS THROUGH THE GATES.
HOW YOU PLAN TO CONVINCE HIM HE'S SAFE ENOUGH TO TRY?

'FORE I SAY ANY MORE 'BOUT IT, THIS IS THE MOST IMPORTANT THING I EVER TRUSTED TO A LIVIN' SOUL. WHAT I'M GONNA DO, SHIT, WHAT I'M GONNA SACRIFICE HERE...
I NEED YOUR WORD THAT YOU WILL SEE THIS THROUGH. THAT YOU WILL KEEP UP YOUR END OF IT.

YOU WANT MY WORD.
LIKE WE'RE SOME KINDA PARTNERS.

YOU WERE A MAN ONCE. NOW YOU'RE SOME-THIN' MORE, OR MAYBE LESS. I AIN'T QUITE SURE.
BUT THERE'S ENOUGH OF A MAN LEFT IN THERE TO KEEP HIS WORD, THAT I KNOW FROM EXPERIENCE.

RECKON THERE'S SOMETHIN' YOU'VE FORGOTTEN, PREACHER.
YOU SEE 'EM OUT THERE?

SEE... WHO?

WELL.
I GUESS YOU DIDN'T KILL 'EM.

LOOK AGAIN.

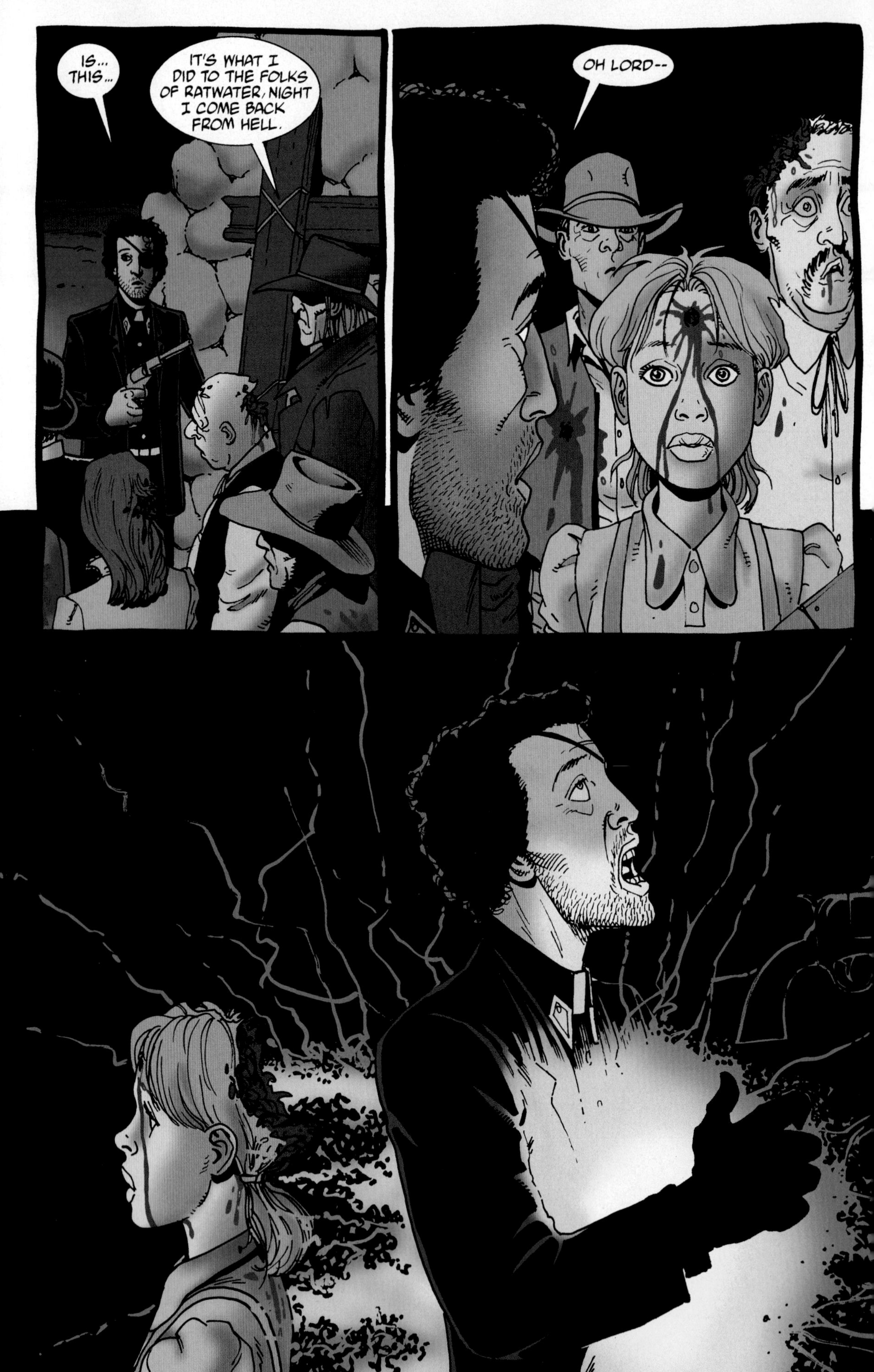
IS... THIS...
IT'S WHAT I DID TO THE FOLKS OF RATWATER, NIGHT I COME BACK FROM HELL.
OH LORD--

HUHH--!
DEAR--
JESUS--
THAT'S WHAT I AM, BOY.
DO WELL TO REMEMBER IT.
THEN BY GOD LET'S TURN YOU LOOSE.

SOME...GOOD NEWS, HERR STARR...
THE FIRST HUMAN PENIS TRANSPLANT HAS BEEN SUCCESSFULLY PERFORMED?
WELL, NO--
ANYTHING ELSE FALLS FAR SHORT OF GOOD NEWS...
JESSE CUSTER WILL BE IN SAN ANTONIO IN ONE WEEK'S TIME?!
WHERE DID THIS COME FROM?
AH, VIA RECEPTION, EARLIER THIS EVENING... THE GIRL SAID THE CALLER HAD A SOUTHERN ACCENT, BUT APART FROM THAT--
FEATHERSTONE. HOOVER.
THESE ARE YOUR ORDERS.

ISSUE A **WORLDWIDE PRIORITY EDICT**: ALL SAMSON PERSONNEL TO ASSEMBLE IN SAN ANTONIO, TEXAS, SEVENTY-TWO HOURS FROM TONIGHT. LOCAL UNIT TO ARRANGE R.V.
BOOK A **VIDEOPHONE CALL** TO THE ELITE COUNCIL AT LE SAINT MARIE--DAY AFTER TOMORROW, OH-EIGHT-HUNDRED THEIR TIME. BUT FIRST HAVE THE SAMSON C.O. THERE CONTACT *ME*, PERSONALLY.
FINALLY: BEGIN TRANSFER OF THIS H.Q. TO SAN ANTONIO.

AT ONCE, HERR STARR!
er...

MISTER STARR, I DON'T KNOW IF YOU REMEMBER MY REPORT--
I SHOT YOUR PATHETIC REPORT, HOOVER. YOU KNOW THAT.

WELL...IF YOU'D ACTUALLY FINISHED READING IT, YOU'D KNOW OUR SAMSON CAPABILITY IS DANGEROUSLY WEAK. AFTER MASADA AND THE VALLEY WE'LL BE LUCKY TO MUSTER TWO DOZEN TROOPERS...

WE HAVE AT LEAST ONE DEEP COVER OPERATIVE SHADOWING EVERY MAJOR WORLD LEADER, DON'T WE?
PULL THEM IN. THEY'LL MAKE UP THE SHORTFALL IN NO TIME.

BUT THEY'VE SPENT YEARS, DECADES, GAINING THE CONFIDENCE OF THEIR TARGETS! IF WE BRING THEM IN NOW IT'LL ALL BE FOR NOTHING!
WHAT ABOUT THE PLAN? WHAT ABOUT ARMAGEDDON?

WHAT ABOUT SHUTTING UP AND DOING AS YOU'RE TOLD?
ARMAGEDDON CAN WAIT, HOOVER.

NOW GET TO IT.

DID YOU...HEAR THAT...?
YES.
THAT VOICE.

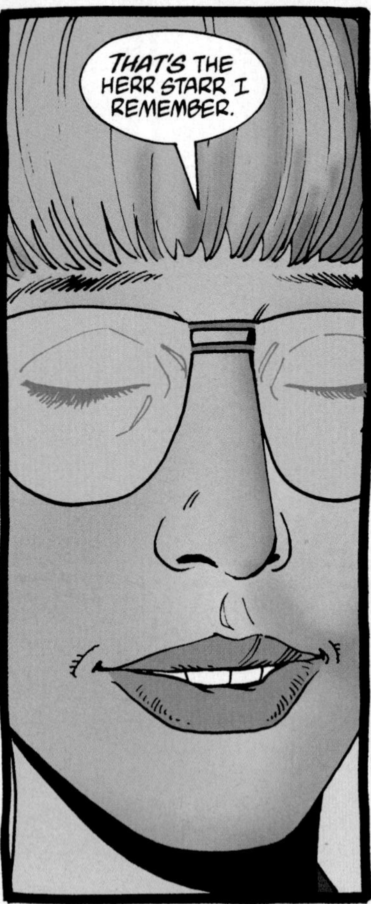
THAT'S THE HERR STARR I REMEMBER.

I GOT NO ILLUSIONS 'BOUT WHAT YOU ARE.
I AIN'T MAKIN' NO DAMN-FOOL PROMISES NEITHER, 'BOUT REDEMPTION, NOR PEACE OF MIND, NOR ANY OF THAT.
NOW MAYBE THIS AIN'T BUT BONES, BUT IT PROVES YOU *WERE* A MAN.
AN' I SURE AS HELL KNOW THERE'S MAN ENOUGH LEFT TO WANT *REVENGE*.
SEE, I KNOW YOUR STORY, MISTER.
MADE BY GOD TO HATE LIKE NOTHIN' AN NO ONE EVER DID BEFORE.
I RECKON THAT'LL DO IT.

OH, YOU GONNA KILL ME? THAT IT?
GODDAMN, YOU THINK BEIN' FUCKED OVER BY THE LORD MAKES YOU *UNIQUE?*

LOOK AT IT! LOOK WHAT HE MADE! ALL THEM YEARS FILLED WITH SUFFERIN' AN' SLAUGHTER, JUST LIKE HE KNEW THEY WOULD BE!
'CAUSE HE WANTS US TO CHOOSE *HIM*, TO LOVE *HIM*, AN' HOW MUCH MORE SATISFYIN' THAT'D BE WHEN THE HELL OF THIS EARTH MAKES THAT CHOICE SO *GOD-DAMNED HARD!*

HELL, I'LL GO YOU ONE BETTER.
HE WANTED THE LOVE OF A POWER GREATER THAN HIS OWN, EVEN THOUGH IT MEANT HE'D HAVE TO FLEE FROM HEAVEN--SO HE CREATED IT.
A DEMON AN' A ANGEL SUDDENLY OVERCOME FUCKIN' *EONS* OF INSTINCT AN' CONDITIONIN', AN' JUST LIKE THAT THEY FALL IN LOVE? BULLSHIT. THAT SERAPHI ASSHOLE SAID IT HIMSELF, ***OUR WILLS WERE NOT OUR OWN...***

I REMEMBER...
A TIME OR TWO, WAY OUT ON THE PRAIRIE...

I'D GET THE FEELIN' SOMETHIN' WAS BEHIND ME.

SOMETHIN' WAITIN' FOR ME TO BECOME IT.

WHAT'S YOUR DAMN PLAN, PREACHER?

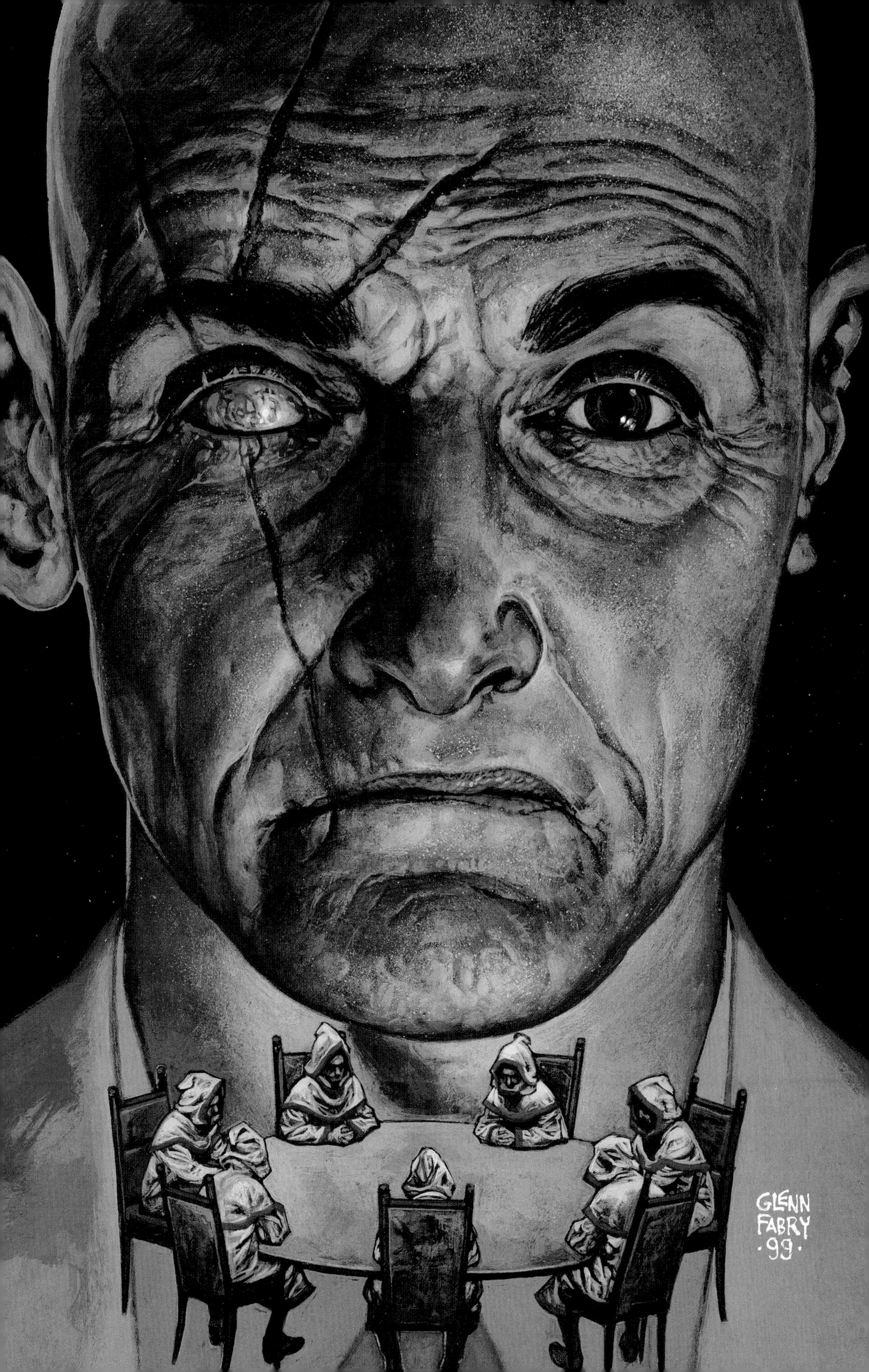
GLENN
FABRY
·99·

"Yes! Look at it! Look at my greatest sacrifice!
Gaze on the face of war!"

WE, THE ELITE COUNCIL OF THE GRAIL, DO GATHER AT YOUR BIDDING...

WE, THE KEEPERS OF THE SACRED BLOODLINE...
WE, WHO BESTOW THE ANCIENT SEAL OF ENABLEMENT...
WE, THE POWER BEHIND THE ALLFATHER...
DO GATHER AT YOUR BIDDING...

BLESSED.
BLESSED.
BLESSED.
BLESSED.
MANY TIMES BLESSED.

ARE WE.
ALLFATHER STARR.

THE WONDER OF YOU

GARTH ENNIS - Writer STEVE DILLON - Artist

PAMELA RAMBO - Colorist CLEM ROBINS - Letterer AXEL ALONSO - Editor

PREACHER created by GARTH ENNIS and STEVE DILLON

DIAMOND MOTEL
THE JEWEL IN THE CRO::N
OF SAN ANTONIO
GODDAMN, GIRL--

WHAT'D YOU BE LIKE AFTER TWO WEEKS?

...SORRY, DID YOU SAY SOME-THING?
NOPE!

YOUR INSULTS ARE...REFRESHING, ALLFATHER.
REALLY.

THEY MAKE A CHANGE FROM SUBTERFUGE.
YOUR ACTION IN ARIZONA WAS A GROSS ABUSE OF POWER, BUT WE SUSPECTED WORSE. THE DESTRUCTION OF MASADA. THE DEATH OF THE CHILD.
YOU?

ME.
YOUR LITTLE GOBLIN EISENSTEIN WOULD HAVE TOLD YOU AS MUCH, IF I HADN'T KICKED HIM OFF A BUILDING. ALSO THAT I PLANNED TO SUBSTITUTE A MORTAL MAN FOR YOUR FARCE OF A MESSIAH, AND HIJACK THE ARMAGEDDON PLAN FOR MY OWN ENDS.

YOU KILLED EISENSTEIN TO MAINTAIN THE SECRETS YOU ARE NOW TELLING US YOURSELF?
ONLY TO BUY TIME. HIS DISCOVERIES ARE ALREADY OUT OF DATE.

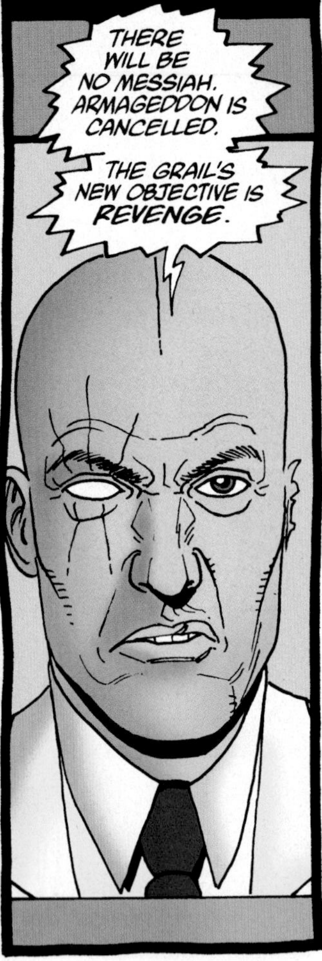
THERE WILL BE NO MESSIAH. ARMAGEDDON IS CANCELLED.
THE GRAIL'S NEW OBJECTIVE IS REVENGE.

HE CONDEMNS HIMSELF--!
BE SILENT.
ARMAGEDDON IS CANCELLED? WHEN YOU'VE ALREADY SAID YOU PLAN TO HIJACK IT?
I SAID PLANNED.

I ONCE BELIEVED I WAS FIGHTING A WAR.
AGAINST CHAOS. FOR HUMANITY.
TO WIN A WORLD OF ORDER.

WITH THE MESSIAH UNDER MY CONTROL, I WOULD SIMPLY SUBVERT YOUR SCHEME TO RULE THE PLANET. I WOULD BUILD THE WORLD I WANTED, INSTEAD OF THE ONE EXPECTED BY THE GRAIL.
BUT WAR DEMANDS SACRIFICE. AND HUMANITY IS NOT WORTH IT.

IT IS NOT WORTH GETTING ONE'S FUCKING EAR SHOT OFF, FOR INSTANCE, OR ONE'S LEG DEVOURED BY CANNIBALS! OR BEING FUCKED UP THE ARSE BY A GIGANTIC ENGLISHMAN! NO!
OR JUST TO GIVE YOU ANOTHER EXAMPLE, HAVING ONE'S HEAD CARVED INTO THE IMAGE OF A A BIG FAT GLEAMING DONG!!

BUT ALL OF THAT PALES INTO INSIGNIFICANCE BESIDE THIS LITTLE ATROCITY! YES! LOOK AT IT! LOOK AT MY GREATEST SACRIFICE!
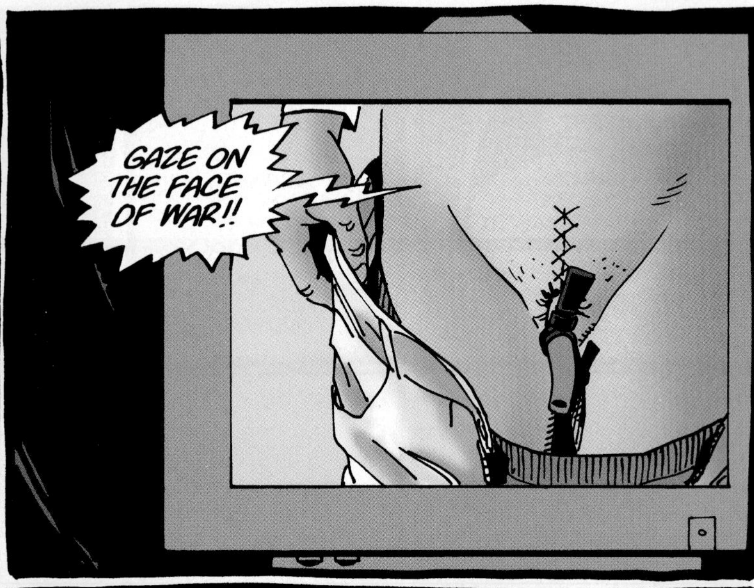
GAZE ON THE FACE OF WAR!!
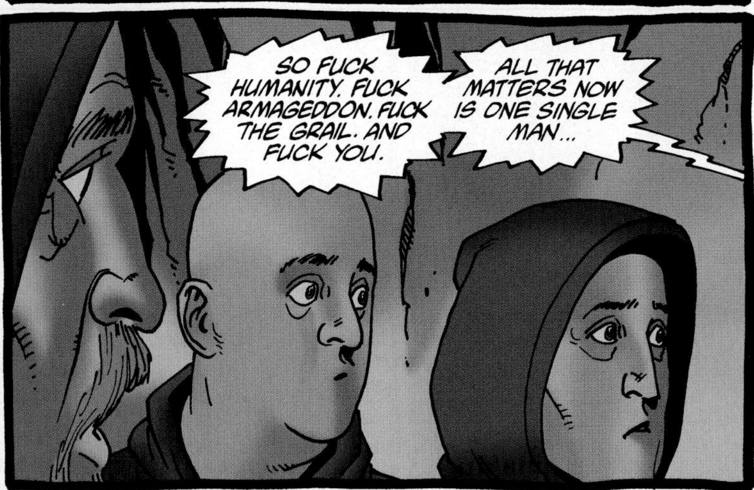
SO FUCK HUMANITY. FUCK ARMAGEDDON. FUCK THE GRAIL. AND FUCK YOU.
ALL THAT MATTERS NOW IS ONE SINGLE MAN...

JESSE CUSTER.
A NAME THAT LIVES IN INFAMY. THAT SET ME DOWN THE ROAD TO THE RUIN YOU SEE BEFORE YOU. THAT BURNS IN MY BRAIN.
THE RESOURCES AND MATERIEL YOU WOULD HAVE PISSED AWAY WILL BRING ABOUT HIS DOOM.

STARR...
YOU ARE THE ONE WHO IS DOOMED.

BRING CAPTAIN GANDER HERE.

AT ONCE.

SO I'M DOOMED, AM I?

TO HELL ITSELF.

MASADA AND THE VALLEY ARE NOTHING. YOU ***SEVERED THE BLOODLINE OF CHRIST,*** STARR. YOU SUCCEEDED WHERE ***HEROD*** FAILED.

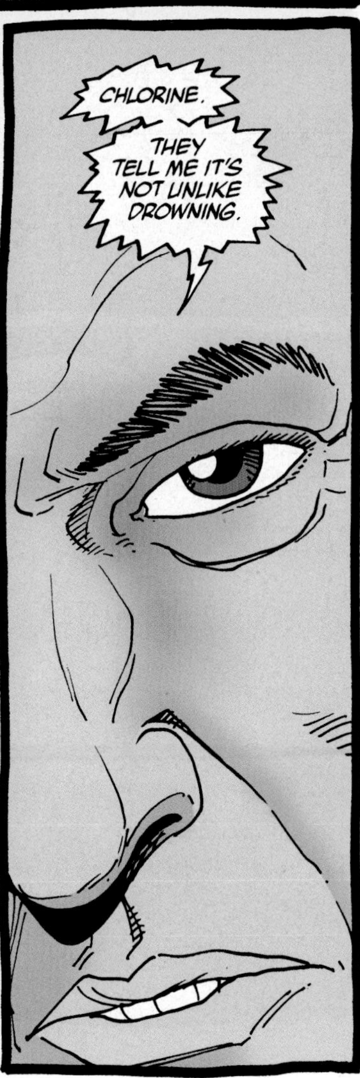

THIS IS ABOUT MANKIND'S SALVATION

THIS IS ABOUT MY GENITALS.

GO ON TO EXTINCTION, HOLY MEN.

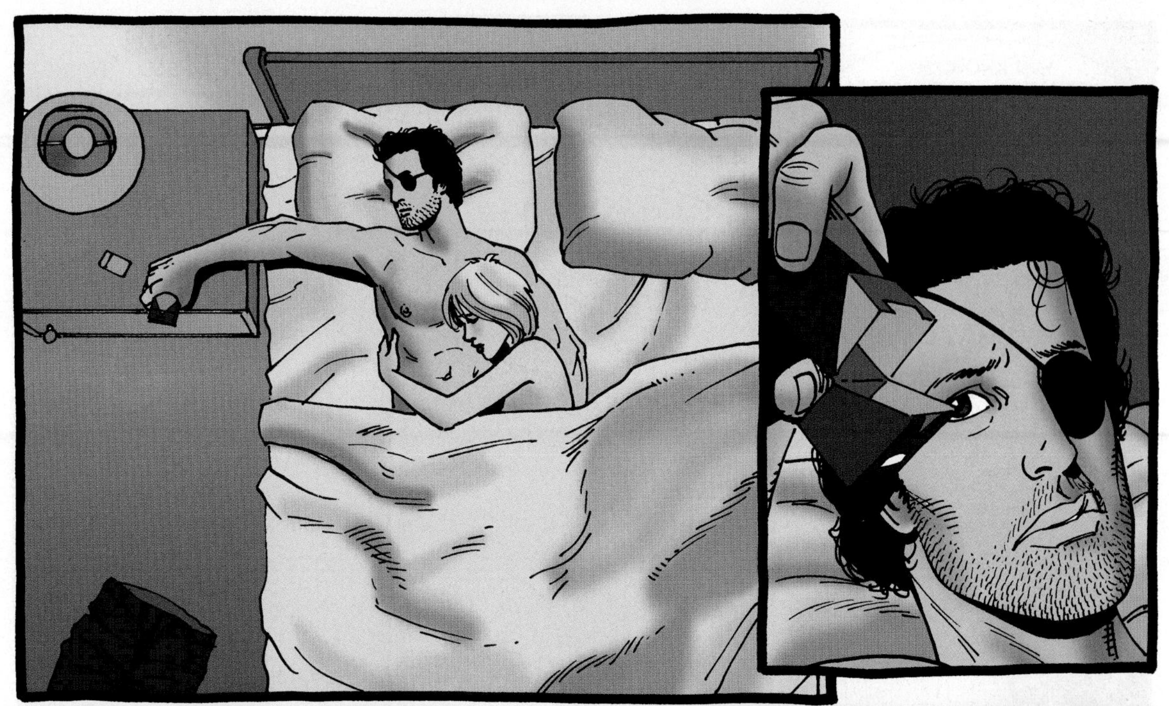

WUFF!

THAT IS SOME DOG.
Uh-huh. EVEN HAD THE GOOD MANNERS TO WAIT OUTSIDE 'TIL ALL THE HOLLERIN' STOPPED.
MM.

I WAS JUST THINKING.
THE LAST TIME THE SEX WAS THIS GOOD AND THIS FREQUENT AND THIS ENERGETIC ALL AT ONCE--

WAS JUST BEFORE YOU RAN OUT ON ME.

YOU KNOW. IN FRANCE. YOU THOUGHT I COULDN'T HANDLE MYSELF, YOU HAD TO KEEP ME AWAY FROM DANGER...
HONEY...!

TULIP, HONEY, LOOK AT ME NOW! HOW COULD YOU EVEN THINK I WOULD DO THAT AGAIN?

AIN'T YOU SHOWN ME TIME AFTER TIME WHAT A FOOL I WAS TO THINK THAT WAY? IN THAT OL' CAJUN CEMETERY? AN' THAT GOD-DAMN BATTLE IN THE DESERT?

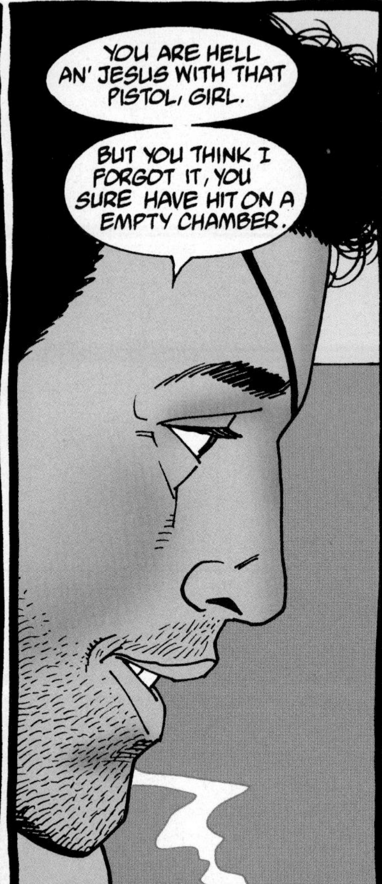
YOU ARE HELL AN' JESUS WITH THAT PISTOL, GIRL.
BUT YOU THINK I FORGOT IT, YOU SURE HAVE HIT ON A EMPTY CHAMBER.

I JUST HAVE TO BE SURE, JESSE.

WELL HONEY, YOU MIGHT RECALL IT AIN'T SO LONG SINCE YOU THOUGHT I WAS DEAD AN' I THOUGHT YOU WERE DONE WITH ME. IT OCCUR TO YOU THAT FINDIN' OUT OTHERWISE MIGHT BE THE CAUSE OF ALL OUR ENTHUSIASM?
POINT.

BUT.

I KNOW YOU'RE GETTING READY TO FINISH THIS. YOU HAVEN'T TOLD ME WHERE YOU'VE BEEN FOR THE LAST WEEK, BUT I KNOW YOU'VE GOT SOME-THING IN MIND.
AND WHATEVER THE DETAILS MIGHT BE, WITH STARR, THE SAINT, THAT PRICK CASSIDY AND GOD ALMIGHTY HIMSELF MIXED UP IN IT--
THIS WON'T HAVE A QUIET ENDING.

TULIP--
JESSE.

PLEASE HEAR AND UNDERSTAND AND BELIEVE ME: I LOVE YOU. I'M YOURS AND YOU'RE MINE.
IT'S THAT SIMPLE. IT'S WHAT'S RIGHT AT THE HEART OF US, IT'S WHY WE WORK, AND IF YOU COULD JUST SEE IT YOU'D NEVER DOUBT ME AGAIN.

NOW, I HAVE A FUCKING *ARSENAL* OUT IN THAT TRUCK AND I WILL USE IT. I WILL FIGHT LIKE HELL TO PROTECT YOU.

TO PROTECT US BOTH. AND THE GOOD LIFE WE HAVE COMING.

YOU FOUND IT? GOOD.
WEAPONS AND AMMUNITION CRATED UNDER THE FLOOR, FOOD IN STORAGE AT THE REAR. NO, NO ONE MENTIONED EXPLOSIVES TO ME.

I DON'T KNOW, CAN'T YOU JUST IMPROVISE? ISN'T THAT WHAT YOU PEOPLE DO? OH, THERE'S NO CALL FOR THAT KIND OF LANGUAGE...!
LOOK, THERE'LL BE MORE UNITS ARRIVING IN THE NEXT DAY OR TWO. MAKE SURE THEY'RE FED AND EQUIPPED, OKAY?
YES, HE'S COMING...

HE'LL BRIEF YOU IN PERSON WHEN HE--

WHAT... WHAT WAS MY SIN...?

FUCKIN' WITH ME AN' MINE.
GET TO IT.

YEAH, YOU REMEMBER **JESUS!!**
AHA HA HA HA **VENGEANCE IS MINE!!**
...
WHO MIGHT YOU BE?

HOW DID YOUR CALL TO THE COUNCIL GO, HERR STARR?
I HAVE THEIR UNWAVERING DEVOTION. DON'T FORGET TO PACK EXTRA COLOSTOMY BAGS.
STILL NO WORD FROM THAT TURD HOOVER?
I'M SURE HE'S FINE.
HE'D FUCKING BETTER BE. IF SAMSON ALPHA AREN'T ON-SITE AND PREPPED IN TIME FOR OUR ARRIVAL IN SAN ANTONIO, HE'S DEAD.
IT'S TIME, HERR STARR.

TIME FOR WHAT?
FOR ME TO TELL YOU THAT I LOVE YOU.

I'VE BEEN WANTING TO SAY IT FOR SO VERY, VERY LONG.

WHEN YOU HAD YOUR ACCIDENT I WORRIED THAT YOU'D LOST YOUR WAY. YOU SEEMED SO DISTANT, SO UNFOCUSED, EVEN A LITTLE UNSTABLE... BUT I KNOW I SHOULDN'T HAVE WORRIED.
YOU'RE STRONG. YOU'LL ALWAYS BE STRONG.
LISTENING TO YOU JUST NOW, I COULD HEAR IT IN EVERY WORD YOU SAID.

YOU LOVE ME.
I SEE.

WELL...YES... I MEAN EVER SINCE WE MET, I'VE-- I'VE SEEN HOW--
YOU HAVE THIS... AMAZING STRENGTH, HERR STARR. YOU HAVE A MISSION, A TASK YOU'VE SET YOURSELF TO SAVE THE WORLD, AND... er...
YOU WON'T LET ANYTHING STAND IN YOUR WAY...
I MEAN--ahrrm-- ALL THE HARDSHIP, THE ADVERSITY, THE PAIN YOU'VE ENDURED... I'VE WEPT FOR EVERY TERRIBLE WOUND YOU'VE SUFFERED...
WHEN YOU WERE LOST AFTER THE BOMB, I--I ALMOST GAVE UP--
er...
WELL.
H-HERR STARR?
FEATHERSTONE, COULD YOU SEE YOURSELF KNEELING BEHIND ME WITH A SAWFISH AND THRUSTING IT INTO MY RECTUM YELLING, "WHO'S THE MAN, WHO'S THE MAN"?

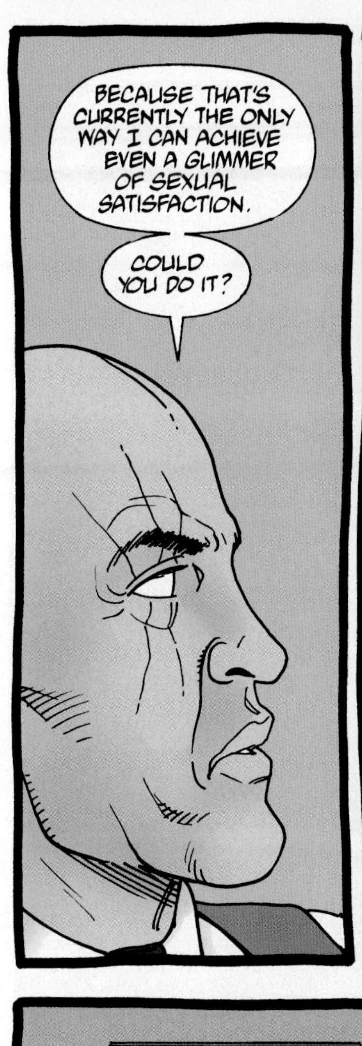
BECAUSE THAT'S CURRENTLY THE ONLY WAY I CAN ACHIEVE EVEN A GLIMMER OF SEXUAL SATISFACTION.
COULD YOU DO IT?

NO, OF COURSE YOU COULDN'T.

YOU MAKE A MUCH BETTER ADJUTANT THAN YOU EVER WOULD A LOVER, FEATHERSTONE.
FINISH PACKING. LET ME KNOW WHEN THE LIMO ARRIVES.

YES...
HERR STARR...

YOU DON'T KNOW ME?
UH-UH.
AFTER WHAT YOU DID, YOU-- YOU DON'T REMEMBER ME?

YOU'RE FUCKING DEAD, WHOEVER YOU ARE! DROP IT!!

YES...
YEAH, YOU'RE ONE'VE STARR'S PEOPLE, AIN'T YOU? FROM CALIFORNIA?
GET IT OVER WITH, WILL YOU?

HUH?
I WOULD HAVE KILLED YOU. GO ON, JUST FINISH ME OFF...

YOU WOULDA KILLED ME.
I SHOT SOMEONE BEFORE. I COULD HAVE DONE IT.
YOU KILLED A DEFENSELESS MAN. COLD BLOOD, BANG, YOU JUST WALKED RIGHT UP AN' SHOT HIM.

WELL NOT EXACTLY...!
BUT YOU LEFT ME ON THAT BEACH, DIDN'T YOU? YOU DID THAT--THING YOU DO WITH YOUR VOICE! YOU JUST LEFT ME THERE AND YOU MADE ME COUNT SAND!
THREE MILLION GRAINS! I WAS STUCK THERE FOR MONTHS! LOOK AT ME!

I KNOW.
I REMEMBER.

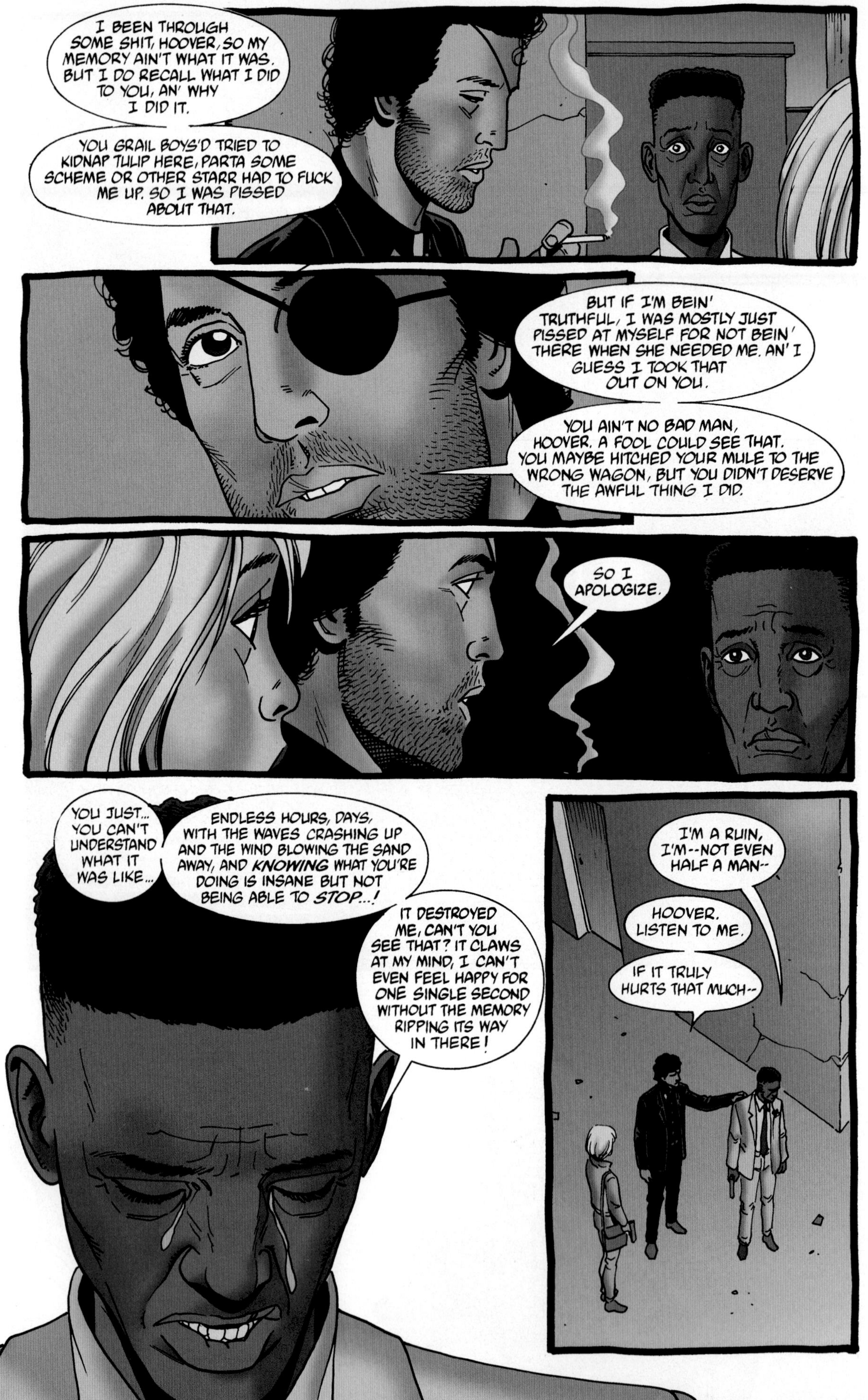

I BEEN THROUGH SOME SHIT, HOOVER, SO MY MEMORY AIN'T WHAT IT WAS. BUT I DO RECALL WHAT I DID TO YOU, AN' WHY I DID IT.

YOU GRAIL BOYS'D TRIED TO KIDNAP TULIP HERE, PARTA SOME SCHEME OR OTHER STARR HAD TO FUCK ME UP. SO I WAS PISSED ABOUT THAT.

BUT IF I'M BEIN' TRUTHFUL, I WAS MOSTLY JUST PISSED AT MYSELF FOR NOT BEIN' THERE WHEN SHE NEEDED ME. AN' I GUESS I TOOK THAT OUT ON YOU.

YOU AIN'T NO BAD MAN, HOOVER. A FOOL COULD SEE THAT. YOU MAYBE HITCHED YOUR MULE TO THE WRONG WAGON, BUT YOU DIDN'T DESERVE THE AWFUL THING I DID.

YOU JUST... YOU CAN'T UNDERSTAND WHAT IT WAS LIKE...

ENDLESS HOURS, DAYS, WITH THE WAVES CRASHING UP AND THE WIND BLOWING THE SAND AWAY, AND *KNOWING* WHAT YOU'RE DOING IS INSANE BUT NOT BEING ABLE TO *STOP*...!

IT DESTROYED ME, CAN'T YOU SEE THAT? IT CLAWS AT MY MIND, I CAN'T EVEN FEEL HAPPY FOR ONE SINGLE SECOND WITHOUT THE MEMORY RIPPING ITS WAY IN THERE!

I'M A RUIN, I'M--NOT EVEN HALF A MAN--

HOOVER. LISTEN TO ME.

IF IT TRULY HURTS THAT MUCH--

JUST FORGET IT.
FORGET... WHAT...?
WELL DIP ME IN HONEY AND THROW ME TO THE LESBIANS.

OH, I GET IT...
HUH?

"AND LO, HE WALKED AMONG THEM, HEALING THE SICK AND THE INFIRM OF MIND, AND YET THEY KNEW HIM NOT..."

"BUT IT CAME TO PASS THAT WORD SPREAD OF HIS PASSING, AND OF THE GREAT MIRACLES HE WAS PERFORMING..."
KNOCK IT OFF...!
"AND SOMEONE SAID--WHOA, BRETHREN, CHECK OUT HIS INITIALS! AND SOMEONE ELSE SAID--FUCK ME, YOU'RE RIGHT!"

"AND IT CAME TO PASS THAT THEY DID PUT TWO AND TWO TOGETHER AND START A RELIGION AROUND HIM, AND IT DID SPREAD FAR AND WIDE ACROSS THE LAND..."
KNOCK IT OFF...!

"WHICH OF COURSE HE SECRETLY KIND OF DUG..."

SALVATION, TX
POP. 1626
GLENN FABRY ·99·
P.798HN

"Lemme get right to it, son.
Would you like to come an' shovel shit for me?"

SALVATION TX.
POPN. 1626

JODIE'S BAR &

...AN' THEN I SAID FUCK ME!!

AND EVERY DOG HIS DAY

GARTH ENNIS - Writer STEVE DILLON - Artist

PAMELA RAMBO - Colorist CLEM ROBINS - Letterer AXEL ALONSO - Editor

PREACHER created by GARTH ENNIS and STEVE DILLON

HELLO, BIRDS!

HELLO, SKY!!

HELLO PEOPLE, PASSING BY!

UH...DUDE. AIN'T YOU THAT GUY OFF TV? WITH LIKE THE FACE?
NUH.*
*NO.

UH'M NUBUHDUH.*
*I'M NOBODY.

HEY! FREAKSHOW!

C'MON, HONEY, LET'S SEE THAT BIG OL' PEEPER!
GODDAMN, GIRL, IS THAT A SPECIAL EFFECT YOU GOT THERE?
GET YOU A JOB IN THE CIRCUS, BITCH--
STOP IT! WHY CAN'T YOU STOP IT!

I CAN'T HELP BEING DIFFERENT!!

STUBBUD!*
WHO THE FUCK!
STUBBUD!*
*STOP IT!
*STOP IT!

STUHB BUHN SUH CRUHHLLL!!*
*STOP BEING SO CRUEL!!

HOLY LIVIN' FUCK! WHAT IS THIS PLACE?
I KNEW WE SHOULDN'TA STOPPED HERE!
RUN!!

...UH YUH UHLRUHD, MUHZ?*
*...ARE YOU ALL RIGHT, MISS?

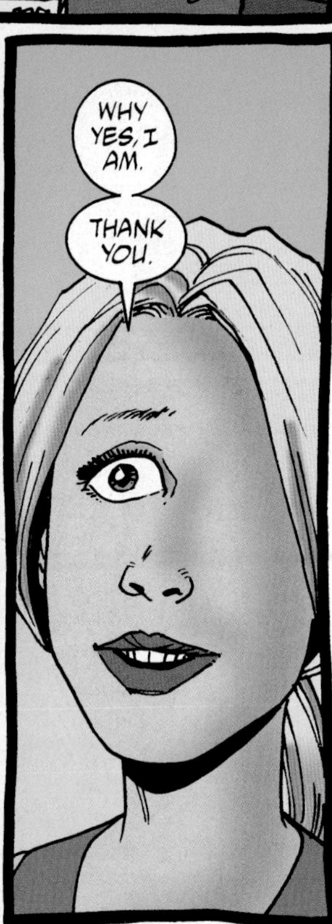
WHY YES, I AM.
THANK YOU.

I'M LORENA BOBBS. PEOPLE CALL ME LORIE.
UHZFUHZ.*
*ARSEFACE.

ARE YOU STAYING IN SALVATION, MR. ARSEFACE?
JUHZ UHZFUHZ. NUH, UHM UNUH PUZZ-UHN THRUH, LURUH.*
*JUST ARSEFACE. NO, I'M ONLY PASSING THROUGH, LORIE.

OH, WELL, YOU'LL HAVE TO HAVE SOMETHING TO EAT BEFORE YOU GET BACK ON THE ROAD. THE FOOD IN JODIE'S IS WONDERFUL.
IT'S THE VERY LEAST I CAN DO...

HEY, CHRISTINA. I JUST GOT A CALL ABOUT TROUBLE OUTSIDE JODIE'S...
OH, HELLO, CINDY. YES, TOBY SAID SOME TRASH FROM OUT OF TOWN WERE BOTHERING LORIE, BUT...

HMMMM.
JODIE'S BAR & GRILL

AND WELCOME TO SAN ANTONIO, BOTH OF YOU! HOW WAS THE FLIGHT?
BUS

FUCKING MARVELOUS.
CHRIST ALMIGHTY, WHAT A LOATHSOME SHITHOLE...
OH, LET ME GET THOSE FOR YOU, FEATHERSTONE!

HERE IS A GOOD ONE! WHY DID THE REDNECKS END UP WORKING FOR THE MEXICAN?
EASY! BECAUSE THEY WERE TOO BUSY MAKING WETBACK JOKES TO ASK IF HE HAD ANY FORMAL EDUCATION--

AND TOO BUSY FUCKING THE BIG FAT CRACKER SOW WHO QUITE OFTEN TOOK THEM ON TWO OR THREE AT A TIME TO NOTICE HIM GOING FOR THE FOREMAN'S JOB AT THE NEW PLANT! AHAHAHAHA!
AAAW-HAAAWW!
AHA HA HA, THAT IS A GOOD ONE!
SURE IS ONE'VE MY FAVORITES!
SAY, LEMME GET YOU ANOTHER DRINK THERE, HECTOR!

...SO THINGS HAVE REALLY CHANGED IN THE LAST FEW MONTHS. THERE'S HARDLY ANY TROUBLE, NOW THAT CINDY'S THE SHERIFF...
RULUH?*
*REALLY?

YES, SHE'S WONDERFUL--OH, HELLO, MR. QUINCANNON!

GOOD EVENIN' TO YOU, LORIE. AN' THIS MUST BE OUR VISITIN' CELEBRITY.
CONAN QUINCANNON, SON. DAMN GLAD TO MEET YOU.

YOU NUH HUHYUM?*
*YOU KNOW WHO I AM?
MOST ANYONE WATCHES TV KNOWS WHO YOU ARE, SON. AN' WORD TRAVELS FAST IN A PLACE THIS SIZE.
HOPE YOU ENJOY YORE TIME IN SALVATION. MAYBE I'LL SEE YOU LATER; RIGHT NOW I'VE A BURNIN' DESIRE FOR ONE'VE THE CHEESEBURGERS THIS PLACE IS GETTIN' FAMOUS FOR.

HUH SUMZ LUHGUH GUD GUH...*
*HE SEEMS LIKE A GOOD GUY...
OH, MR. QUINCANNON'S A SAINT!

HE HAD THIS AWFUL BROTHER WHO USED TO RUN A FACTORY NEAR HERE--HE WAS A TERRIBLE MAN, HE ALMOST BURNED THE WHOLE TOWN DOWN ONCE! CAN YOU IMAGINE?
BUT HE'S DEAD. WHEN OUR MR. QUINCANNON CAME ALONG, HE OPENED A NEW FACTORY. EVERYONE'S GETTING JOBS THERE, IT REALLY IS SO MUCH NICER...
HE'S SORT OF THE MAN WHO SAVED SALVATION, I SUPPOSE.

SO YOU WERE ON TV? I DON'T WATCH IT MUCH, IT KIND OF CONFUSES ME...
UH WUZ SUHD UV UH RUG STUH, UH SPUZ. BUHD THUHZ ULL UVUH NUH.
DUHD UN BURUD, YUZ SUH...*
*I WAS SORT OF A ROCK STAR, I SUPPOSE. BUT THAT'S ALL OVER NOW.
DEAD AND BURIED, YES SIR.

A ROCK STAR.
I THOUGHT IT WOULD BE SOMETHING LIKE THAT.

WHAT ARE YOUR PLANS NOW?
WUHL, UH... UH DUNNUH, RULUH. UHV GUHD NUH MUNUH, NUH JUHB...UH DUNNUH HUHDA DUH UNUHTHUNG...
UH DUNH WUHNA BUH UH RUG STUH UNUNMUH, UHNYWUH.*
*WELL, I...I DON'T KNOW, REALLY. I'VE GOT NO MONEY, NO JOB...I DON'T KNOW HOW TO DO ANYTHING...
I DON'T WANT TO BE A ROCK STAR ANYMORE, ANYWAY.

UH UHM THRUH WUTH FUHM.*
*I AM THROUGH WITH FAME.

WOULD YOU EXCUSE ME FOR A MOMENT? YOU COULD GET US A COUPLE MORE PLATYPUSES, I'LL BE RIGHT BACK...
UH, UKUH.*
*OH, OKAY.

TWO MORE?
YUHZ, PLUZ.
PUHDUN MUH, BUHD... WUZ WRUNG WUH LURUHZ UHH?*
*YES, PLEASE.
PARDON ME, BUT... WHAT'S WRONG WITH LORIE'S EYE?

NOTHING. IT'S HOW SHE WAS BORN.
UH NUH! NUH, UH DUHDUN MUHN THUDD!
NUH, SHUH SUHMZ TUH KUHB SUHYUNG THUNGZ UHD UND THUH..!*
*OH NO! NO, I DIDN'T MEAN THAT!
NO, SHE SEEMS TO KEEP SEEING THINGS THAT AREN'T THERE...

WELL, THAT'S JUST A LITTLE CONDITION. HER BRAIN SOMETIMES GETS DIFFERENT SIGNALS FROM HER EYE THAN IT'S SUPPOSED TO.
SO SHE SEES A HOUSE, SAY, BUT HER EYE TELLS HER BRAIN SHE'S LOOKING AT A HERD OF HOGS. AND SO ON.

BUT DON'T LET THAT FOOL YOU: LORIE IS A BRIGHT, BRIGHT GIRL.

WITH A GOOD, GOOD HEART.
YOU MIGHT DO WELL TO REMEMBER THAT.

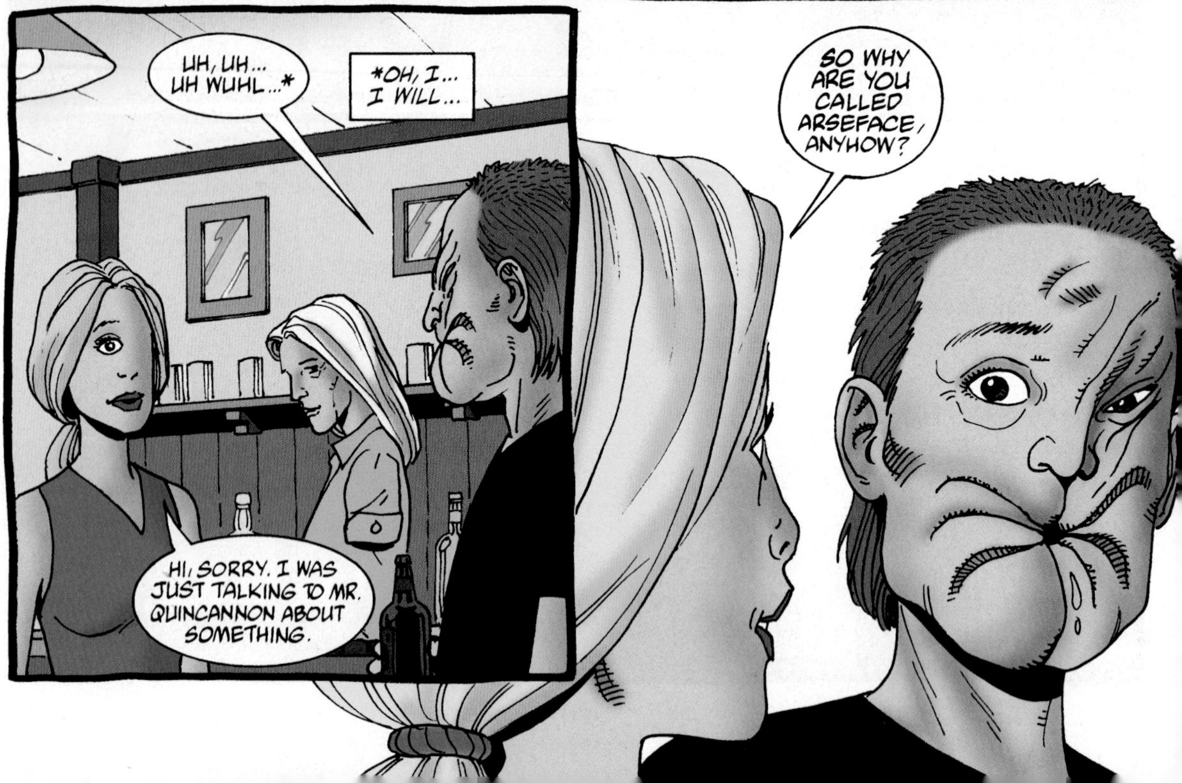

UH, UH... UH WUHL...*
*OH, I... I WILL...
HI, SORRY. I WAS JUST TALKING TO MR. QUINCANNON ABOUT SOMETHING.

SO WHY ARE YOU CALLED ARSEFACE, ANYHOW?

TEL
DOOM COCK...

DOOM COCK...
IS IT BIG ENOUGH FOR YOU, FEATHERSTONE?

MM...?
THE ROOM! HAVE YOU GOT ENOUGH SPACE AND EVERY-THING?
I MEAN I KNOW IT'S HARDLY THE RITZ, BUT I HAD TO BOOK ACCOMMO-DATIONS AT RATHER SHORT NOTICE...

OH...YES. THE ROOM.
IT'S FINE, HOOVER. I'M JUST SORRY HERR STARR SWORE AT YOU SO MUCH WHEN WE GOT HERE.

NEVER MIND HIM, FEATHERSTONE.
WE'VE MORE IMPORTANT THINGS TO TALK ABOUT.

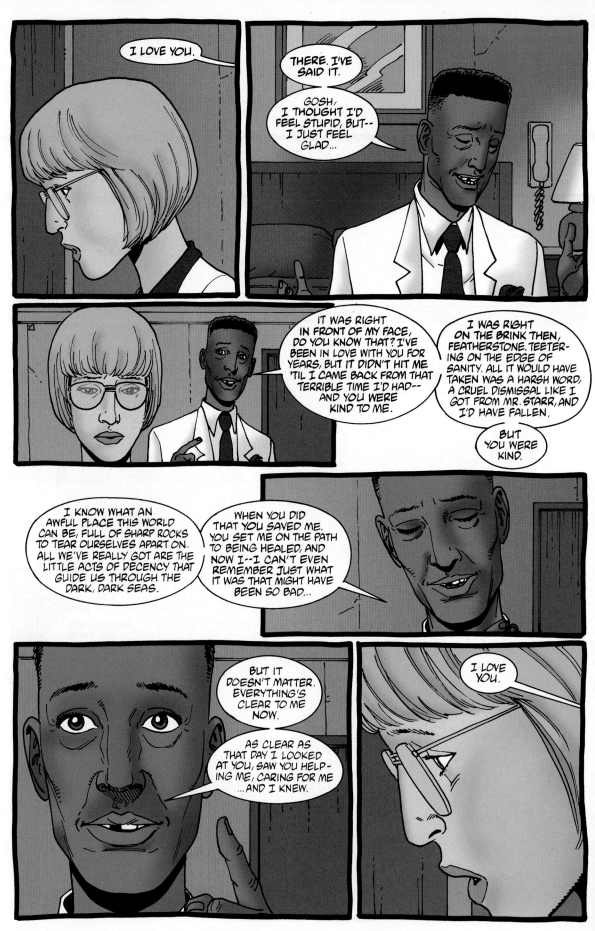

I LOVE YOU.

THERE. I'VE SAID IT.
GOSH, I THOUGHT I'D FEEL STUPID, BUT-- I JUST FEEL GLAD...

IT WAS RIGHT IN FRONT OF MY FACE, DO YOU KNOW THAT? I'VE BEEN IN LOVE WITH YOU FOR YEARS, BUT IT DIDN'T HIT ME 'TIL I CAME BACK FROM THAT TERRIBLE TIME I'D HAD-- AND YOU WERE KIND TO ME.
I WAS RIGHT ON THE BRINK THEN, FEATHERSTONE. TEETERING ON THE EDGE OF SANITY. ALL IT WOULD HAVE TAKEN WAS A HARSH WORD, A CRUEL DISMISSAL LIKE I GOT FROM MR. STARR, AND I'D HAVE FALLEN.
BUT YOU WERE KIND.

WHEN YOU DID THAT YOU SAVED ME. YOU SET ME ON THE PATH TO BEING HEALED, AND NOW I--I CAN'T EVEN REMEMBER JUST WHAT IT WAS THAT MIGHT HAVE BEEN SO BAD...
I KNOW WHAT AN AWFUL PLACE THIS WORLD CAN BE, FULL OF SHARP ROCKS TO TEAR OURSELVES APART ON. ALL WE'VE REALLY GOT ARE THE LITTLE ACTS OF DECENCY THAT GUIDE US THROUGH THE DARK, DARK SEAS.

BUT IT DOESN'T MATTER. EVERYTHING'S CLEAR TO ME NOW.
AS CLEAR AS THAT DAY I LOOKED AT YOU, SAW YOU HELPING ME, CARING FOR ME ...AND I KNEW.

I LOVE YOU.

...WHAT?

I'M SORRY, HOOVER, I TUNED OUT COMPLETELY THERE. WHAT WAS IT YOU WERE TALKING ABOUT?

NOTHING

OH, OKAY.
BETTER GET SOME SLEEP. HERR STARR WANTS TO INSPECT SAMSON ALPHA AT OH-SIX-THIRTY.
RIGHT

GOODNIGHT, HOOVER.
GOODNIGHT

I'VE COME TO FIND OUT ABOUT DRINKING.
WELL, YOU'VE COME TO THE RIGHT PLACE.
BIGUNS!
ANAL RAMPAGE
ANAL RAMPAGE
WOW
OUT NOW!!

YOU MIND IF I JOIN YOU, SON?

MUZDUH KWUHNCUHNUN... NUH, BUH MUH GUZZD.*
*MISTER QUIN-CANNON... NO, BE MY GUEST.
THANK YOU.
SUH THUH TUHL MUH YUH UHN UH FUHGDRUH?*
*SO THEY TELL ME YOU OWN A FACTORY?

YES I DO, SON. I'M IN SHIT.

OH, YOU CAN DRESS IT UP, CALL IT LIQUID WASTE MANAGEMENT OR EFFLUENT DISPOSAL, BUT IT ALL COMES DOWN TO SHIT.
PLACE I RUN PROCESSES SEWAGE, SEE, TREATS IT WITH CHEMICALS, TURNS IT INTO FERTILIZER, GETS RID OF IT ONE WAY OR ANOTHER. KEEPS IT FROM STINKIN' THINGS UP.
A SHIT PLANT.

AN' THAT'S WHAT I WANTED TO TALK TO YOU ABOUT.
I GOT A KINDA PROPOSITION FOR YOU.

NOW, WOULD I BE RIGHT IN SAYIN' YOU'D LIKE TO PUT THE PAST BEHIND YOU? MAYBE SETTLE DOWN SOMEWHERE KINDA QUIET... FORGET ABOUT SOME THINGS YOU AIN'T TOO PROUD OF...
THUZ--THUZ UD UGZUGLUH!*
*THAT'S--THAT'S IT EXACTLY!
YEAH.
SEE, WHEN I FIRST CAME HERE IT WAS IN THE WAKE OF THE AWFUL THINGS MY BROTHER DID. HE WAS A DEVIL TO THE GOOD FOLKS OF THIS TOWN, THE PAIN AN' SUFFERIN' HE CAUSED WAS UNFORGIVABLE...
I KNEW I HAD TO DO SOMETHIN'--I FELT LIKE I OWED SALVATION. I HAD TO OPEN UP MY SHIT PLANT RIGHT AWAY.
HELL, LISTEN TO ME. I GUESS ALL I'M SAYIN' IS I KNOW A LITTLE BIT ABOUT ESCAPIN' FROM THE PAST, ABOUT MAKIN' A FRESH START...
LEMME GET RIGHT TO IT, SON.
WOULD YOU LIKE TO COME AN' SHOVEL SHIT FOR ME?
YUH BUDYUH!!*
*YOU BETCHA!!

LURUH!!*
*LORIE!!

MM?
LURUH, YUHL NUVUH BUHLUV UHD! MUZDUH KWUHNCUHNUHN GUV MUH UH JUHB!*
*LORIE, YOU'LL NEVER BELIEVE IT! MISTER QUINCANNON GAVE ME A JOB!

I KNOW.
I ASKED HIM TO.
YUH DUHD? BUHD... WUH?*
*YOU DID? BUT...WHY?

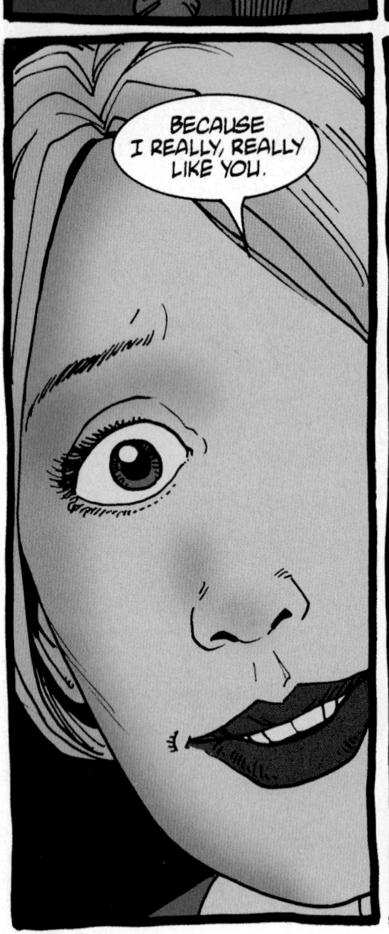
BECAUSE I REALLY, REALLY LIKE YOU.

BUT--BUT--
YOU'RE NOT HIDEOUS, ARSEFACE!
I MEAN NOT FROM WHERE I'M STANDING.

SSHHHLLSSSSSHHPP

SO IF HOOVER'S HERE, I SUPPOSE THAT MEANS STARR MUST BE TOO.

I GUESS SO, HON.
SO HOW WOULD THEY KNOW WE'D BE IN SAN ANTONIO...?

WELL, IT'S THE GRAIL, TULIP. GOT SPIES EVERY-WHERE.
YOU KNOW.

IT'S GOING TO MAKE THINGS DIFFICULT.
SO WHEN DO I GET TO HEAR YOUR BIG PLAN, ANYWAY? I MEAN EVERY TIME I ASK, YOU EVER-SO-SUBTLY DEFLECT THE QUES-TION BY BANGING MY BRAINS OUT--NOT THAT I'M COMPLAINING--
TELL YOU TOMORROW, BABY. I PROMISE.

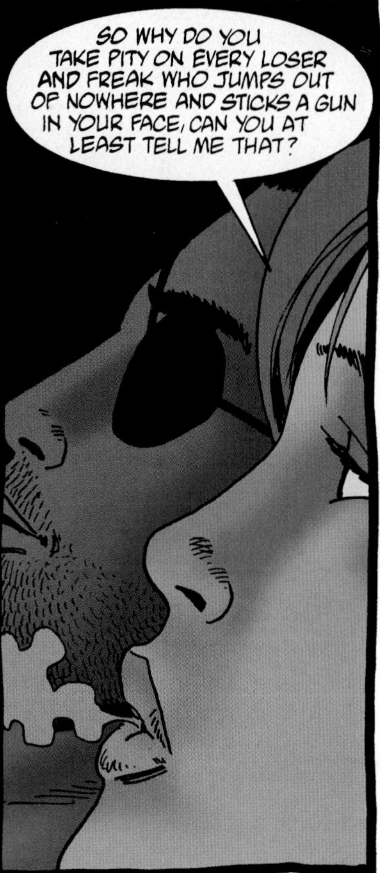
SO WHY DO YOU TAKE PITY ON EVERY LOSER AND FREAK WHO JUMPS OUT OF NOWHERE AND STICKS A GUN IN YOUR FACE, CAN YOU AT LEAST TELL ME THAT?

GODDAMN, THAT TIME WITH ARSEFACE! I CLEAN FORGOT ABOUT THAT...!
IT'S JUST, YOU KNOW, I'VE SEEN THE THINGS YOU'VE DONE TO MOST OF THE PEOPLE WHO'VE MESSED WITH YOU...

WELL THEY WERE FUCKS, HON.
BUT ARSEFACE AN' OL' HOOVE--BOYS LIKE THAT AIN'T GOT NO EVIL IN 'EM. THEY'RE INNOCENTS AN' THEY MADE DUMB CHOICES, AN'... HELL.
I GUESS EVERY-ONE DESERVES A SECOND CHANCE TO GET THINGS RIGHT, WHEN YOU GET DOWN TO IT.

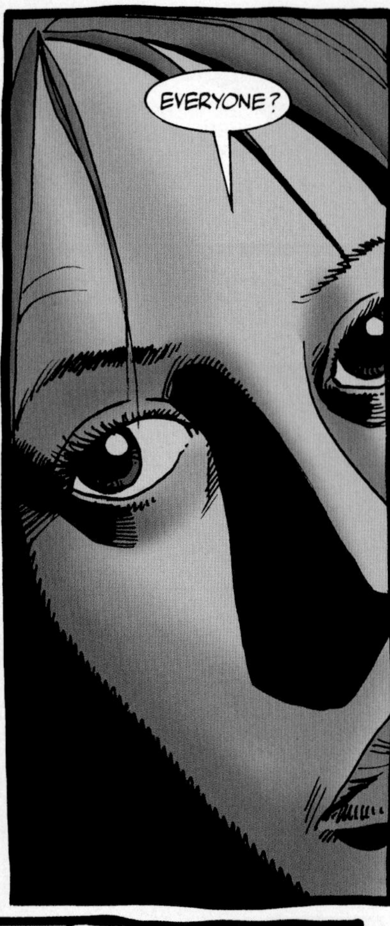
EVERYONE?

GOODNIGHT, JESSE.

GLENN FABRY ·99·

"But why would God save me, Jesse?
You know as well as I do: God's a bastard."

THE BEST DAY OF MY LIFE?
ANY ONE SPENT WITH YOU, I GUESS.
FLATTERER.
WHAT ABOUT THE WORST?
KINDA SPOILT FOR CHOICE, AIN'T I?
IF YOU HAD TO CHOOSE.
...THE TIME JODY SHOT YOU.
THAT WAS 'BOUT AS BAD AS IT GETS, SEEIN' HIM STEP UP AN'... I MEAN RIGHT THERE IN FRONTA ME, YOUR PRECIOUS LIFE JUST CANCELLED OUT...
GODDAMN. THANK CHRIST YOU MADE IT, BABY.
I DIDN'T.

HUH?
I DIDN'T MAKE IT.

JODY SHOT ME BETWEEN THE EYES AT POINT BLANK RANGE. THE BACK OF MY HEAD WAS GONE. YOU SAW IT HAPPEN, JESSE.
HOW COULD I POSSIBLY HAVE SURVIVED THAT?

TULIP... HONEY, WHAT'RE YOU TALKIN' 'BOUT?
YOU KNOW WHAT HAPPENED. GOD BROUGHT YOU BACK. IT WAS A WARNIN'; HE SAVED YOU SO I'D LEAVE HIM BE...

BUT WHY WOULD GOD SAVE ME, JESSE?

YOU KNOW AS WELL AS I DO:

GOD'S A BASTARD.

JEEEEZUS--!

JESSE'S GIRL

GARTH ENNIS - Writer STEVE DILLON - Artist

PAMELA RAMBO - Colorist CLEM ROBINS - Letterer AXEL ALONSO - Editor

PREACHER created by GARTH ENNIS and STEVE DILLON

BINOCULARS, HOOVER.
AT ONCE, MR. STARR.

WHAT ABOUT SAMSON ALPHA?
AWAITING YOUR INSPECTION.
THE SAN ANTONIO AUTHORITIES?
YOUR CALL TO THE MAYOR WORKED WONDERS. THE POLICE WON'T INTERFERE.

WELL FUCKING GET ON WITH IT THEN...!

WHAT'S THE MATTER WITH YOU TODAY, FEATHERSTONE? I'M ENGINEERING THE DOWNFALL OF OUR GREATEST ADVERSARY AND YOU'RE STANDING THERE LIKE A ZOMBIE!
FOR CHRIST'S SAKE, EVEN HOOVER'S PULLED HIS HEAD OUT OF HIS ASS FOR ONCE...

WHAT? WHAT THE FUCK ARE YOU STARING AT?
I--I--

WHAT IS IT, FEATHERSTONE?
N-N-NOTHING--!

RIGHT! SO LET'S GO AND HAVE A LOOK AT OUR SAMSON TEAM, SHALL WE?
THEY'RE SOLDIERS; AT LEAST I CAN RELY ON THEM TO TAKE THINGS SERIOUSLY...

WANT TO GO GET SOME BREAKFAST?
THREE IN THE AFTERNOON, I GUESS WE OUGHTTA.

WE WILL KEEP GETTING BACK IN BED...
GOT AS FAR AS THE SHOWER A COUPLE TIMES. YOU WANT YOUR WATER?
THANKS. PARCHED.

WHAT'RE YOU READING, ANYWAY?
BOOK I TOOK OFF THE OATLASH WOMAN. FIGHTER PLANES. BOYS AN' THEIR TOYS, THAT KINDA THING.
AXIS EAGLES

I USED TO WANT TO BE A FIGHTER PILOT. I BET I WOULD'VE BEEN GREAT.
WELL, YOU CAN TAKE A LOOK AT THIS IF YOU WANT, MAYBE REVISIT YOUR DREAMS'VE GLORY.

WAS ONE THING I THOUGHT WAS KINDA NICE, THIS POEM A JAP KAMIKAZE BOY WROTE. LITTLE BIT SAD, I GUESS.
LEMME SEE:

"I AM AN EMPTY DREAM..."

"...LIKE SNOW LEFT ON THE MOUNTAINS IN SUMMER. I FEEL MY WARM BLOOD MOVING INSIDE OF ME AND I AM REMINDED THAT I AM LIVING."
"MY SOUL WILL HAVE ITS HOME IN THE RISING OF THE SUN.
"IF YOU FEEL SAD, LOOK AT THE DAWN WITH ALL OF ITS BEAUTY."

"YOU WILL FIND ME THERE."

...THAT IS A LITTLE BIT SAD.

YEAH.
C'MERE, HONEY.

BEST DAY OF MY LIFE WAS WHEN I TURNED AROUND AN' SAW YOU FOR THE VERY FIRST TIME.
WHY JESSE, WHAT BROUGHT THAT ON...?

JESSE?
I AM SO SORRY.
SORRY THIS IS ALL I COULD THINK OF.

THIS IS SAMSON ALPHA?

THIS IS EVERYONE WE'VE GOT, IS THAT WHAT YOU'RE TRYING TO TELL ME? THE GRAIL'S ENTIRE MILITARY CAPABILITY CONSISTS OF TWO DOZEN MEN?
WE LOST NINETY PERCENT OF OUR SAMSON FORCE AT MASADA, MR. STARR. MONUMENT VALLEY TOOK CARE OF THE REST.
WHAT YOU HAVE HERE ARE CAPTAIN GANDER'S TEAM FROM LESAINT MARIE, AND THE FEW DEEP COVER OPERATIVES WHO ACTUALLY BOTHERED TO SHOW UP.

WHAT?
WELL... MOST OF THEM DIDN'T EVEN ACKNOWLEDGE YOUR PRIORITY EDICT. THOSE WHO DID MENTIONED CONCERNS ABOUT GRAIL POLICY, LOSS OF FAITH IN THE CURRENT LEADERSHIP...

BUT READING BETWEEN THE LINES, I THINK THE PROBLEM IS THAT THEY ALL RATHER LIKE DEEP COVER.
I MEAN YOU'RE TALKING ABOUT PEOPLE WHO MOVE IN THE HIGHEST ECHELONS OF POLITICAL POWER AS THEY SHADOW THEIR TARGETS, PEOPLE WHO LIVE IN THE LAP OF LUXURY... YOU CAN SEE HOW THEY MIGHT NOT BE ALL THAT KEEN TO LEAVE IT...
THOSE FUCKERS--!

THEY'LL PAY, OH YES, I'LL MAKE THEM FUCKING PAY...
RIGHT. I'M GOING TO GO AND FEED THESE IDIOTS THE APPROPRIATE BULLSHIT. YOU TWO WAIT OUTSIDE.

OH GOD.
HEE!

HOOVER, WHAT THE HELL WERE YOU THINKING? ARE YOU *INSANE*?
DEFINITELY WORKING ON IT!
HE'S THE ALLFATHER OF THE GRAIL, FOR GOD'S SAKE! HE'S GOING TO LOOK RIDICULOUS!

SO WHY DIDN'T YOU STOP HIM?
HE'D HAVE *KILLED YOU*--!

HE PROBABLY STILL WILL. COME ON, I DON'T WANT TO MISS THIS.
WE'LL WATCH FROM THE DOOR AND THEN I'LL MAKE MYSELF SCARCE FOR AN HOUR OR TWO...

JESUS CHRIST.
...AND WHAT DID HE MEAN, *APPROPRIATE BULLSHIT*?

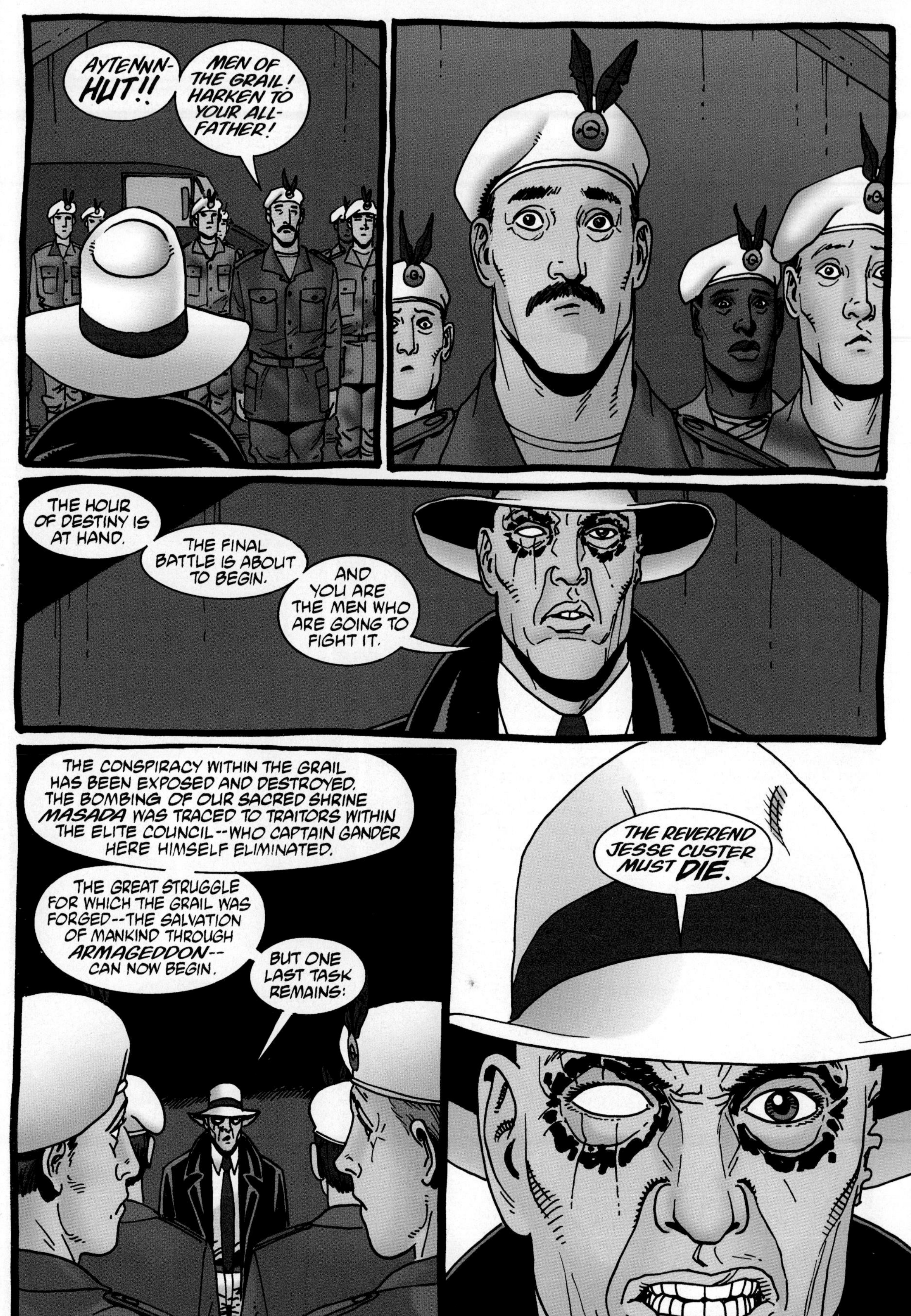
AYTENNN-HUT!!
MEN OF THE GRAIL! HARKEN TO YOUR ALL-FATHER!
THE HOUR OF DESTINY IS AT HAND.
THE FINAL BATTLE IS ABOUT TO BEGIN.
AND YOU ARE THE MEN WHO ARE GOING TO FIGHT IT.
THE CONSPIRACY WITHIN THE GRAIL HAS BEEN EXPOSED AND DESTROYED. THE BOMBING OF OUR SACRED SHRINE MASADA WAS TRACED TO TRAITORS WITHIN THE ELITE COUNCIL--WHO CAPTAIN GANDER HERE HIMSELF ELIMINATED.
THE GREAT STRUGGLE FOR WHICH THE GRAIL WAS FORGED--THE SALVATION OF MANKIND THROUGH ARMAGEDDON--CAN NOW BEGIN.
BUT ONE LAST TASK REMAINS:
THE REVEREND JESSE CUSTER MUST DIE.

THIS MAN IS OUR MOST LETHAL ENEMY. THE BLOOD HE HAS SPILLED--THE TOLL HE HAS TAKEN OF YOUR COMRADES-IN-ARMS--CANNOT GO UNAVENGED.

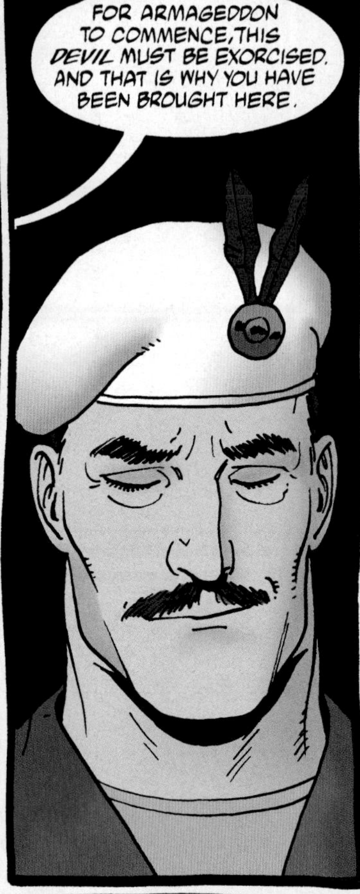
FOR ARMAGEDDON TO COMMENCE, THIS DEVIL MUST BE EXORCISED. AND THAT IS WHY YOU HAVE BEEN BROUGHT HERE.

TO THIS END, YOU WILL DRAW WEAPONS AND AMMUNITION AND PROCEED TO A SPECIFIC LOCATION IN DOWNTOWN SAN ANTONIO. THERE YOU WILL POSITION YOURSELVES DISCREETELY AND COMMENCE COVERT SURVEILLANCE.
ONCE CUSTER ARRIVES--AND WE HAVE EVERY REASON TO BELIEVE HE WILL--YOU WILL ALLOW HIM ACCESS TO THE AREA AND THEN SEAL OFF ALL EXITS. PHOTO I.D. ON CUSTER AND HIS ASSOCIATES WILL OF COURSE BE PROVIDED.

CAPTAIN GANDER AND I WILL HANDLE THE ACTUAL KILL. YOUR PRIORITY IS PERIMETER SECURITY.
THIS OPERATION IS CLASSIFIED ULTRA-SECRET. LOCAL LAW ENFORCEMENT HAS BEEN TAKEN CARE OF; IT IS VITAL THAT NO PUBLIC INTERFERENCE OR OBSERVATION BE PERMITTED.
USE OF LETHAL FORCE IS THEREFORE APPROVED.

FURTHERMORE, YOU MUST--
MUST...

CAPTAIN GANDER?
MM?

CAPTAIN.
GANDER.

ALLFATHER?

WOULD YOU MIND TELLING ME.
CAPTAIN.
EXACTLY WHAT THE

FUCK!!!

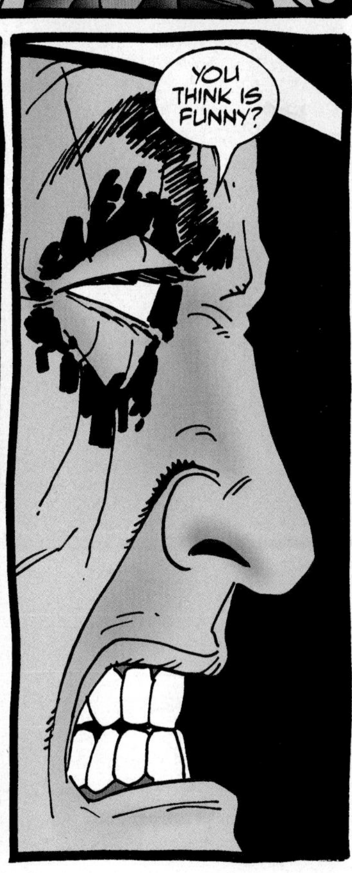
YOU THINK IS FUNNY?

YOU'RE STAYIN' TOO, SKEETER.
WUFF!
I AIN'T GETTIN' YOU KILLED NEITHER. YOU GOTTA STAY AN' LOOK AFTER HER NOW.
TULIP
I HATE THIS.
I HATE THIS 'CAUSE IT'S A LIE.
I TOLD HER I TRUSTED HER. I SAID I KNEW SHE COULD HANDLE HERSELF, I DIDN'T THINKA HER AS NO WEAK LITTLE GAL--HELL, I DON'T. I BELIEVED WHAT I WAS SAYIN' TO HER, I TRULY DID.
BUT NOW, WITH THE SHIT 'BOUT TO START FLYIN'...
JESUS.
I TRULY HATE A GODDAMNED LIE.

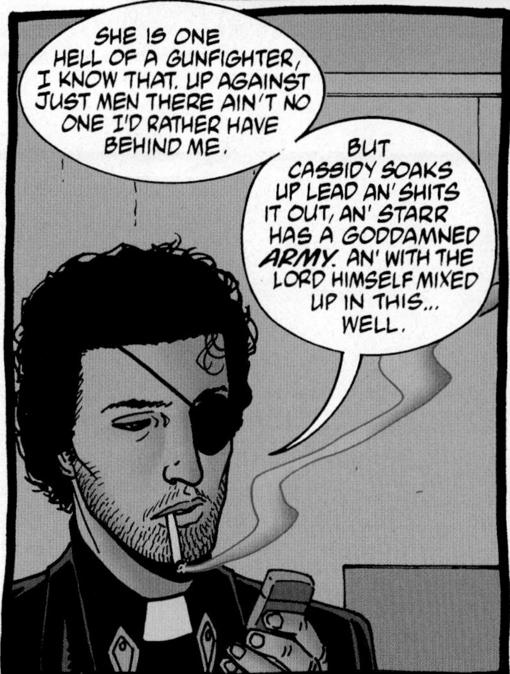
SHE IS ONE HELL OF A GUNFIGHTER, I KNOW THAT. UP AGAINST JUST MEN THERE AIN'T NO ONE I'D RATHER HAVE BEHIND ME.
BUT CASSIDY SOAKS UP LEAD AN' SHITS IT OUT, AN' STARR HAS A GODDAMNED ARMY. AN' WITH THE LORD HIMSELF MIXED UP IN THIS... WELL.

I SEEN HER DIE FOR REAL ONE TIME, AN' A HUNDRED MORE IN MY NIGHTMARES.
THERE IT IS.

DAMN, HOW COME DOIN' RIGHT AN' SHOOTIN' STRAIGHT'S SO EASY, EXCEPT WHEN IT COMES TO HOW YOU DEAL WITH WOMEN?

WELL, PILGRIM--

AIN'T A MAN ALIVE KIN GIVE YA THE ANSWER TO THAT'N.

HERR STARR--!

LOOK, I KNOW WHAT YOU MUST BE THINKING AND I REALLY WAS GOING TO STOP YOU, BUT YOU WERE IN SUCH A HURRY AND I JUST COULDN'T SEEM TO FIND THE OPPORTUNITY...
AND I MEAN, YOU KNOW, YOU HAVE TO ADMIT--

SO I GUESS YA FIGGERED OUT HOW TA... FINISH THIS FIGHTA YERS AT LONG LAST...
YEAH...

YEAH, I CAME UP WITH A KINDA IDEA. ALREADY KICKED THE LID OFF IT, AS A MATTER'VE FACT.
FUNNY THING IS, ONLY WAY I COULD SEE IT WORKIN'...
WAS IF I DIDN'T COME THROUGH IN ONE PIECE.

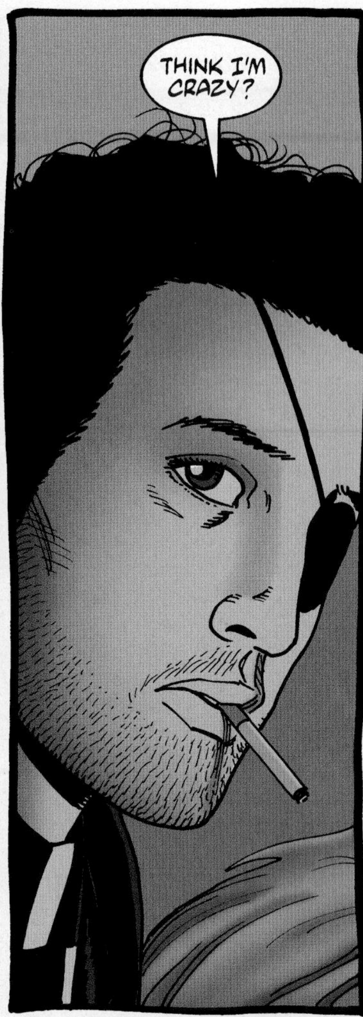
THINK I'M CRAZY?

THINK YA OUGHTA... MAKE SURE THE BULLET-HOLES'RE IN YER FRONT.

YA STILL RECALL THEM THINGS YER DADDY TOLD YA?
YOU KNOW I DO.

THEN LET'S HEAR 'EM, LOUD AN' CLEAR.

...
DON'T TAKE NO SHIT OFF FOOLS...

AN' YOU JUDGE A PERSON BY WHAT'S IN 'EM, NOT HOW THEY LOOK.

AN' YOU DO THE RIGHT THING.

YOU GOTTA BE ONE OF THE GOOD GUYS, SON:

'CAUSE THERE'S WAY TOO MANY OF THE BAD.

THINK YA LIVED UP TA THEM WORDS, PILGRIM? THINK YA BEEN ONE'VE THE GOOD GUYS?

I DON'T KNOW.
I AIN'T GOT THE SLIGHTEST IDEA.

GOOD ANSWER.

BEEN WATCHIN' OVER YA A LONG TIME NOW, I GUESS. TRIED TA HELP YA WHEN I COULD, BUT... MOSTLY JUST BIN WATCHIN'.
SAW YA LEARN TA FOLLOW YER HEART, AN' NOT TA QUIT NER DUCK A FIGHT. SAW YA LEARN TA BE A MAN.

BUT THERE AIN'T NO MORE THAT I CAN TELL YA. I GOTTA...GO ON NOW, LEAVE YA TA FINISH IT.
THIS LAST THING YA GOTTA DO ALONE.

I GUESS I'M... BURNIN' DAYLIGHT...
HEY.

I WANT TO THANK YOU.

THANK ME FER WHAT...?

FOR BEIN' A GODDAMNED HERO.

HELL, PILGRIM, I'M JUST A... BROKE-DOWN, WORE-OUT OL' COWBOY...

BUT THIS BROKE-DOWN, WORE-OUT OL' COWBOY WANTED YA TA KNOW:

HE'S PROUDA YA.

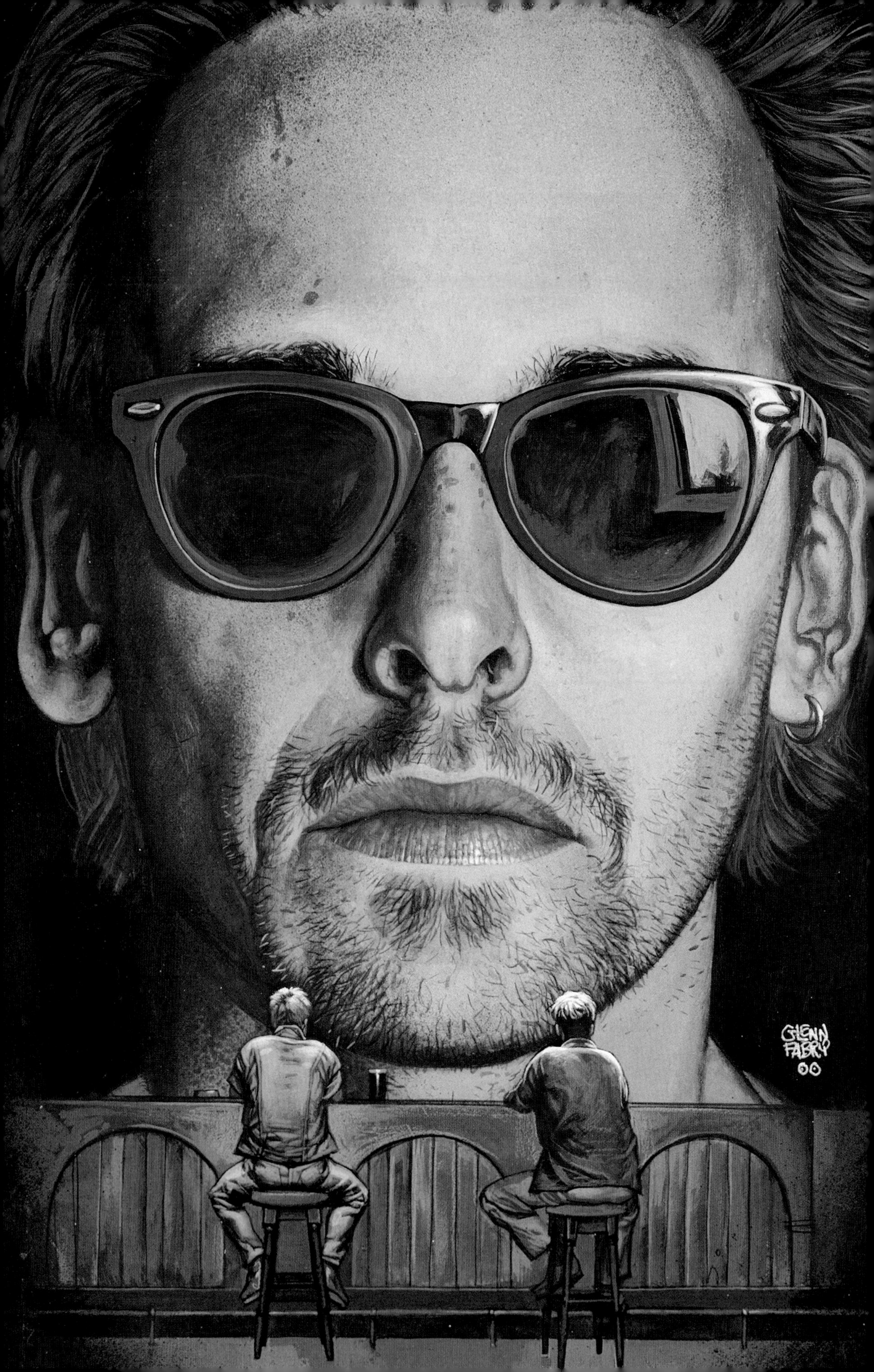
GLENN
FABRY
00

"No, I wouldn't be able to look at me either..."

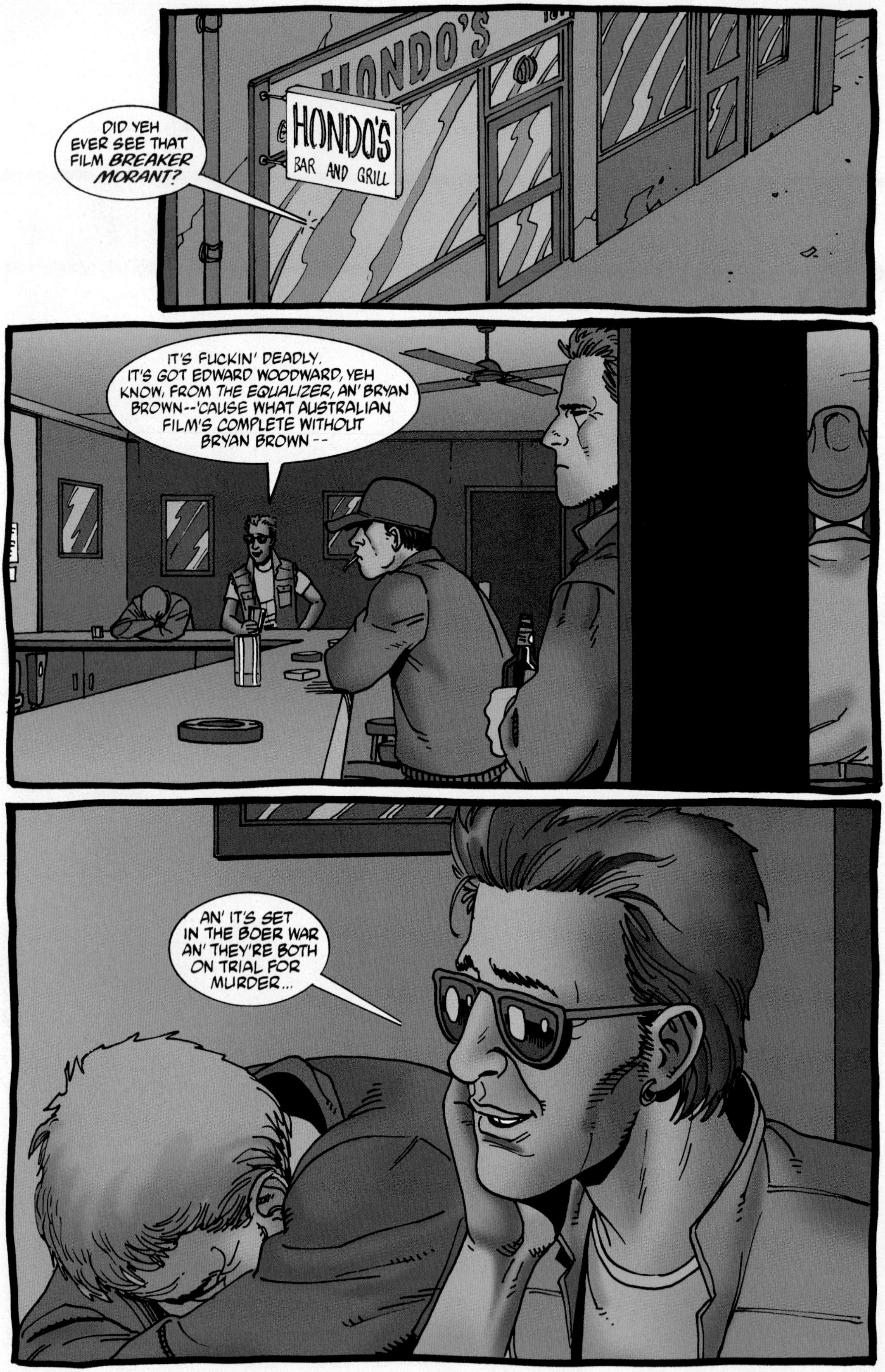

AN' IT'S SET IN THE BOER WAR AN' THEY'RE BOTH ON TRIAL FOR MURDER...

NOW THEY'RE BEIN' FRAMED-- WELL, THEY DID IT, BUT...
WELL IT'S SORT'VE COMPLICATED, YEH KNOW? YEH'LL HAVE TO WATCH THE MOVIE, I DON'T WANT TO RUIN IT FOR YEH.

BUT THEY'RE FOUND GUILTY AN' THEY'RE GONNA BE SHOT, AN' THE NIGHT BEFORE THE EXECUTION ONE'VE EDWARD WOODWARD'S MATES COMES ROUND TO BUST HIM OUT...

AND THIS IS ME FAVORITE BIT, I ALWAYS LOVE THIS--

'CAUSE, uh...
'CAUSE EDWARD WOODWARD DOESN'T WANNA GO.

SO HIS MATE'S SAYIN' COME ON, HE CAN GET A BOAT AN' GET OUT'VE THERE, HE CAN GO OFF AN' SEE THE WORLD...!
NAH, HE SAYS.

IF I KNEW THE WAY I'D GO BACK HOME

GARTH ENNIS - Writer STEVE DILLON - Artist

PAMELA RAMBO - Colorist CLEM ROBINS - Letterer AXEL ALONSO - Editor

PREACHER created by GARTH ENNIS and STEVE DILLON

I'LL GET THIS...
I CAN BUY MY OWN WHISKEY.

NICE WEE PLACE.
BIT OF A JOB FINDIN' IT, LIKE. APPARENTLY THEY SAY SAN ANTONIO WAS LAID OUT BY A BLIND SPANIARD--
RIDIN' A DRUNK MULE, YEAH. I HEARD THAT'N.

WELL... CAN I HAVE A CIGARETTE?
YOU BRING YOUR OWN LIGHTER?

WHAT?
IT'S A JOKE.

OH...!
SO LOOK, I'VE GOT TO ASK: HOW THE FUCK DID YEH SURVIVE FALLIN' OUT'VE THAT PLANE?
THE GOOD LORD SAVED MY ASS. KINDA MY LAST CHANCE TO BACK OFF AN' LEAVE HIM BE.

JAYSIS. AN' NO DOUBT YEH'RE STILL HUNTIN' THE BASTARD, TOO.
D'YEH EVER WONDER IF YEH'RE WASTIN' YER TIME? YEH KNOW, RUNNIN' ROUND AFTER GOD ALMIGHTY HIM-FUCKIN'-SELF WHEN IT MAYBE WON'T MAKE A PICK'VE DIFFERENCE?
I MEAN YOU THINK ABOUT IT: GOD'S QUIT, THE WORLD'S MENTAL. BIG FUCKIN' SURPRISE...

WE HERE TO TALK ABOUT ME?

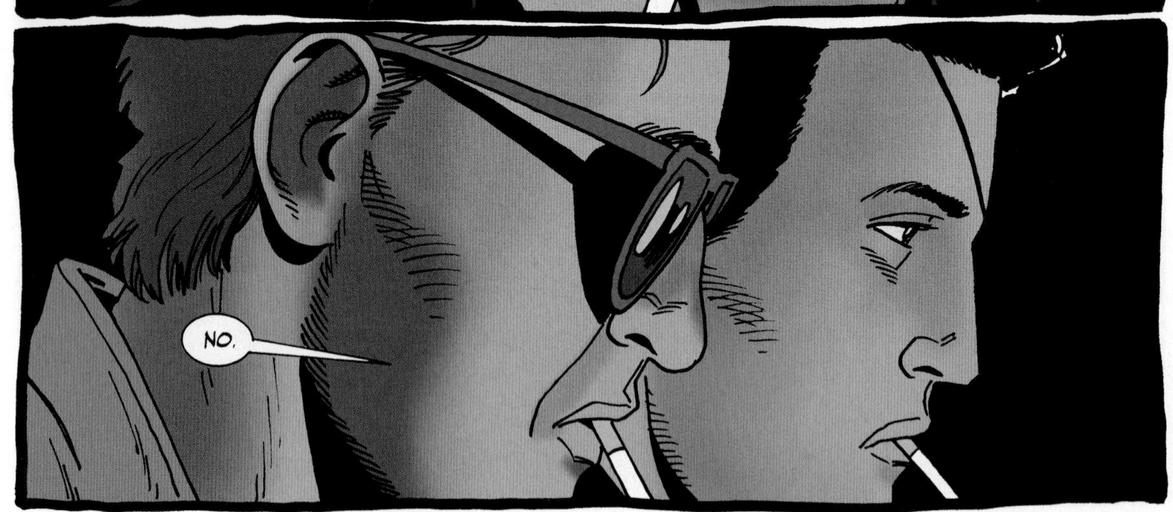
NO.

RRARF
RRARF RRARF
RRARF

MM...?

McCANN'S LONG GONE. AN' I KNOW GILLY'S DEAD, I WAS AT HER FUNERAL IN EIGHTY-NINE.
SO WITH WHAT YEH WERE SAYIN' THE LAST TIME, I'D IMAGINE YEH'VE PROBABLY BEEN TALKIN' TO SALLY.

YEP.
SO HOW IS SHE?
DEAD.

AH, JAYSIS. POOR OUL' SALLY.
I MUST'VE KNOWN HER TWENTY YEARS. WE NEVER REALLY GOT TOGETHER, BUT. SHE WAS ALWAYS TOO SMART FOR ME.

I MEAN SHE LIKED ME, BUT... SHE HAD THIS WAY OF SMILIN' AT ME: "I KNOW YOU, CASSIDY. DON'T EVEN TRY IT."
IT'S FUNNY, YEH KNOW WHO SHE WAS A BIT LIKE?
WHO?

uh... NO ONE YOU KNOW. SORRY, I WAS THINKIN'VE SOMEONE FROM YEARS AGO.

SO I GUESS THE POINT IS YOU WERE NEVER CLOSE. SO SHE DIDN'T GET HOOKED ON SMACK WITH YOU TRYNNA DRINK HER BLOOD TO STAY ALIVE.
DIDN'T GET HER JAW BROKE, NEITHER.

SHE TOLD YOU ABOUT JOANIE, TOO.
uh-huh.
I NEVER HIT JOANIE.
LUCKY OL' HER.

DO YOU THINK HITTIN' A WOMAN IS THE KIND'VE THING YEH JUST WALK AWAY FROM?

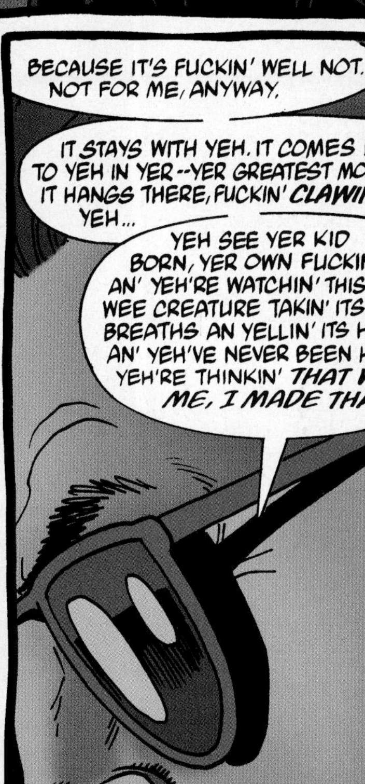

BECAUSE IT'S FUCKIN' WELL NOT. NOT FOR ME, ANYWAY.
IT STAYS WITH YEH. IT COMES BACK TO YEH IN YER--YER GREATEST MOMENTS. IT HANGS THERE, FUCKIN' CLAWIN' AT YEH...
YEH SEE YER KID BORN, YER OWN FUCKIN' KID, AN' YEH'RE WATCHIN' THIS AMAZIN' WEE CREATURE TAKIN' ITS FIRST BREATHS AN YELLIN' ITS HEAD OFF-- AN' YEH'VE NEVER BEEN HAPPIER, YEH'RE THINKIN' THAT WAS ME, I MADE THAT--

AN OUT'VE FUCKIN' NOWHERE YEH REMEMBER THE IMPACT'VE YER FIST ON SOME WEE GIRL'S JAW AN HOW IT TRAVELLED UP YER ARM TO YER SHOULDER AN' YEH REMEMBER YEH'RE FUCKIN' DAMNED...!

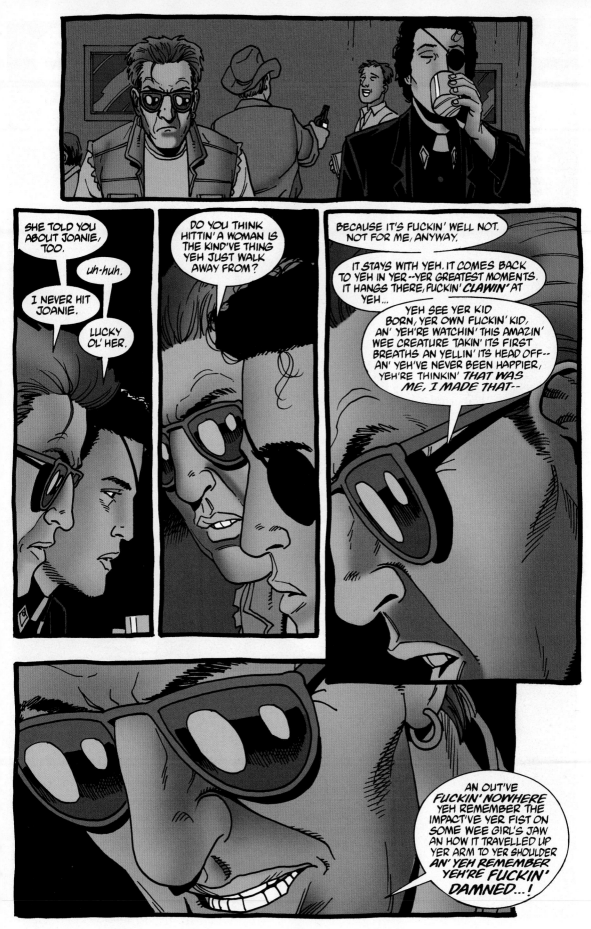

NEVER KNEW YOU HAD A KID.
A COUPLE. I'VE LOST TOUCH WI' THEIR MOTHERS.
I KNOW, I KNOW, LUCKY THEM...

I WAS TO MAKE EVERY CHEAP SHOT YOU'RE SETTIN' UP FOR ME, WE'D STILL BE HERE A GODDAMN YEAR FROM NOW.
JUST SAY YOUR PIECE.

ALL I'M TRYNNA TELL YEH IS I KNOW THAT IT'S WRONG. IT'S LIKE BREAKIN' ONE'VE THE RULES. THE RULE.
YEH'RE NOT SUPPOSED TO HIT WOMEN.

YEH DO IT AN' YEH'RE ONE'VE THE MONSTERS, YEH'RE DOOMED AN' YEH'RE FUCKED--BUT YEH KNOW WHAT? YEH WAKE UP THE NEXT MORNIN' AN' YEH'RE STILL ALIVE. AN' YEH'RE THINKIN', WELL, JAYSIS, WHAT'M I SUPPOSED TO DO NOW...?
YEH CAN'T GO OFF AN' LIVE LIKE A HERMIT OR SOME-THIN', SO YEH JUST KEEP GOIN'. YEH SORT YERSELF OUT A BIT, AN'... WELL, EVENTUALLY THERE'S MORE LIGHT IN YER LIFE THAN DARK. AN' A WEE TINY PART'VE YEH STARTS TO BELIEVE IN A SECOND CHANCE.

AN' THEN YOU DO IT AGAIN.

THE LAST TIME WAS IN NEW ORLEANS WI' A WEE GIRL CALLED DEE.
I'D BEEN ON THE STRAIGHT AN' NARROW FOR MOST'VE THE EIGHTIES, AN' THEN I WENT THERE AN' GOT MIXED UP WI' *LES ENFANTS DU SANG*. THERE WAS ONE EEJIT IN PARTICULAR, THIS SORT'VE ARCH-BOLLICKS OF A FELLA...
BUT DEE WAS GREAT. I REALLY THOUGHT SHE'D HELP ME PUT THAT SORT'VE SHITE BEHIND ME, ALL THESE AWFUL OUL' MEMORIES THE WANKERS'D STIRRED UP-- BUT YEH'VE BEEN TO THE QUARTER. YEH KNOW WHAT IT'S LIKE.
THEY'RE SELLIN' TEMPTATION ON EVERY CORNER.

D'YEH REMEMBER YEH ONCE TOLD ME I DIDN'T KNOW ME OWN STRENGTH?
WELL, WHEN I THUMPED DEE IN THE SIDE'VE HER HEAD, HER EYE-BALL BURST.

AFTER THAT I WAS ON ME OWN FOR A LONG, MISER-ABLE TIME...
BUT WHAT'RE YOU S'POSED TO DO, HUH? YOU CAN'T LIVE LIKE A HERMIT.
YOU START TO BELIEVE IN A SECOND CHANCE.

WELL YEH... YEH CAN'T FEEL DAMNED FOREVER...
BUT AYE, THE YEARS WENT BY, AN' SLOWLY BUT SURELY THINGS WERE LOOKIN' UP. AN' ONE NIGHT I'M DRIVIN' OUT'VE DALLAS AN' ALL OF A SUDDEN THIS CRAZY WOMAN RUNS UP AN' STICKS A GUN IN ME FACE...

WELL NOW WE'RE GETTIN' TO IT.

FEATHERSTONE, I AM SO SORRY...!
JUST POUR, HOOVER.

I MEAN HOW COULD HE DO THAT? WHO DOES HE THINK HE IS?
THAT-- THAT--
MOTHERFUCKER?
FEATHERSTONE--!
IT'S STILL JUST A WORD, HOOVER. IT ALWAYS WILL BE.

YOU GET STRESSED AND YOU SAY ASSHOLE OR COCKSUCKER OR MOTHER-FUCKER, AND THEY'RE ALL JUST WORDS. THE WORLD DOESN'T END WHEN THEY'RE UTTERED ALOUD.
BUT YOU FEEL A TINY, TINY BIT BETTER, IF ONLY BECAUSE YOU KNOW THAT SAYING THOSE WORDS IS THE ONE FREEDOM YOU'LL ALWAYS HAVE.

WHAT'D YOU DO BEFORE YOU JOINED THE GRAIL?

WELL...I WAS A LIFEGUARD AT A SWIMMING POOL ACTUALLY.
WERE YOU ANY GOOD?

NOT REALLY. SOMEONE DROWNED.
I TAUGHT SUNDAY SCHOOL. I WAS *GREAT* AT IT.

I BELIEVED VERY STRONGLY IN WHAT I WAS DOING. I WAS COMMITTED TO TEACHING CHILDREN JESUS' MESSAGE, TRYING TO PREPARE THEM SPIRITUALLY AND MORALLY FOR LIFE.
THEN ONE DAY I CAME HOME TO THE APARTMENT I SHARED WITH MY SISTER, WHERE I FOUND HER RAPED AND BUTCHERED BODY DUMPED IN THE BATHTUB.

NO ONE WAS EVER CAUGHT.

I DIDN'T GIVE UP ON GOD. A LOT OF PEOPLE EXPECTED ME TO, BUT I'D NEVER BEEN THAT NAIVE.
I'D KNOWN LIFE WAS FRAGILE. CHAOS AND RANDOM HORROR WERE NEVER MORE THAN A BAD DAY AWAY FROM ANYONE. YOU ONLY HAD TO WATCH THE NEWS TO SEE THAT.
BUT GOD HAD A PLAN, I KNEW, AND OUR SUFFERING ON EARTH WOULD BE REWARDED IN HEAVEN.

IT WAS ONLY WHEN I SAW JENNY LYING DEAD IN A TUB FULL OF BLOOD THAT I THOUGHT GOD MIGHT NEED A BIT OF A HELPING HAND.

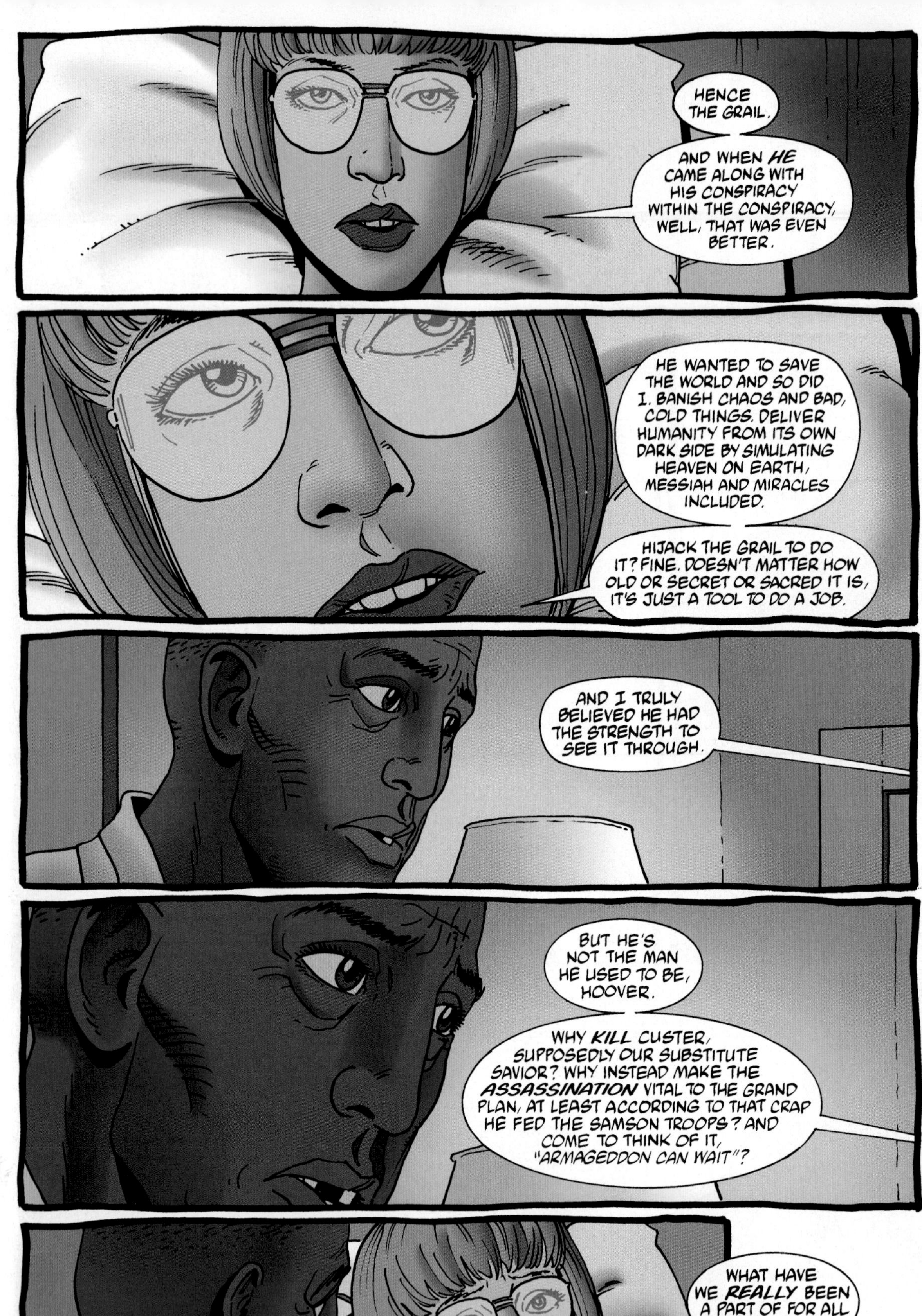
HENCE THE GRAIL.
AND WHEN HE CAME ALONG WITH HIS CONSPIRACY WITHIN THE CONSPIRACY, WELL, THAT WAS EVEN BETTER.
HE WANTED TO SAVE THE WORLD AND SO DID I. BANISH CHAOS AND BAD, COLD THINGS. DELIVER HUMANITY FROM ITS OWN DARK SIDE BY SIMULATING HEAVEN ON EARTH, MESSIAH AND MIRACLES INCLUDED.
HIJACK THE GRAIL TO DO IT? FINE. DOESN'T MATTER HOW OLD OR SECRET OR SACRED IT IS, IT'S JUST A TOOL TO DO A JOB.
AND I TRULY BELIEVED HE HAD THE STRENGTH TO SEE IT THROUGH.
BUT HE'S NOT THE MAN HE USED TO BE, HOOVER.
WHY KILL CUSTER, SUPPOSEDLY OUR SUBSTITUTE SAVIOR? WHY INSTEAD MAKE THE ASSASSINATION VITAL TO THE GRAND PLAN, AT LEAST ACCORDING TO THAT CRAP HE FED THE SAMSON TROOPS? AND COME TO THINK OF IT, "ARMAGEDDON CAN WAIT"?
WHAT HAVE WE REALLY BEEN A PART OF FOR ALL THIS TIME?

I SUPPOSE WHAT I WANTED... REALLY...

WAS FOR HER TO GROW TO LIKE ME MORE AN' MORE, AN' EVENTUALLY JUST... WELL...CHOOSE ME.
BUT FOR IT TO BE OKAY WI' YOU ANYWAY. SO WE'D ALL STILL BE MATES.

WELL.
THAT HAS TO BE ABOUT THE DUMBEST, MOST PATHETIC THING I HEARD IN MY ENTIRE LIFE.

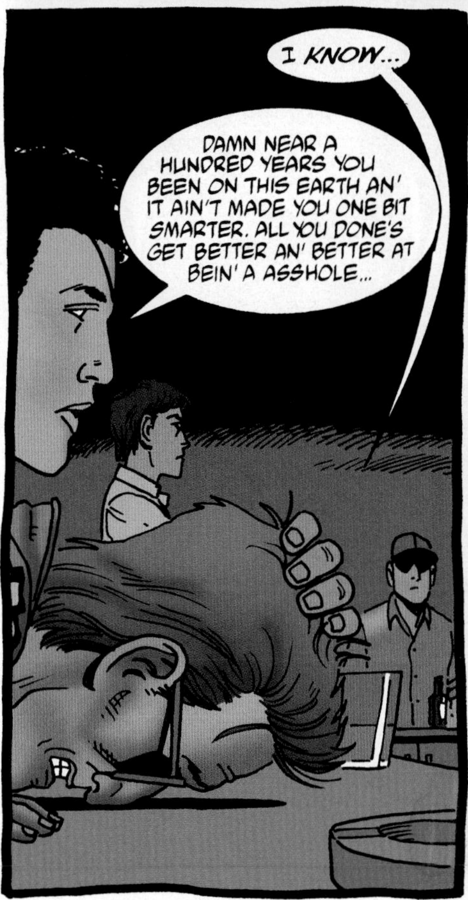
I KNOW...
DAMN NEAR A HUNDRED YEARS YOU BEEN ON THIS EARTH AN' IT AIN'T MADE YOU ONE BIT SMARTER. ALL YOU DONE'S GET BETTER AN' BETTER AT BEIN' A ASSHOLE...

LOOK.
GIRLS LIKE TULIP'RE ONE IN A MILLION, RIGHT? YEH DON'T NEED ME TO TELL YEH THAT. BUT--
GIRLS LIKE TULIP NEVER SEEM TO *GO FOR ME*...

SO WHAT ELSE CAN YOU DO BUT STICK A KNIFE IN YOUR BUDDY'S BACK, RIGHT?

BUT SHE DON'T CHOOSE YOU, WAY YOUR SMOOTH LITTLE PLAN WAS S'POSED TO WORK OUT.
THEN YOU KEEP ON MAKIN' IT WORSE, BUT 'FORE THINGS CAN COME TO A HEAD I FALL OUT'VE A GODDAMN AIRPLANE. AFTER THAT ALL YOU GOTTA DO'S KEEP HER DOPED UP AN' LEAVE THE LIQUOR BOTTLE LYIN' AROUND.
NO, I WOULDN'T BE ABLE TO LOOK AT ME EITHER...

BUT IT WASN'T JUST *LIKE* THAT...!
I MEAN I THOUGHT YEH WERE DEAD, WE BOTH THOUGHT YEH WERE DEAD! AN' SHE *ASKED ME* FOR THE BLEEDIN' PILLS--
FUCK YOU.

...AYE.
SHE NEEDED THEM AT FIRST BUT I SHOULD'VE GOT HER OFF THEM. I SHOULD'VE--
BUT I DIDN'T WANT HER SOBER, OH *JAYSIS*...

AND WHAT ELSE'S THE LIFE AN' SOULA THE PARTY BEEN DOIN' ALL THEM YEARS, I WONDER.
WHAT ELSE YOU COVERED UP WITH A SMILE AN' A SLAP ON THE BACK AN' *HOW'RE YEZ, GOD BLESS ALL HERE*...

OH, YEH THINK YEH KNOW IT ALL, DON'T YEH?
BUT YOU CAN'T EVEN IMAGINE.

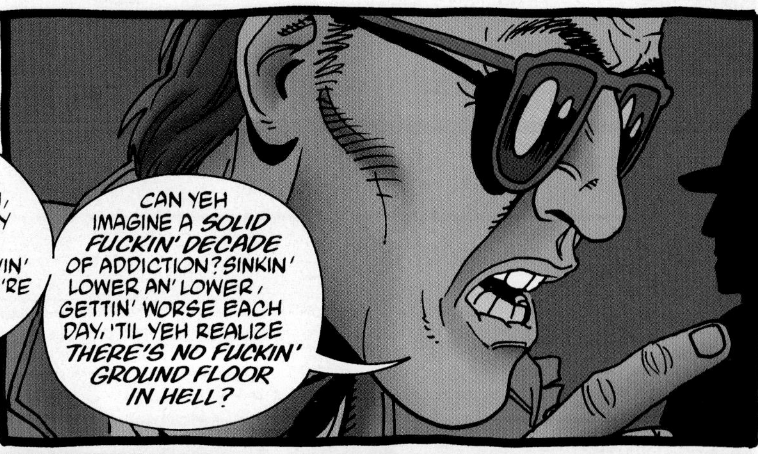
CAN YEH IMAGINE GETTIN' BUGGERED FOR MONEY? OR BEATIN' YER GIRL-FRIEND WHO FUCKIN' LOVES YEH, OR KILLIN' A MAN AN' THEN ONLY REMEMBERIN' YEH DID IT TWO YEARS LATER? WHAT ABOUT HAVIN' YER BODY WASTE AWAY 'TIL YEH'RE CLAWIN' WORMS OUT'VE THE GROUND TO EAT?
CAN YEH IMAGINE A SOLID FUCKIN' DECADE OF ADDICTION? SINKIN' LOWER AN' LOWER, GETTIN' WORSE EACH DAY, 'TIL YEH REALIZE THERE'S NO FUCKIN' GROUND FLOOR IN HELL?

I O.D.ED THIS ONE TIME, SOMEWHERE NOBODY KNEW ME. SO I WOKE UP IN THE COFFIN' AN' I HAD TO SPIT OUT THE EMBALMIN' FLUID AN' PULL THE STITCHES OUT'VE ME EYELIDS, BUT THERE WAS NO FUCKIN' BLOOD TO DRINK...!
I HAD TO WAIT A MONTH DOWN THERE 'TIL ALL THE MEAT GREW BACK! AN' THEN I'D TO DIG ME WAY OUT'VE ME OWN FUCKIN' GRAVE!

WAY YOU MAKE IT SOUND, YOU HAD ALLA THAT DONE TO YOU. 'STEADA YOU BEIN' THE ONE THAT DID IT.

...
WHAT NEXT?

WELL, I BEEN THINKIN' ABOUT THAT. AN' I RECKON WHAT I'M GONNA DO IS TAKE YOU OUT IN THE STREET AN' BEAT THE LIVIN' SHIT OUTTA YOU.
THEN I NEVER WANNA HEAR FROM YOU AGAIN.

WHAT?
YOU HEARD.

I WANT YOU TO KNOW HOW IT FEELS TO BE BEATEN AN' HELPLESS. TO HAVE FISTS CRASHIN' DOWN ON YOU AN' NOT A GODDAMN THING YOU CAN DO ABOUT IT.
TO BE THE VICTIM FOR THE FIRST FUCKIN' TIME IN YOUR LIFE.

JESSE... I'M AS STRONG AS FIFTY MEN...
THEN I'LL KICK YOUR ASS FIFTY TIMES.

BUT--I MEAN--THIS IS STUPID, I DON'T HAVE TO FIGHT YEH! I CAN JUST FUCK OFF, OR, OR STAND THERE WHILE YEH WEAR YERSELF OUT, OR--
WHEN THE TIME COMES, BOY--

YOU BETTER FIGHT LIKE HELL.

SAY! I BET MAH BUDDY BIG JOHN FIVE DOLLARS YOU TWO FAGGOTS GOT LOST AN' COME IN HERE BY ACCIDENT--AN' I WAS TO EVEN TALK TO YA, YA'D HIGHTAIL IT OUT THE DOOR AN' NOT DARE SAY A GODDAMN WORD!
SO WHAT'S IT GONNA BE, LADIES?!

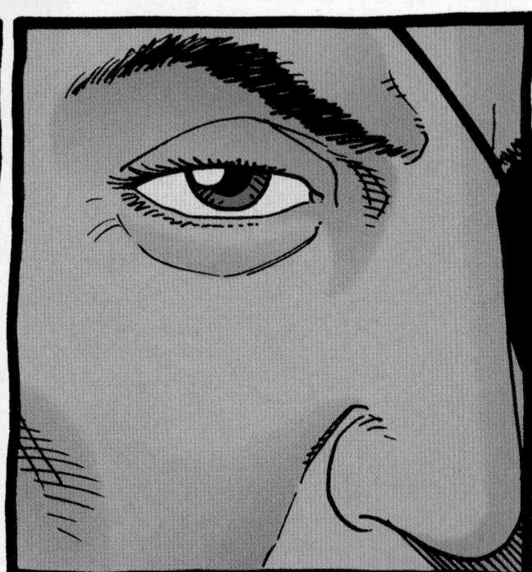

I'M GOING TO SAVE HIS STUPID FUCKING LIFE FOR HIM--

AND THEN I'M GOING TO KILL HIM.

THE TRUCK'S STILL IN THE LOT SO HE HASN'T LEFT TOWN. HE'S ON FOOT. GOT NEARLY A THREE-HOUR START.

...JUST LIKE OLD TIMES, WHA'?
YEAH.

YOU READY?

NOW?

AW, C'MON...!
I MEAN CAN WE NOT SIT DOWN AN' HAVE ANOTHER DRINK OR TWO YET? MAYBE TALK A WEE BIT MORE?
THERE AIN'T NOTHIN' MORE TO BE SAID.
WELL THEN COULD YEH JUST LEAVE ME ALONE FOR A COUPLE'VE HOURS?
ALL I WANNA DO'S HAVE A PINT AN'... AN' THINK. THEN I'LL MEET YEH WHEREVER YEH WANT.
JESSE, WHAT DIFFERENCE'LL IT MAKE?
...
I'LL BE WAITIN' IN FRONTA THE ALAMO. FIVE A.M.
DON'T MAKE ME COME LOOKIN' FOR YOU.

SO ANY-WAY.

THE NEXT MORNIN' EDWARD WOODWARD AN' BRYAN BROWN'RE MARCHED OUT TO BE SHOT. AN' THEY STICK THEM IN FRONT'VE THE FIRIN' SQUAD AN' WAIT FOR THE SUN TO COME UP...

SHOT AT DAWN, YEH KNOW? IT'S SORT'VE TRADITIONAL.
SO IT'S READY... AIM... AN' THEY'RE JUST ABOUT TO FIRE...

AN' EDWARD WOODWARD CALLS OUT *SHOOT STRAIGHT YOU BASTARDS, DON'T MAKE A MESS OF IT...*

AN' THE PAIR'VE THEM ARE BLASTED TO FUCK.

THE END.

GLENN
FABRY

"It's a simple question.
What side of the Goddamn grave are you on?"

HEY...
TAKE YOUR SHADES OFF.

WELL HOUL' ON, ARE WE JUST GONNA START GOIN' AT IT?
JESSE?

TAKE 'EM THE FUCK OFF.

JESSE--
YOUR CHOICE, PARDNER.
FOR FUCK'S SAKE, JESSE--

...Custer! His name reverberates like the clang of a sword.
Evan S. Connell
Son of the Morning Star

WHAT THE HELL...?

PERFECT SHOT ON CUSTER, ALLFATHER. JUST GIVE THE WORD.
HOLD YOUR FIRE. STAY ON TARGET.

ALLFATHER?
SIR, I KNOW THE SAN ANTONIO P.D. IS KEEPING CLEAR, BUT PEOPLE WILL SOON BE--
STAY ON FUCKING TARGET, CAPTAIN.

I WANT TO SEE THIS.

YOU KNOW WHAT'S WEIRD, SKEETER?
I HAVEN'T SEEN A COP CAR IN MAYBE TWENTY BLOCKS...

WUFF?

STAY.

GODDAMN, I THINK I SEE WHY YOU WEAR THEM THINGS...

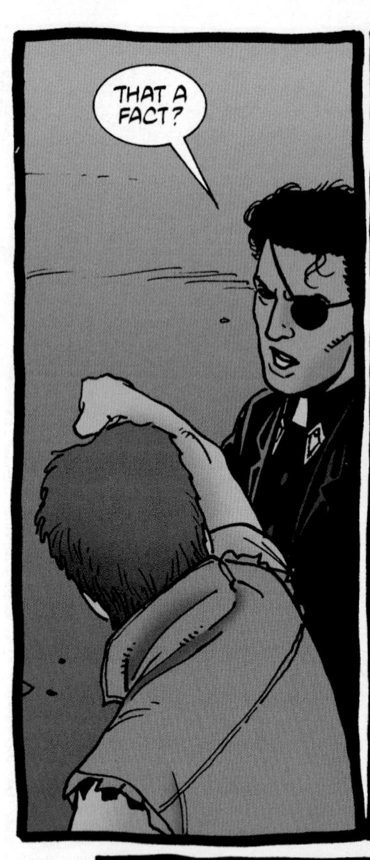
THAT A FACT?

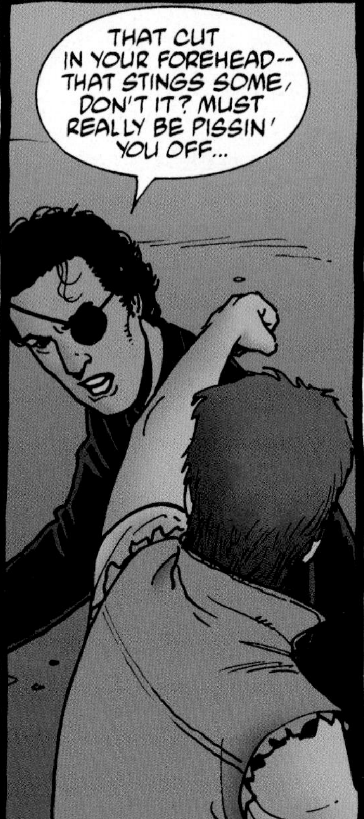
THAT CUT IN YOUR FOREHEAD-- THAT STINGS SOME, DON'T IT? MUST REALLY BE PISSIN' YOU OFF...

EYES FILLIN' UP WITH BLOOD... GETTIN' HARDER AN' HARDER TO SEE...

I CAN STILL FUCKIN' *SMELL YEH*--

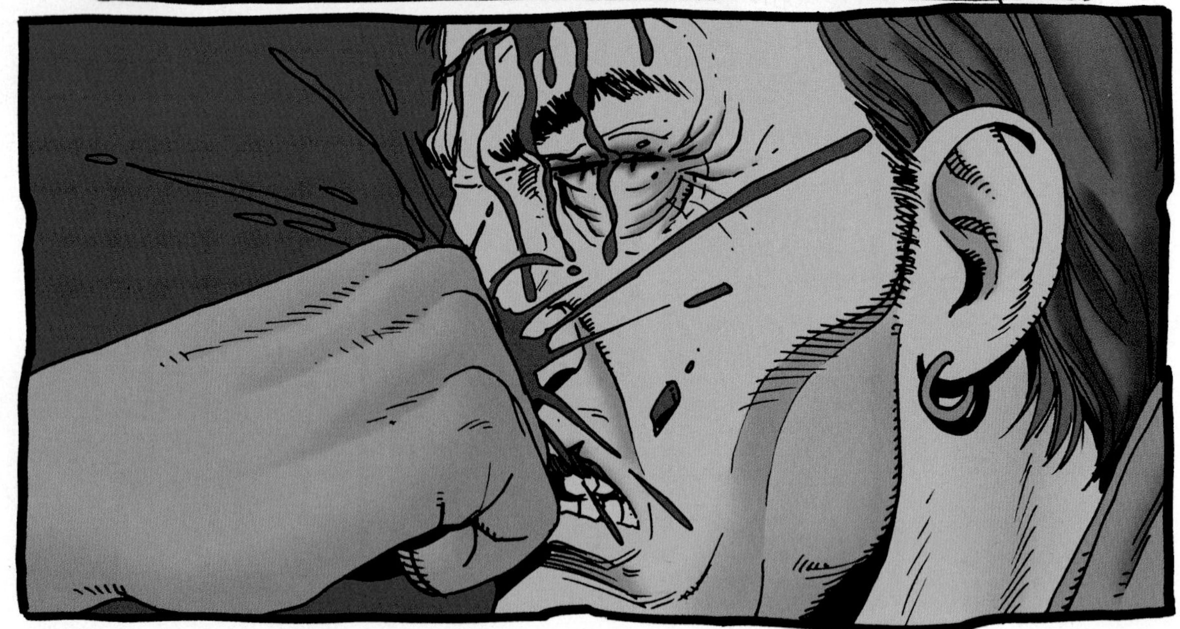

WHAT'S GOING ON?
WHAT'S GOING ON...
TWO GOOD AND DEAR FRIENDS ARE FIGHTING LIKE ANIMALS. TRADING LOVE AND HONOR AND RESPECT FOR HATRED. THROWING EVERY CHERISHED MOMENT OF THEIR FRIENDSHIP DOWN THE TOILET.
AND I'M FUCKING LOVING IT, FEATHERSTONE.
NOW GET BACK DOWNSTAIRS WITH HOOVER. YOU'RE SUPPOSED TO BE COORDINATING THE SAMSON TROOPS.
GOD...
YOU REALLY ARE A MONSTER, AREN'T YOU?

YES, I SUPPOSE I AM.

I BECAME ONE A LONG TIME AGO.
AT FIRST IN ORDER TO SAVE THE WORLD. NOW MERELY FOR THE SAKE OF VENGEANCE.

I MEAN LOOK AT ME: MY HEAD LOOKS LIKE A PENIS, I'VE GOT ONE LEG, ONE EAR, ONE EYE, AND MY COCK'S BEEN REPLACED WITH A RUBBER TUBE. YOU CAN'T SAY I DON'T LOOK THE PART.

SO I'M THE VILLAIN. I'M THE MONSTER. AND ALL I WANT IS MY REVENGE ON JESSE CUSTER.
THE WORLD WILL HAVE TO LOOK ELSEWHERE FOR ITS SAVIOR, FEATHERSTONE.

SO WILL YOU.

OH, YOU BASTARD.
YOU BASTARD.

YOU KNOW YOUR PROBLEM?

YOU GOT THE STRENGTH--

AN' THE SPEED--

BUT YOU DON'T KNOW HOW TO--
PUT 'EM TOGETHER, DO YOU?
'COURSE, THAT'S PRETTY MUCH THE STORY OF YOUR LIFE, WHEN YOU GET RIGHT DOWN TO IT...

THIS THING YOU ARE--

THE ADVANTAGES IT GIVES YOU--

YOU NEVER EARNED NONE'VE IT, DID YOU?
OH, YOU JUST LIE THERE A SPELL, BOY...

YOU DIDN'T EARN IT AN' YOU DIDN'T LEARN IT. YOU NEVER HAD TO, HELL, WHY SHOULD YOU LEARN TO FIGHT WHEN YOU'RE STRONG AS A GODDAMN OX? YOU HAD YOUR WHOLE LIFE HANDED TO YOU ON A PLATTER.
AN' YOU WANDER IN AN' OUTTA OTHER FOLKS' WITH NO IDEA'VE THE TROUBLE YOU CAN MAKE FOR 'EM, 'CAUSE YOU DON'T KNOW ANY MORE 'BOUT PEOPLE THAN YOU DO 'BOUT FIGHTIN'.
FELLA TAUGHT ME TO FIGHT WAS THE SAME PIECE OF SHIT SHOT MY DADDY DEAD IN FRONTA MY EYES.
THAT'LL TEND TO FOCUS YOUR CONCENTRATION.

HA!!

AAAWWWHHHH...!
THAT HURT, HUH?

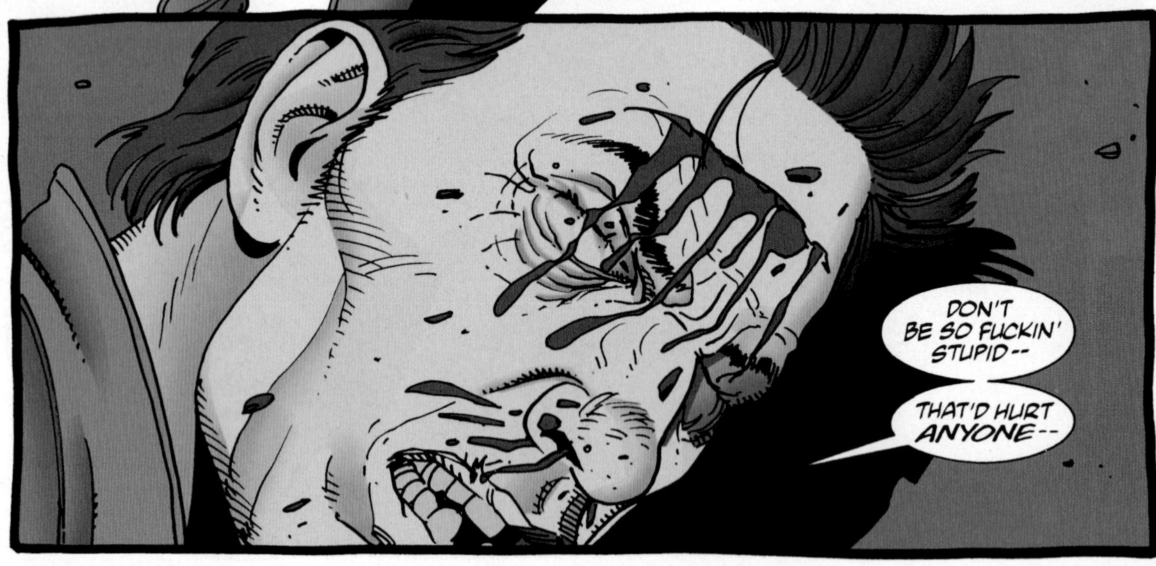
DON'T BE SO FUCKIN' STUPID--
THAT'D HURT ANYONE--

I CAN'T BELIEVE THAT MORON HOOVER DIDN'T THINK TO FILL IT UP...
HURRY UP IN THERE!

OKAY, I THINK I'VE GOT IT! TRY IT NOW!
RIDICULOUS LEVEL OF INCOMPETENCE I HAVE TO PUT UP WITH... HONESTLY...

MY GOD--!
ALL UNITS CONVERGE ON THAT! NOW!
WHAT IN JESUS' NAME--?
WHO CARES?
THE SAMSON TEAM WILL DEAL WITH IT. YOU MAKE SURE YOU STAY ON TARGET.

CHRIST IN HEAVEN, WHAT HAPPENED...?
I DON'T KNOW, I...
IS THAT THE VAN IN THERE--?

JESUS!

WHO THE--
SHOOT BACK AT HER, DAMN YOU!

FUCKERS--

GOD ABOVE US, WHO IS THIS WOMAN?

YOU FUCKERS--

OH LORD!
NO!!

YOU FUCK WITH ME, I'LL SHOW YOU WHO YOU'RE FUCKING WITH--

AAAH--!

STARR'S HERE. STARR HAS TO BE HERE. WHERE?
OH NO-- PLEASE NO--
WHERE?
ROOFTOP FACING THE ALAMO! PLEASE!

PLEASE--

WHAT THE FUCK...?
AIN'T NONE'VE YOUR CONCERN. I WAS YOU, I'D BE MORE WORRIED 'BOUT THAT KNEECAP YOU GOT HANGIN' OFF YOU THERE.
TELL ME SOMETHIN': ARE YOU ALIVE OR ARE YOU DEAD?

...AM I *WHAT*?

IT'S A SIMPLE QUESTION. WHAT SIDE OF THE GODDAMN GRAVE ARE YOU ON?

DO YOU KNOW WHAT IT MEANS TO BE A HUMAN BEING? DO YOU UNDERSTAND THINGS LIKE GIVIN' YOUR WORD, AN' STICKIN' BY THE FOLKS YOU GIVE IT TO? ALL THE SHIT WE PULLED EACH OTHER OUT'VE, DOES THAT *MEAN* ANY-THIN' TO YOU?
OR ARE YOU JUST A CORPSE STITCHED INTO THE SHAPE'VE A MAN, SOME KINDA BLOODSUCKIN' MONSTER DON'T EVEN KNOW IT'S DEAD...?
'CAUSE THE WAY YOU BEEN GOIN' THROUGH LIFE, I DON'T THINK YOU'RE TOO SURE YOURSELF.

C'MON THEN! C'MON!
I'LL FUCKIN' SHOW YEH--
BEHIND YOU, YOU DUMB SHIT.

RRAAAAHH!
REMEMBER SI?

WHUH?
YOU KNOW. YOUR BUDDY IN NEW YORK, THE PRICK TURNED OUT TO BE A SERIAL KILLER.
I WAS THINKIN' 'BOUT WHAT YOU SAID TO ME AFTER-WARDS, THAT WHOLE SPEECHA YOURS 'BOUT WHEN YOU THINK YOU GOT A GOOD FRIEND AN' YOU LET 'EM IN, YOU LET 'EM GET RIGHT IN YOUR HEART--BUT THAT'S OKAY, 'CAUSE YOU FIGURE YOU GOT 'EM THE SAME--

AN' IT TURNS OUT THEY'RE JUST ANOTHER FUCKER?
DID YOU MEAN SI? OR WERE YOU, SOME PARTA YOU, TRYNNA WARN ME?

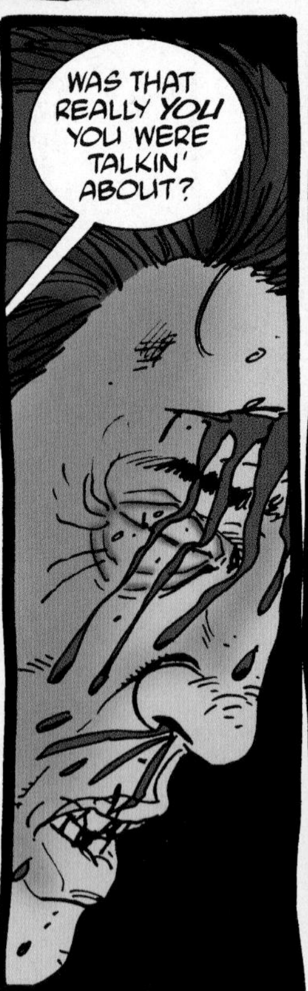
WAS THAT REALLY YOU YOU WERE TALKIN' ABOUT?

IT WAS NOT! IT FUCKIN' WELL WAS NOT! THAT'S NOT ME!
WHO THE FUCK DO YOU THINK YOU ARE, SAYIN' THESE FUCKIN' THINGS! WHO THE FUCK ARE YOU TO JUDGE ME?!

WHY, I'M JUST THE SON OF A BITCH NEVER BEAT UP NO WOMAN, CASS.
GODDAMN YOU!!
YOU ASSHOLE!!
WHY THE FUCK DID YOU LET ME DOWN SO BAD!!!

ALLFATHER, I'M GETTING MORE AND MORE UNEASY ABOUT THIS...
STAY ON TARGET.
BUT WHAT'S GOING ON, EXACTLY? WHAT WAS THAT YOU SAID TO YOUR ADJUTANT, THAT BUSINESS ABOUT--
STAY ON TARGET.
MOTHERFUCKER.
YOU EVIL, TWISTED MOTHER-FUCKER.

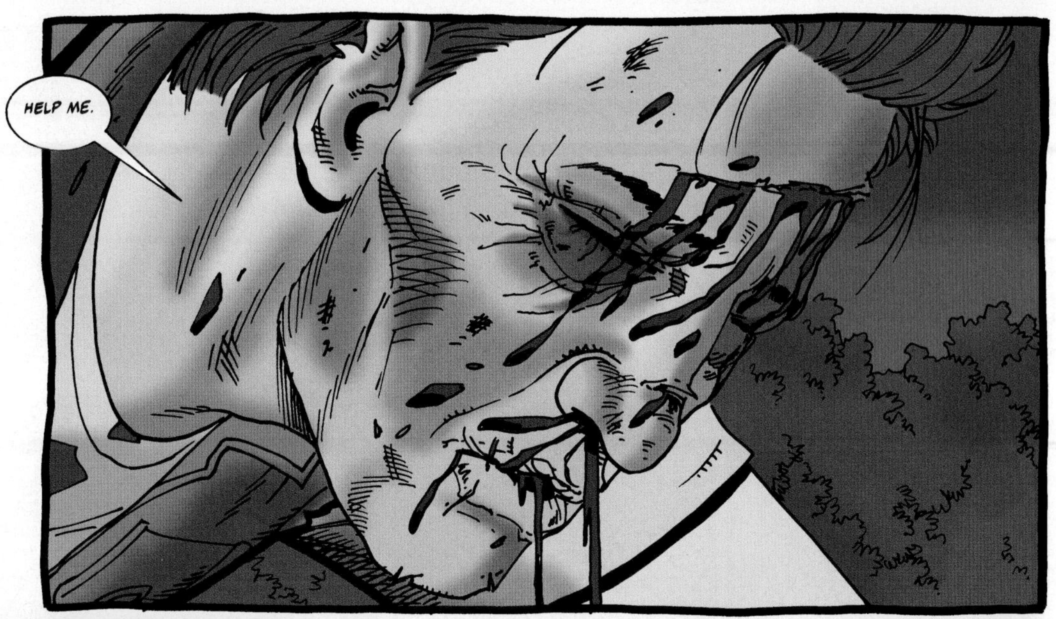
HELP ME.

WHAT?

HELP ME, I SAID.
YEH'RE THE ONLY ONE THAT CAN.

WHAT THE FUCK'RE YOU--
NO. NO, LISTEN TO ME NOW. MY TURN TO SPEAK.

BE TOTALLY FUCKIN' HONEST NOW.
THE FIRST TIME WE MET, BY THAT ROADSIDE, WHEN THE COPS WERE AFTER YOU AN' TULIP.
YEH LOOKED ME IN THE EYES LIKE YEH WERE WEIGHIN' UP WHAT SORT'VE A FELLA I WAS, AN' YEH ASKED IF YEZ COULD HAVE A RIDE WHEN YEH COULD'VE JUST TAKEN ME TRUCK, AN' THEN YEH LET ME STICK AROUND LATER, TOO...

TOTALLY... FUCKIN'... HONEST.
WHY?

BECAUSE--
...

BECAUSE I THOUGHT I WAS LOOKIN' AT A GOOD GUY.

AN' YOU SUCH A BRILLIANT JUDGE OF CHARACTER, TOO.
THERE'S A RUMOR GOIN' ROUND THAT NOBODY'S PERFECT.

SO I HEAR.
BUT DO YEH KNOW SOMETHIN'? I CAME BACK TO RESCUE YEH LATER, AFTER WE BOTH TOLD EACH OTHER TO FUCK AWAY OFF. 'CAUSE I KNEW THE SAINT WAS COMIN' TO GET YEH. 'CAUSE I THOUGHT YOU WERE A GOOD GUY.
AN' IT TURNED OUT TO BE THE FIRST DECENT THING I'D DONE IN YEARS.

AS I RECALL, YOU FUCKED UP THE RESCUE...
AW, I FUCK EVERYTHING UP! THAT'S NOT THE POINT AN' YOU KNOW IT!

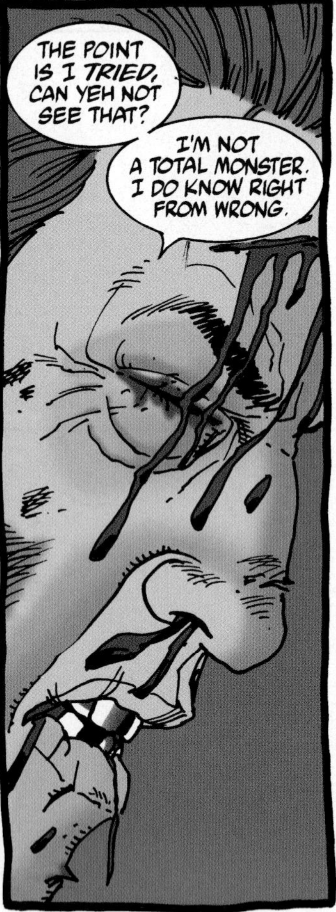
THE POINT IS I TRIED, CAN YEH NOT SEE THAT?
I'M NOT A TOTAL MONSTER. I DO KNOW RIGHT FROM WRONG.

AN' YOU THINK KNOWIN' YOU'RE A BASTARD IS SOME KINDA EXCUSE FOR IT? THAT LETS YOU OFF THE HOOK FOR PREYIN' ON PEOPLE, TREATIN' THEM LIKE TRASH, ALLA THAT SHIT?
NO...!

ALL I THINK IS THERE'S MAYBE A SPARK OF HOPE.

BUT I'M GONNA NEED HELP IF I'M GONNA MAKE ANYTHING OF IT.

...
FUCK YOU.

FUCK YOU, NO, NO FUCKIN' WAY, I CAN'T BELIEVE YOU GOT THE BALLS TO SAY THAT TO ME!
I OUGHTA RIP YOUR FUCKIN' HEAD OFF JUST FOR--FOR--

WHAT THE FUCK IS THIS, ARE YEH MADE'VE FUCKIN' STONE OR SOME-THIN'? LOOK AT ME! LOOK AT ME!
I'M YER FRIEND AN' I'M ASKIN' YEH FOR HELP!!

OH JESUS.
I NEED YER HELP OR I'M DAMNED, JESSE.
I NEED TO BE FORGIVEN. I NEED TO BE DRAGGED OUT'VE THIS AWFUL FUCKIN' NIGHTMARE I LIVE IN.
YOU ALWAYS USED TO GO ON ABOUT THIS COUNTRY GIVIN' PEOPLE A SECOND CHANCE-- WELL, WHERE'S MINE?
DO I GET A SECOND CHANCE, JESSE?
CAN YEH REACH OUT A HAND TO A FRIEND?
YOU HAD A THOUSAND CHANCES.
YOU'RE THE ONE WHO MADE YOUR LIFE INTO A NIGHTMARE.
FUCK YOURSELF.
JESSE FUCKIN' CUSTER...!
IT'S NOT SO EASY TO STAND BY YER FRIENDS WHEN THEY'RE STUCK ON THE ROAD TO HELL, IS IT?

GOD DAMMIT, CASSIDY.

ALL YOU EVER HAD TO DO WAS ACT LIKE A MAN.

ROOF
ACCESS

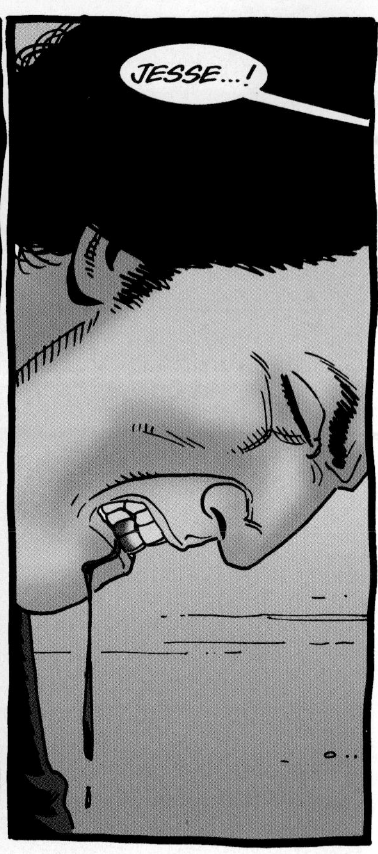

LET'S GO.

JAYSIS...

WHAT THE FUCK DO THEY *MAKE* LADS LIKE YOU FROM?

AH, FUCK, WOULD YEH LOOK AT THE STATE'VE THE PAIR'VE US...

WHAT THE FUCK-- *HNNGH*--
WHAT'RE YOU *DOIN'*..?
ME TIMIN'S A WEE BIT OFF. BUT THEN I WASN'T EXPECTIN' TO GET SUCH A FUCKIN' KICKIN' FROM YEH.

I DON'T *DESERVE* TO BE YER FRIEND, JESSE. I'LL ALWAYS BE AN ARSEHOLE, I'LL NEVER BE SOMEONE YEH CAN RELY ON. THAT SHOULD BE PAINFULLY OBVIOUS NOW.
I DON'T DESERVE YER FRIENDSHIP, AN' I DON'T DESERVE SALVATION...
AN' I MEAN THE KIND'VE THINGS I'VE DONE--*HITTIN' WOMEN,* FOR JAYSIS' SAKE--YEH CAN'T BE FORGIVEN FOR EVIL LIKE THAT.

YEH'VE GOT TO BURN IT OUT.
NO!!

CASSIDY, YOU ASSHOLE --
DON'T--

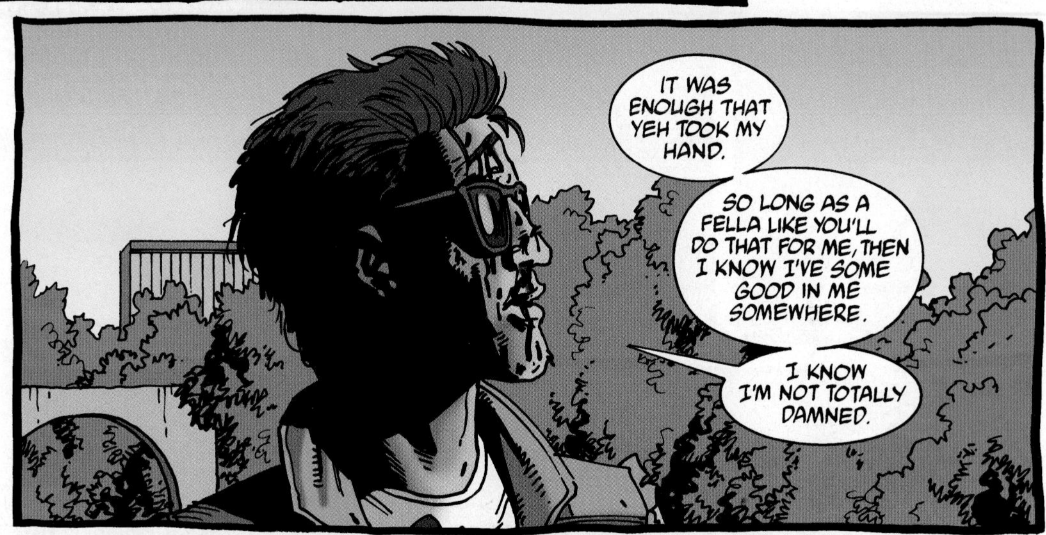
IT WAS ENOUGH THAT YEH TOOK MY HAND.
SO LONG AS A FELLA LIKE YOU'LL DO THAT FOR ME, THEN I KNOW I'VE SOME GOOD IN ME SOMEWHERE.
I KNOW I'M NOT TOTALLY DAMNED.

DON'T DO THIS! DON'T BE SO FUCKIN' CRAZY!
YOU GOTTA GET OUTTA THE SUN...!
I'LL TELL YEH THE FUNNY THING ABOUT AMERICA, JESSE. AN' I SHOULD KNOW, I'VE SPENT MOST'VE A CENTURY SEEIN' IT.

IT IS A BRILLIANT FUCKIN' PLACE. IF YEH'RE SMART ABOUT IT, IT'LL GIVE YEH EVERY-THING.

BUT JAYSIS, IT'D WEAR YEH OUT.

CHEERS, MATE.
NO.
CASSIDY-- AAAAH--!
DON'T! YOU DON'T HAVE TO! I DON'T WANT THIS, I SWEAR TO FUCKIN' GOD!
CASSIDY, NO!!
HELLO THERE.
YEH BIG BLONDE BITCH.

CASSIDYYYY!!!

GENESIS.

WH...
WHAT WAS...

RRRAAAAHHH!!

HUHH!!
AAA--!
I'LL KILL YOU, YOU WHORE! I'LL KILL YOU!
I'LL KILL EVERY LAST ONE OF YOU BITCHES, YOU TOOK MY FUCKING COCK!!
AAAOW!!

AARRRHHH, FUCK YOU!

TOO LATE! AAAAH! TOO FUCKING LATE!
I'VE FUCKING GOT YOU NOW--

KLIK

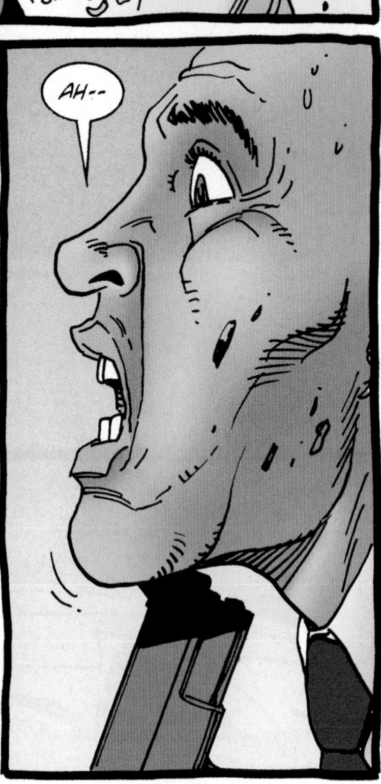
AH--

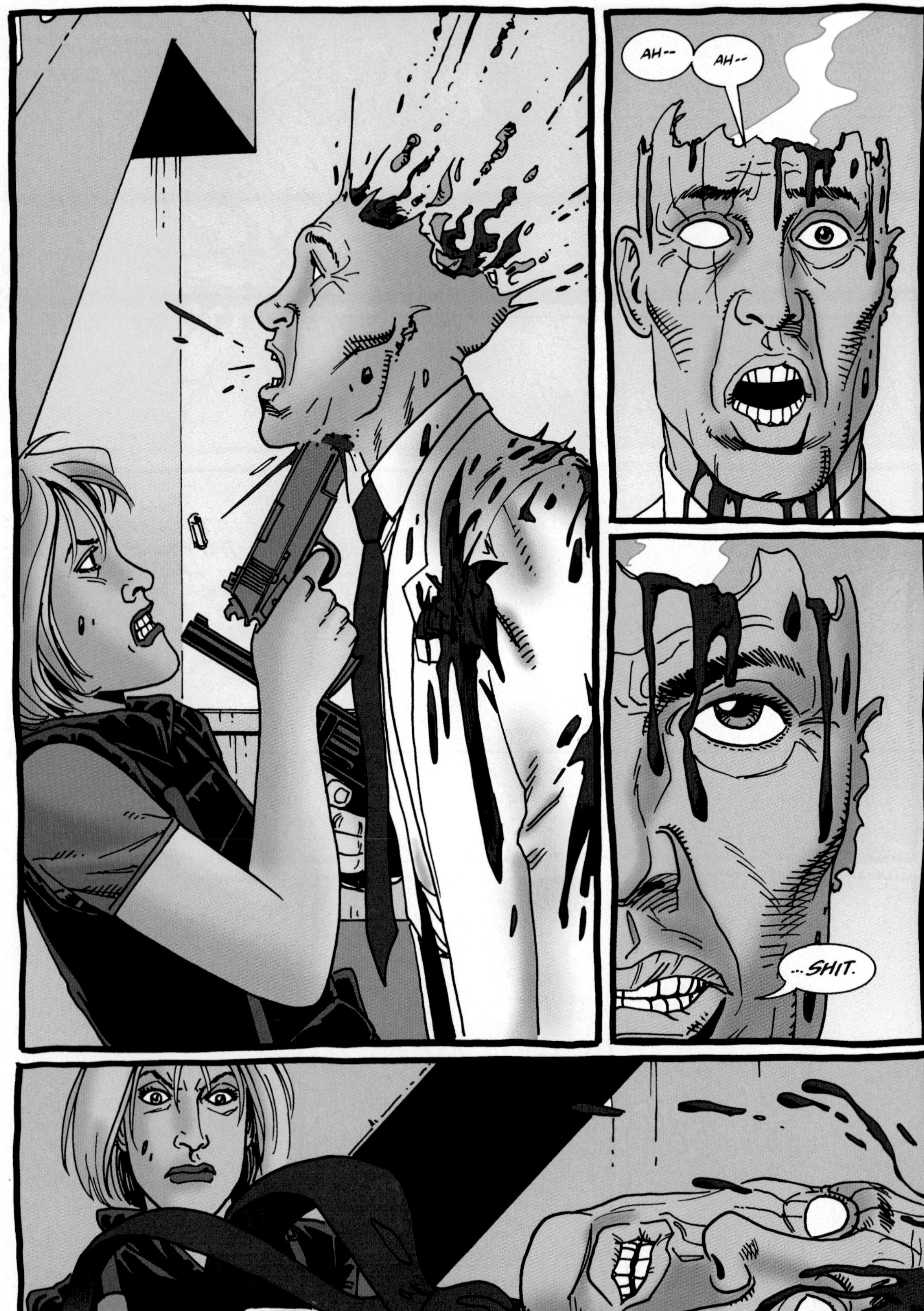
AH--
AH--
...SHIT.

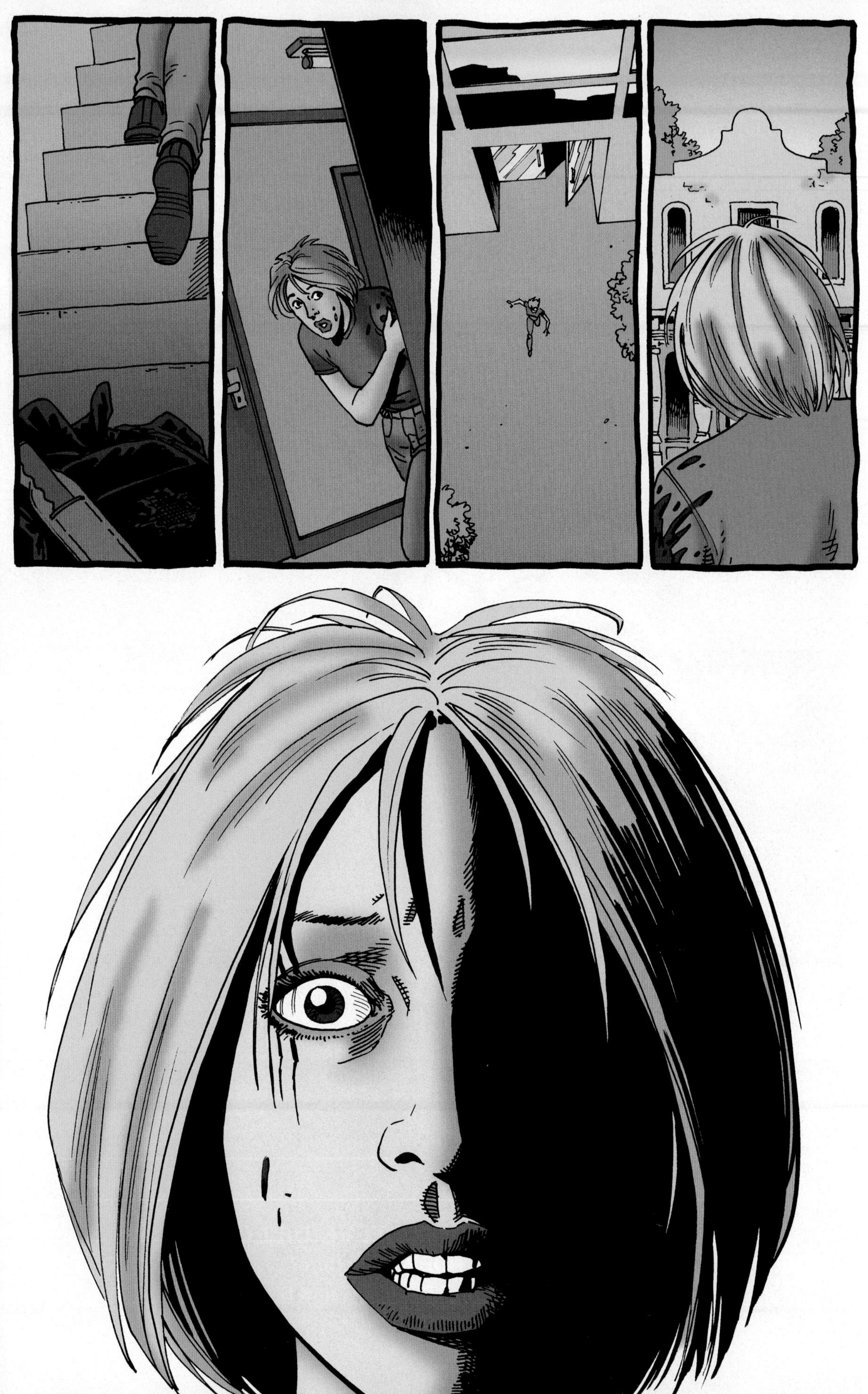

AND THAT WAS HOW THEY KILLED HIM, COVERED IN THE ASHES OF HIS DEAREST FRIEND.

SHOOT STRAIGHT YOU BASTARDS

GARTH ENNIS - Writer STEVE DILLON - Artist

PAMELA RAMBO - Colorist CLEM ROBINS - Letterer AXEL ALONSO - Editor

PREACHER created by GARTH ENNIS and STEVE DILLON

GLENN
FABRY
00

"I think I'll try actin' like a man."

"But Captain," the boy said, "They say you were the most famous Ranger. They say you've carried Captain McCrae three thousand miles just to bury him. They say you started the first ranch in Montana. My boss will fire me if I don't talk to you. They say you're a man of vision."

"Yes, a hell of a vision," Call said. He was forced to put spurs to the dun to get away from the boy, who stood scribbling on a pad.

—Larry McMurtry, *Lonesome Dove*

So we banged the drum slowly and we played the fife lowly
And silently wept as we bore him along
For we all loved our comrade, so brave and handsome
We all loved our comrade, although he'd done wrong.

— *The Cowboy's Lament*

I was told when I grew up I could be anything I wanted: a fireman, a policeman, a doctor — even President, it seemed. And for the first time in the history of mankind, something new, called an astronaut. But like so many kids brought up on a steady diet of Westerns, I always wanted to be the avenging cowboy hero — that lone voice in the wilderness, fighting corruption and evil wherever I found it, and standing for freedom, truth and justice. And in my heart of hearts I still track the remnants of that dream wherever I go, in my endless ride into the setting sun.

— Bill Hicks, *Revelations*

MY DARLING,

I GUESS THE FIRST THING YOU'LL THINK IS, WELL, THIS OUGHT TO BE PRETTY GODDAMN GOOD. BUT THIS ISN'T ANY KIND OF EXCUSE LIKE THE LAST TIME. IT'S JUST THE DUMB SON OF A BITCH YOU FELL IN LOVE WITH TELLING YOU THE EVEN DUMBER THING HE'S DONE.

I KNOW YOU'LL TAKE THIS HARD, BUT WHEN IT CAME TO IT I COULDN'T FACE WHAT I HAD TO WITH YOU BY MY SIDE. I WAS SCARED YOU'D GET HURT OR KILLED, AND THE THOUGHT OF YOU DYING WAS MORE THAN I COULD STAND. SO YES, I'VE RUN OUT ON YOU AGAIN. WORSE, I'VE DRUGGED YOU SO YOU'LL SLEEP THROUGH WHAT'S ABOUT TO HAPPEN. HERE IS WHY.

WHEN ALL THIS CRAZINESS BEGAN I TOOK ON A TASK THAT I COULD NOT IGNORE. I SWORE TO FIND THE LORD GOD AND FORCE HIM TO CONFESS TO HIS PEOPLE THE SIN HE COMMITTED AGAINST THEM: TO HIS BETRAYAL OF MANKIND BY ABANDONING HIS PLACE IN HEAVEN. IF I DID NOT TRY TO SET THIS TERRIBLE THING TO RIGHTS, THEN I WOULD BE NO KIND OF MAN AT ALL.

BUT WHAT SEEMED SO EASY TO FIGURE BACK THEN HAS BECOME A HELL OF A LOT MORE COMPLICATED. YOU AND I HAVE BOTH SEEN GOD FACE TO FACE, AND WHAT HE SAID THOSE TIMES SET ME TO THINKING. WHEN I LEARNED WHAT GENESIS ITSELF KNEW—AND HALF THE SECRETS OF HEAVEN ARE LOCKED INSIDE THIS DAMN SPOOK OF MINE—I KNEW I HAD AN EVEN HARDER JOB TO DO.

THE LORD IS NOT THE LOVING GOD HE SWORE TO US HE WAS. INSTEAD HE'S JUST A GOD WHO FEEDS ON LOVE. THE CREATION OF MANKIND WAS THE ACT OF AN EGOMANIAC, PLAIN AND SIMPLE—TO CHOOSE TO FOLLOW GOD WOULD BE A CONSCIOUS ACT, AND THEREFORE ALL THE MORE PLEASING TO HIM. THE RESULT WAS A WORLD THAT CAN NEVER KNOW PEACE, BUT I GUESS THAT NEVER BOTHERED HIM.

CAUSING A WAR BETWEEN HIS ANGELS WAS NOTHING BUT A CHEAP, STUPID TEST OF WHO WOULD CHOOSE HIM OR REJECT HIM, AND ENGINEERING THE RISE OF A POWER BEYOND HIS OWN IN GENESIS—WELL, THAT'S WHERE HE WENT LOOKING FOR LOVE SOMEWHERE VERY, VERY BAD, AND WHAT IT GOT HIM WAS HAVING TO RUN FOR HIS LIFE. WHAT IT GOT THE WORLD WAS A NIGHTMARE.

THESE ARE NOT THE ACTIONS OF A LOVING GOD. THEY ARE THE FUCKED-UP, TWISTED MACHINATIONS OF A BEING DANGEROUSLY SET ON BEING ADORED, AND I BELIEVE HUMANITY MUST BE FREE OF HIM, IF WE'RE TO HAVE ANY CHANCE OF MAKING IT AT ALL.

NOW MAYBE I COULD HAVE HUNTED DOWN THE LORD, BUT I DOUBT IT VERY MUCH, NOT EVEN IN A HUNDRED LIFETIMES. AND MAYBE I COULD HAVE FORCED HIM TO CONFESS WHAT HE'D DONE—I GUESS I HAVE THE POWER, AFTER ALL. BUT THE REAL TROUBLE RUNS A LOT DEEPER THAN THAT. AND HERE'S WHERE I SKIN THIS THING DOWN TO THE BONE.

WOULD FOLKS BUY IT? WOULD THEY BELIEVE THEY'D SEEN GOD? WOULD THEY ACKNOWLEDGE THAT THEY'D HEARD HIS VOICE? OR WOULD THEY SAY IT WAS ONE BIG SPECIAL EFFECT, AND GO ON BELIEVING EXACTLY WHAT SUITED THEM?

BECAUSE IF THERE WAS ONE THING I LEARNED IN THOSE FIVE GODAWFUL YEARS AS PREACHER TO THAT SHITHOLE TOWN OF ANNVILLE, IT'S THAT FOLKS NEVER BELIEVE MORE THAN WHAT'S CONVENIENT. WHAT THEY CALL THEIR FAITH IS JUST A HOOK: THEY HANG THEIR HOPES ON IT AT THE BEST OF TIMES, THEY HANG THE BAD STUFF

THEY DO TO OTHER FOLKS ON IT AT THE WORST. AND WHILE THEY WORSHIP A GOD THAT SUITS THEIR NEEDS, THE REAL GOD THRIVES ON THEIR STUPID, MISDIRECTED LOVE, AND DOES BAD, BAD THINGS TO THIS WORLD WITH THE POWER IT GRANTS HIM.

SO GOD HAS GOT TO GO, TULIP. HE DESERVES IT FOR THE THINGS HE'S DONE, BUT MORE THAN THAT THE WORLD JUST PLAIN NEEDS TO BE RID OF HIM. WHICH IS WHY I MADE A DEAL WITH THE SAINT OF KILLERS.

THE SAINT IS GOING TO KILL THE LORD ALMIGHTY.

NOW HE CAN ONLY DO IT IF HE'S GOT GOD IN HIS SIGHTS, AND THE ONE PLACE HE CAN BE SURE OF FINDING GOD IS IN HEAVEN. BUT GOD WON'T GO BACK THERE UNTIL HE KNOWS THAT GENESIS IS GONE, BECAUSE HE KNOWS THAT I COULD USE ITS POWER TO HUNT HIM EVEN THERE. AND HE CAN'T BE SURE THAT GENESIS IS GONE UNLESS HE KNOWS THAT I AM DEAD.

I SENT WORD TO OUR OLD FRIEND STARR THAT I'LL BE IN SAN ANTONIO TONIGHT, SO HE'LL COME RUNNING WITH THAT BUNCH OF ASSHOLES HE CALLS AN ARMY. I HAVE BUSINESS OF MY OWN WITH CASSIDY, WHICH BY GOD IS ONE THING I INTEND TO TAKE CARE OF WITH MY OWN TWO HANDS. AND THEN I GUESS STARR'S BOYS WILL TAKE CARE OF ME, AND THE SAINT WILL TAKE CARE OF THEM, AND THEN HE'LL GO ON TO HEAVEN AND SETTLE THINGS WITH GOD.

BUT YOU, MY PRECIOUS ANGEL, WILL SLEEP THROUGH THE WHOLE GODDAMN AFFAIR.

I WISH LIKE HELL I COULD HAVE COME UP WITH SOMETHING BETTER, SOMETHING SMARTER, BUT THIS WAS THE ONLY WAY I COULD THINK OF TO DISCHARGE THE RESPONSIBILITY I TOOK ON. NOT JUST THE TASK I SET MYSELF, BUT IN A STRANGE KIND OF WAY THE OBLIGATION OF A PREACHER TO SERVE THE LORD AS BEST HE CAN. I WILL TRADE MY LIFE FOR HIS, AND IN DOING SO I WILL PUT AN END TO HIM.

MY GREATEST REGRET—MY ONLY TRUE REGRET, BECAUSE I HAVE LIVED ONE HELL OF A LIFE BY ANY MAN'S RECKONING—IS THAT I WILL NEVER SEE YOU AGAIN. YOU WERE THE ONE CONSTANT IN THE TIME I SPENT ON THIS EARTH. IN A WORLD THAT SOMETIMES SEEMED LIKE HELL AND SOMETIMES LIKE A FREAK SHOW, THAT BROKE MY HEART A HUNDRED TIMES, YOU WERE THE ONE WHO NEVER LET ME DOWN. I ONLY WISH I COULD SAY I DID THE SAME FOR YOU.

OH, I SWEAR. I'M WRITING THIS AS EVENING DRAWS ON AND I'M WATCHING YOU SLEEP IN THE TWILIGHT, AND YOU ARE SO BEAUTIFUL IT CUTS ME LIKE A KNIFE. IF I COULD CRY, IF THE TRASH WHO KILLED MY DADDY HADN'T TAKEN THAT FROM ME, I WOULD.

I LOVE YOU, TULIP.

ALWAYS, ALWAYS, ALWAYS.

JESSE

P.S.: THIS IS A SMALL THING, BUT I HOPE IT WILL BE OF HELP. THIS KEY FITS A LOCKER IN THE BUS STATION IN DALLAS. IN THERE IS ALL THE MONEY LEFT FROM THE OLD DAYS, FROM OUR MISSPENT YOUTH WITH AMY, THAT I WAS SAVING FOR US WHEN WE COULDN'T DO WITHOUT IT. IT'S NO GREAT FORTUNE, BUT MAYBE YOU CAN FIND A USE FOR IT.

AND SO OF COURSE HE CAME BACK TO LIFE, JUST AS SHE HAD--AND JUST AS SHE HAD, HE FELT
LESS.

KINDA... DIMINISHED, EVEN.
LIKE I'M ALIVE BUT I KNOW I WAS DEAD, AN'IT'S SOME-THIN' I CAN'T PUT BEHIND ME.
THAT'S PRETTY MUCH HOW I FELT, TOO.

I WASN'T SURE IF I'D CATCH YOU...
YOU DIDN'T. I'M OUT OF HERE. YOU'RE NEVER GOING TO SEE ME AGAIN.

DO NOT TRY TO PERSUADE ME OTHERWISE.

I WOULDN'T DARE.
I NO LONGER HAVE THE RIGHT.

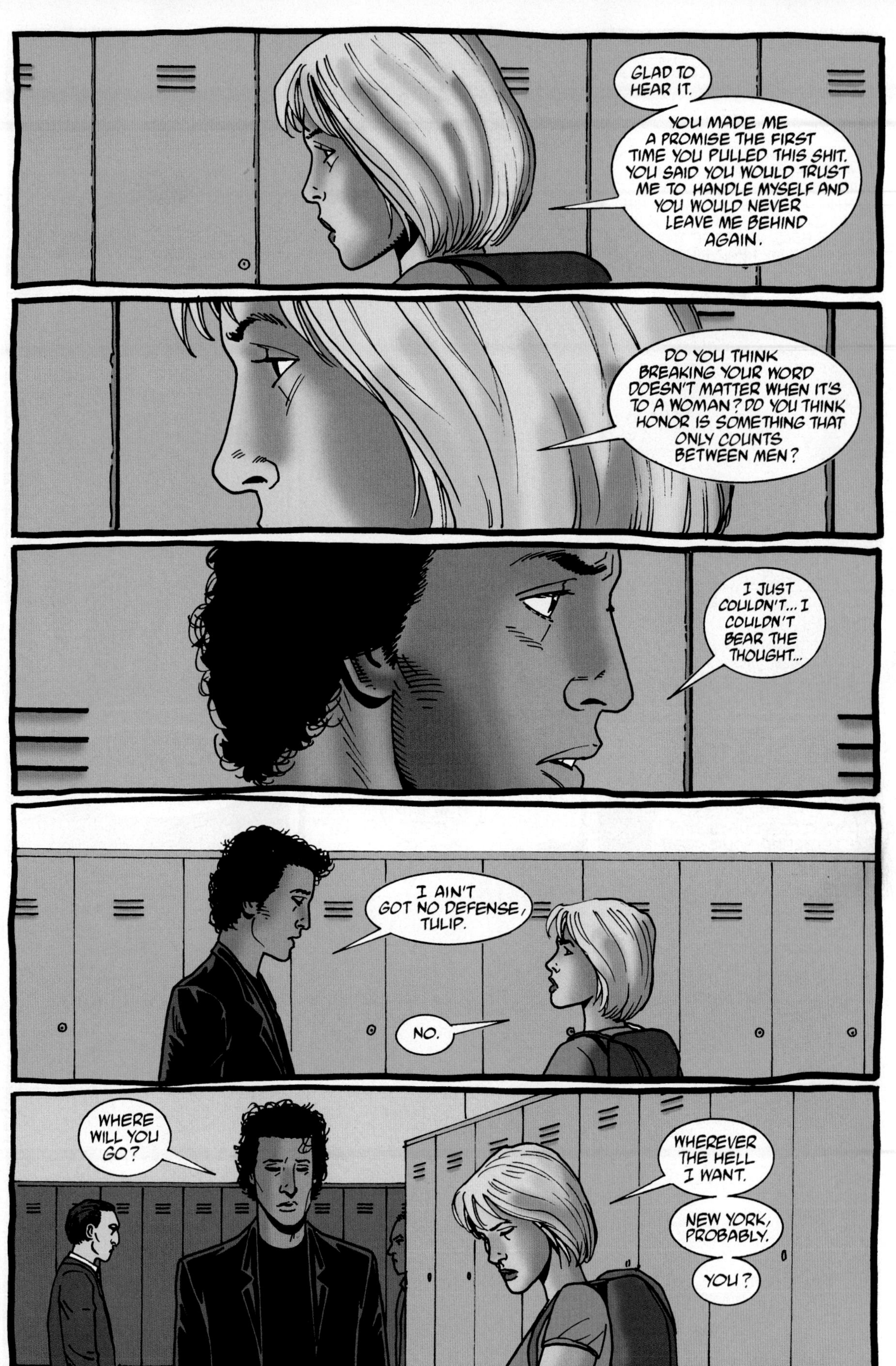
GLAD TO HEAR IT.
YOU MADE ME A PROMISE THE FIRST TIME YOU PULLED THIS SHIT. YOU SAID YOU WOULD TRUST ME TO HANDLE MYSELF AND YOU WOULD NEVER LEAVE ME BEHIND AGAIN.
DO YOU THINK BREAKING YOUR WORD DOESN'T MATTER WHEN IT'S TO A WOMAN? DO YOU THINK HONOR IS SOMETHING THAT ONLY COUNTS BETWEEN MEN?
I JUST COULDN'T... I COULDN'T BEAR THE THOUGHT...
I AIN'T GOT NO DEFENSE, TULIP.
NO.
WHERE WILL YOU GO?
WHEREVER THE HELL I WANT.
NEW YORK, PROBABLY.
YOU?

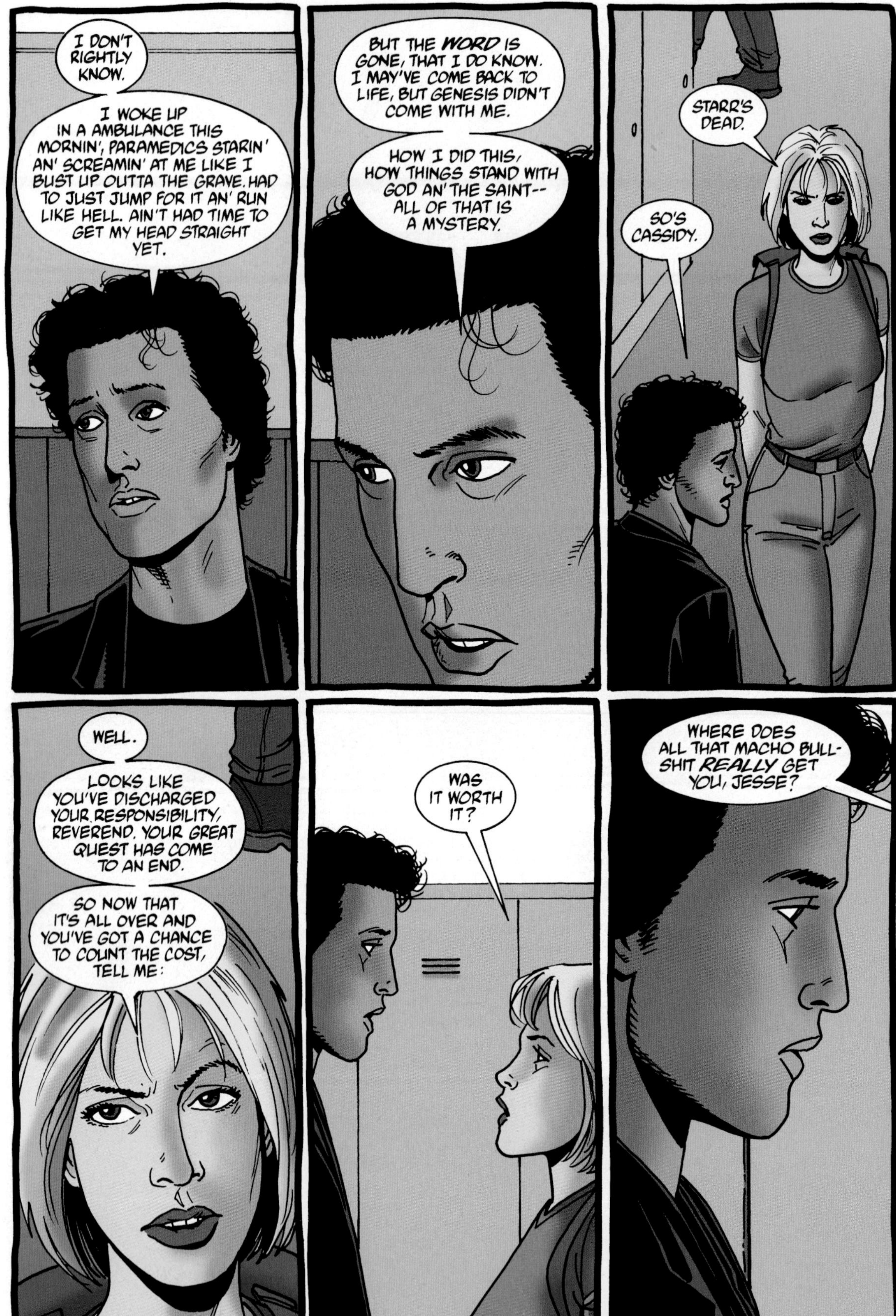
I DON'T RIGHTLY KNOW.
I WOKE UP IN A AMBULANCE THIS MORNIN', PARAMEDICS STARIN' AN' SCREAMIN' AT ME LIKE I BUST UP OUTTA THE GRAVE. HAD TO JUST JUMP FOR IT AN' RUN LIKE HELL. AIN'T HAD TIME TO GET MY HEAD STRAIGHT YET.
BUT THE WORD IS GONE, THAT I DO KNOW. I MAY'VE COME BACK TO LIFE, BUT GENESIS DIDN'T COME WITH ME.
HOW I DID THIS, HOW THINGS STAND WITH GOD AN' THE SAINT-- ALL OF THAT IS A MYSTERY.
STARR'S DEAD.
SO'S CASSIDY.
WELL.
LOOKS LIKE YOU'VE DISCHARGED YOUR RESPONSIBILITY, REVEREND. YOUR GREAT QUEST HAS COME TO AN END.
SO NOW THAT IT'S ALL OVER AND YOU'VE GOT A CHANCE TO COUNT THE COST, TELL ME:
WAS IT WORTH IT?
WHERE DOES ALL THAT MACHO BULL-SHIT REALLY GET YOU, JESSE?

STAY.

WUFF...

WAY IT'S GOTTA BE, SKEET.
I JUST DON'T DESERVE HER NO MORE.

?

JESSE

Dear Jesse,

If you're reading this it means you reached out your hand to me. Now that might not sound like a big deal to you, but it bloody well is for me, I'm telling you. I suppose by the time you get this I'll have found out if it saved me.

But do you know, in a way I don't really care about that. If there's something bad coming I can hardly say I don't deserve it, can I? It was enough that a guy like you would be my friend, and when it came to it, when the shite really hit the fan, you couldn't find it in you to give up on me.

I wish I'd been a better mate to you than I was--but Jesus, we could write an entire fucking book on that one. A million apologies wouldn't cover it, and sitting here in this wee bar waiting for you I've only the time for one. So I'm truly sorry. And I know it's one thing to take my hand, but quite another to forgive me.

The only thing left to say is Thank You.

And Goodbye, mate.

Cassidy

ps: This is a weird wee thought, and I'm probably just being a dick and flattering myself, but I can't help wondering if maybe the big job you took on wasn't really about God and everything, about saving the world or whatever. If maybe it was more about saving me.

Isn't it funny when you think your story's going one way, and it turns out it was going another way all along?

WELL GOODBYE TO YOU, MY GOOD FRIEND.

I AM THE ALPHA.
I AM THE OMEGA.
I AM THE BRIGHT MORNING STAR.
THE LORD OF HOSTS.
YOUR GOD.

RETURNED AT LAST TO HEAVEN.
MY RIGHTFUL PLACE.
AND ONCE BACK UPON THE THRONE OF PARADISE, MY RIGHTFUL POWER WILL BE REGAINED.

OH MY CHILDREN, I AM NOT SOME MONSTER.
I AM NOT THE BEAST THE PREACHER MADE OF ME, TO JUSTIFY HIS HUNTING ME.
THE WAYS OF GOD ARE NOT FOR MEN TO KNOW.
AND YET KNOW THIS, THAT THE TRUTH IN WHAT I SAY TO YOU BE CLEAR.
WHEN THIS ONE CAME INTO MY HOUSE, AND SAID

I WAS WONDERIN' IF YEH'D BE INTERESTED IN MAKIN' A DEAL.

AND SO I SPOKE TO HIM, AND HE EXPLAINED.
YEH CAN'T RELAX AS LONG AS JESSE CUSTER'S GOT THIS POWER OF HIS. AN' HE CAN'T RELAX 'TIL HE'S DONE WHAT HE THINKS HE'S GOTTA DO.
SO I WANT YEH OUT OF HIS LIFE. I CAN SET HIM UP FOR YEH, I CAN KNOCK THE FUCK OUT OF HIM SO HE CAN'T RESIST, AN' YEH CAN STEP IN AN' GET RID'VE THE WORD AN' GENESIS AN' ALL OF THAT.

AND IN RETURN, I ASKED?
HE LIVES, NO MATTER WHAT.

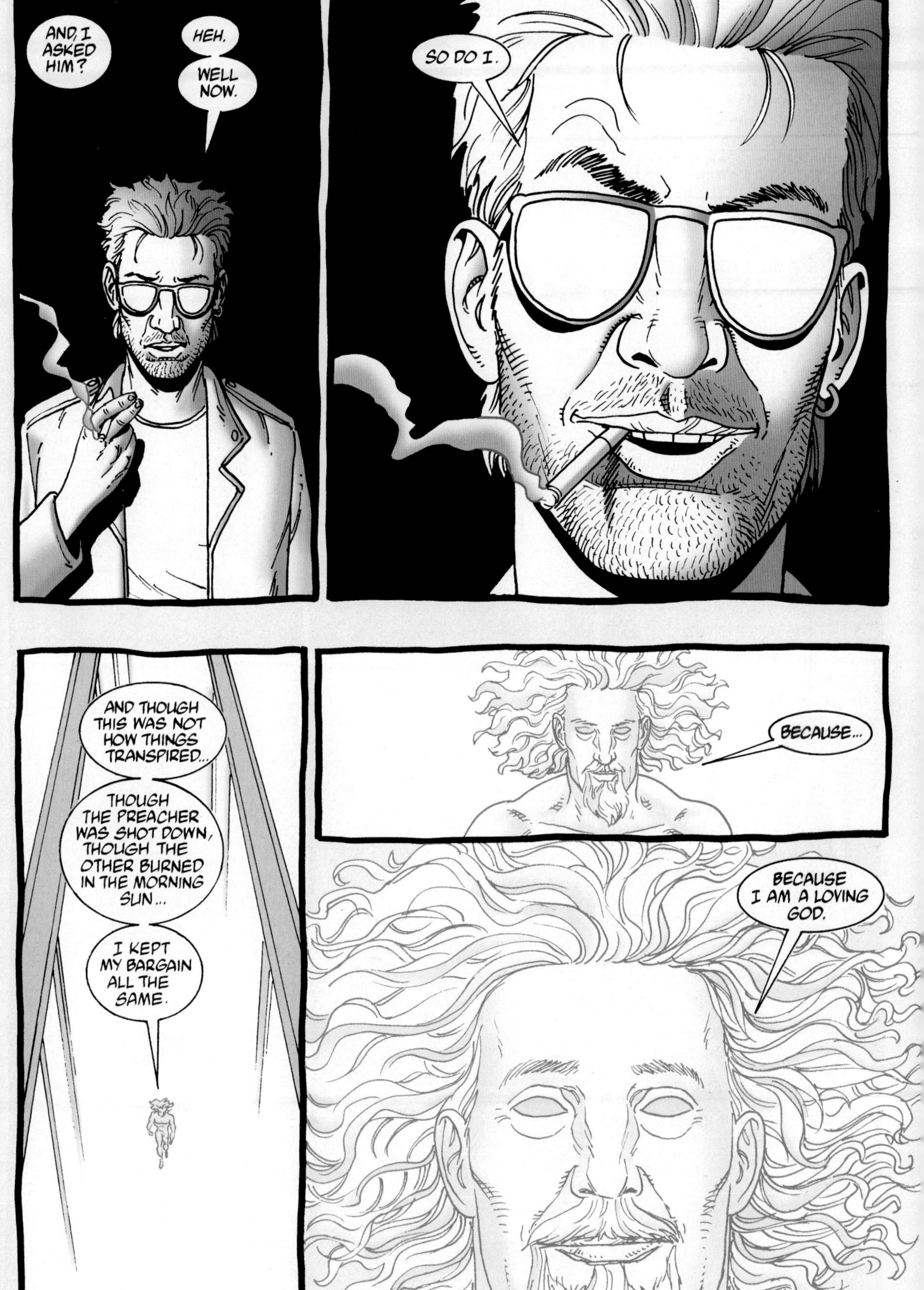
AND, I ASKED HIM?
HEH.
WELL NOW.
SO DO I.
AND THOUGH THIS WAS NOT HOW THINGS TRANSPIRED...
THOUGH THE PREACHER WAS SHOT DOWN, THOUGH THE OTHER BURNED IN THE MORNING SUN...
I KEPT MY BARGAIN ALL THE SAME.
BECAUSE...
BECAUSE I AM A LOVING GOD.

YOU KNOW... IF I DON'T GO AFTER HER...
THEN ALLA THIS HAS BEEN FOR NOTHIN', AN' NOTHIN' GOOD COMES OUT OF IT, JUST BLOOD AN' LOSS AN' HORROR.
WUFF! WUFF!

BUT--
I JUST DON'T THINK--
WUFF...!

...

WUFF! WUFF! WUFF!
I KNOW, I KNOW, IT'S FATE-- BUT IT'S HORSETHEFT, SKEETER! AN' IF THERE'S ONE THING I CANNOT DO--

YOU STUPID FUCKIN' NAG, STRAYIN' OFF AGAIN! ALL THIS DAMAGE IS GONNA COME OUTTA MY PAY!!

THEN AGAIN...

SNAP OUT OF IT...!

TULIP
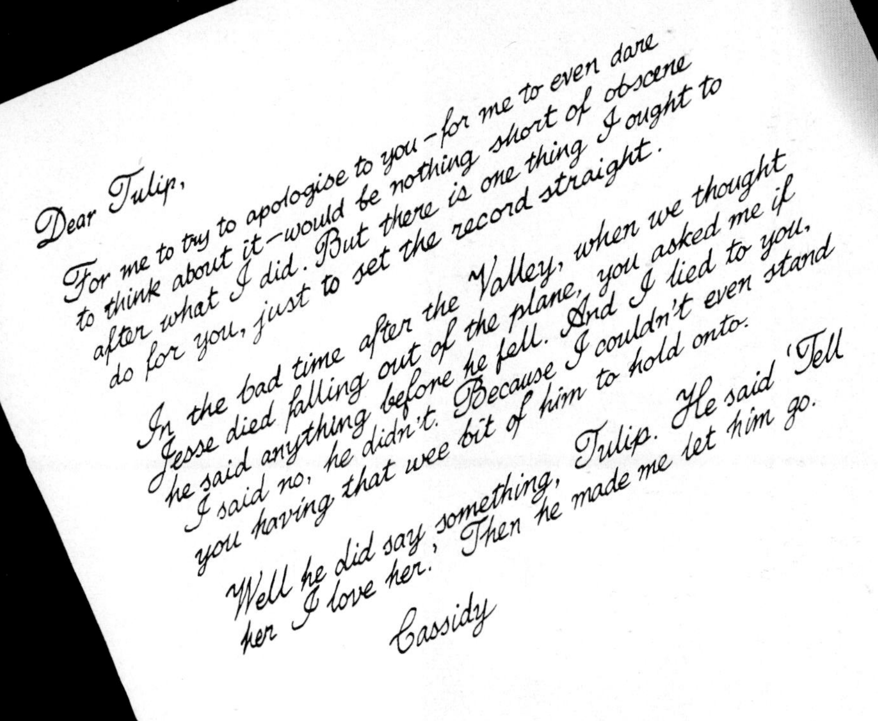
Dear Tulip,
For me to try to apologise to you—for me to even dare to think about it—would be nothing short of obscene after what I did. But there is one thing I ought to do for you, just to set the record straight.
In the bad time after the Valley, when we thought Jesse died falling out of the plane, you asked me if he said anything before he fell. And I lied to you. I said no, he didn't. Because I couldn't even stand you having that wee bit of him to hold onto.
Well he did say something, Tulip. He said 'Tell her I love her.' Then he made me let him go.
Cassidy

TULIP

HEY.

YOU CAME AFTER ME.

I HAD TO.
PEOPLE LIKE YOU AN' ME DON'T FIND EACH OTHER TOO OFTEN IN THIS DAMN WORLD.

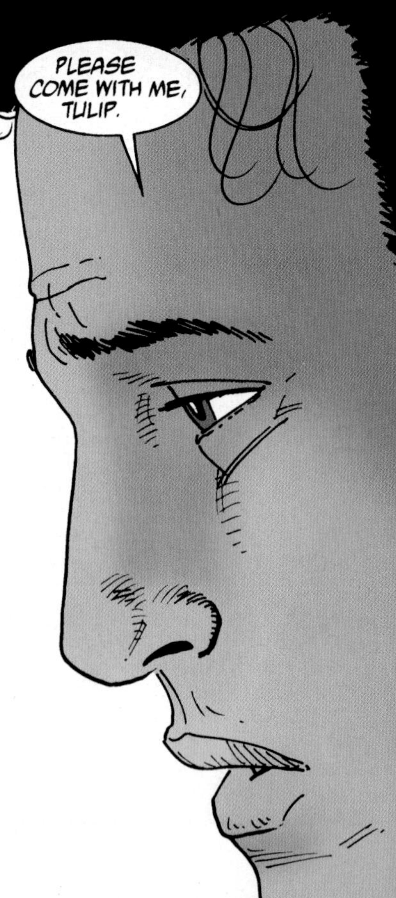
PLEASE COME WITH ME, TULIP.

NO. NO, THAT'S NOT FAIR.
YOU HAVEN'T THE RIGHT TO SAY THAT TO ME, AND YOU KNOW IT...

YOU'LL HURT ME AGAIN, YOU'LL BREAK ANOTHER PROMISE, YOU'LL--
CAN'T YOU SEE IT MAKES NO SENSE FOR ME TO COME WITH YOU...!

OH TULIP, OF COURSE IT DON'T.
WHAT WE HAVE AIN'T BORN OF REASON OR LOGIC 'CAUSE LOVE NEVER IS. IT'S STUPID AN' CRAZY AN' IRRATIONAL, 'CAUSE IT COMES FROM IN HERE, AN' THAT IS ONE THING THAT NEVER MAKES NO SENSE.

BUT I DO KNOW THAT I HAVE GOT TO CHANGE A LITTLE, IF THIS MACHO BULLSHIT YOU TALKED ABOUT IS GONNA KEEP GETTIN' IN THE WAY.
WE DON'T GOTTA JUST ACCEPT THE WAY THINGS ARE. JUST LIKE WE DON'T GOTTA LET OURSELVES BE LESSENED BY DEATH OR ANY OTHER DAMN THING. JUST LIKE WE DON'T NEED NO GOD TO SHAPE THE WORLD FOR US.
WE CAN MAKE OUR LIVES THE WAY WE WANT THEM--

OR WE AIN'T WORTH NOTHING.
NOW TAKE MY HAND AN' I SWEAR I'LL LOVE YOU 'TIL THE GODDAMN STARS GO OUT.

YOU'RE--
CRYING--

I GUESS I MUST BE LEARNIN'.

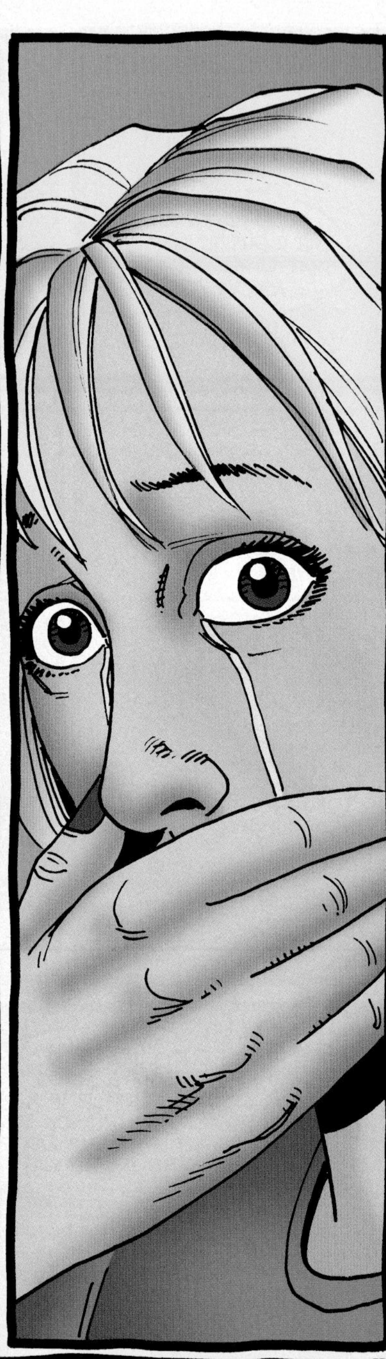

YOU.
ME.

YOU SLAUGHTERED THE ENTIRE HOST...?
FOOLS GOT IN MY WAY.

YOU GOT THIS COMIN', BOY.
MORE'N ANYONE, YOU GOT THIS COMIN'.

YOUR WIFE AND CHILD?

THEM.
THEM AN' THE HELL YOU MADE OF THIS WORLD.

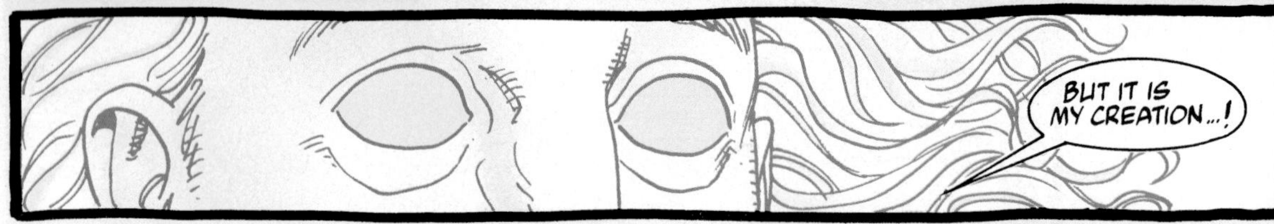
BUT IT IS MY CREATION...!

IT'S OUTGROWN YOU.
YOU SHOULDA FOUND THE SAND TO FACE THE PREACHER. THAT POWER OF HIS OR NO, YOU MIGHTA HAD A CHANCE AGAINST HIM.
NOW YOU'VE NONE.

YOU DO NOT HEAR ME, SAINT OF KILLERS.
THIS WORLD IS MY CREATION, TO DO WITH AS I PLEASE.
AND IT IS GIVEN UNTO NONE TO JUDGE ME, TO STAND AGAINST ME, TO--
PLEASE DON'T.
YOU DO NOT UNDERSTAND. YOU CANNOT KNOW WHAT IT WAS LIKE TO BE THE CREATOR IN THE TIME BEFORE CREATION.
THERE *HAD* TO BE A WORLD. IT *HAD* TO BE THE WAY IT WAS. MEN *HAD* TO CHOOSE TO LOVE ME.
I WAS ALONE.
I WANTED TO BE LOVED.

BUT NO MATTER HOW DARK THIS WORLD IS, I *AM* A LOVING GOD. I *DO* GOOD. I KEPT TO MY BARGAIN, AND BROUGHT THE PREACHER BACK TO LIFE.

JUST LET ME PAST TO TAKE MY THRONE ONCE MORE, AND I WILL HAVE THE POWER TO DO SOME GOOD FOR YOU AS WELL.

I CAN GIVE YOU ANYTHING. YOUR HEART'S DESIRE. YOUR WIFE AND DAUGHTER, ALIVE ONCE MORE.

LOWER THE WEAPON.

LET ME PAST.

PLEASE. THINK WHAT I AM OFFERING. IMAGINE IT.

DO NOT KILL ME, I IMPLORE YOU...!

PLEASE...

PLEASE...

WHAT IS IT THAT YOU *WANT*...?

TO REST.

WHERE WILL WE LIVE?

AMERICA.
WHAT WILL WE DO?

I AIN'T TOO SURE, HONEY. I FIGURE WE'LL KINDA MAKE IT UP AS WE GO.
I DON'T KNOW IF I TOLD YOU, BUT I NEVER REALLY WANTED TO BE A PREACHER...

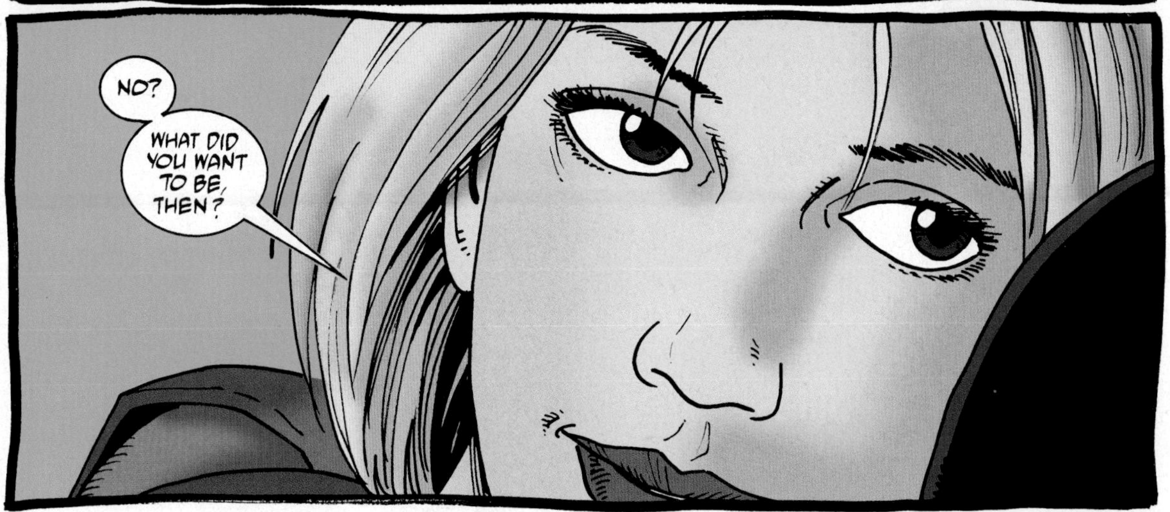
NO?
WHAT DID YOU WANT TO BE, THEN?

HELL, GIRL.

CAN'T YOU GUESS?

I THINK YEH WERE RIGHT, JESSE.

I THINK I'LL TRY ACTIN' LIKE A MAN.

A HELL OF A VISION

GARTH ENNIS - Writer STEVE DILLON - Artist

PAMELA RAMBO - Colorist CLEM ROBINS - Letterer AXEL ALONSO - Editor

PREACHER created by GARTH ENNIS and STEVE DILLON

CLOSING TIME

Final PREACHER Portraits by Glenn Fabry

Dustjacket art for the cover collection
PREACHER: DEAD OR ALIVE
381-383

Cover art for the first trade paperback edition of
PREACHER VOL. 9:
ALAMO
384

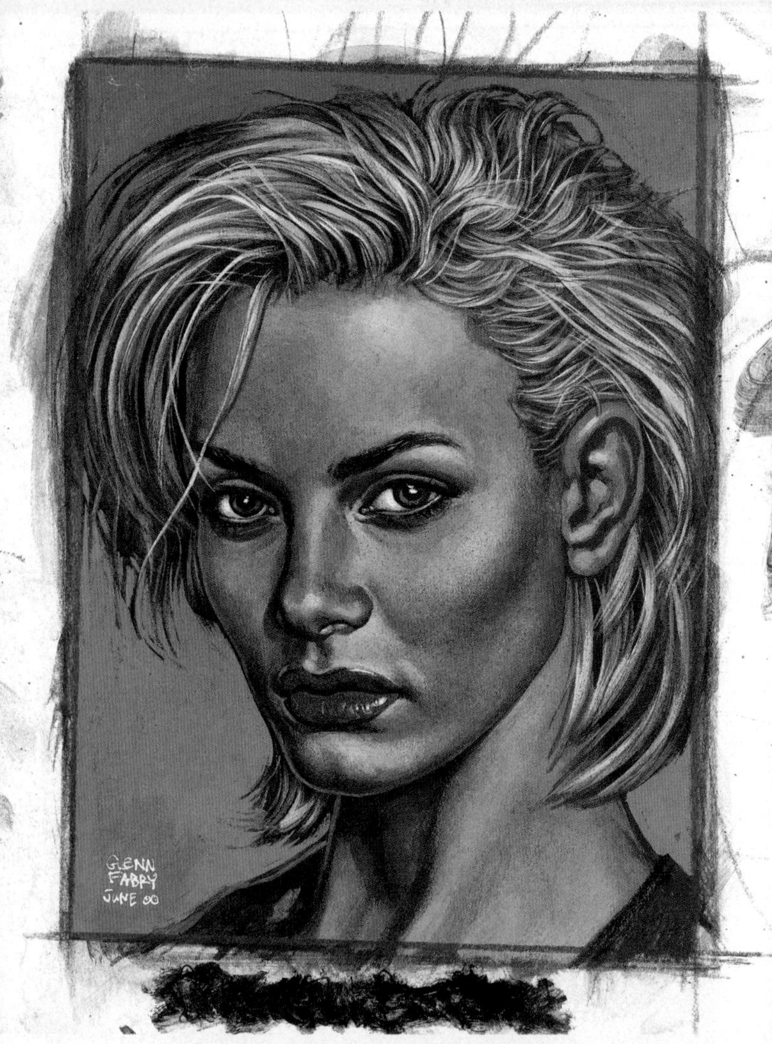
GLENN FABRY
JUNE 00

GLENN
FABRY
MAY 00